MW00931011

HYPNOTHERAPY CDs

Achieving Mental Focus for Swimming Through Hypnosis
Introduction to Close Encounters
Changing Enabling Behavior Through Hypnosis
Healing Stress and Anxiety Through Guided Visualization and Hypnosis
Hypnosis/Guided Visualization for Improving Golf
Hypnotherapy for Hoarding
Hypnotherapy for Improving Swimming
Hypnotherapy for Improving Tennis
Hypnotherapy for Pain Management
Hypnotherapy for Patients with Thoracic Outlet Syndrome
Hypnotherapy for Procrastination
Hypnotherapy for Self-Esteem and Self Confidence
Hypnotherapy for Sports
Hypnotherapy for Stress
Hypnotherapy for Test Anxiety
Learning to Love Yourself Using Visualization and Hypnosis
Spiritual Healing Through Hypnosis
Time Travel Through Hypnosis and Visualization
Using Hypnosis/Visualization to Stop Road Rage
What is Hypnosis?

MEDITATION CDs

Achieving Higher Levels of Consciousness Through Meditation
Meditation to Connect to Cosmic Consciousness

HYPNOSIS PROGRAMS

Hypnotherapy to Stop Smoking

E-BOOKS

Sacred Geometry Review

Our New Chakra System

OTHER BOOKS BY JUDITH CAMERON

Caught Between Two Worlds: A Journey Through Time

All of the above are available by visiting Judy's website:
http://www.worldwidewhoswho.com/judithcameron
If you wish to contact Dr. Judy her e-mail
address is: etdiplomat@gmail.com
Cosmicangelenterprisesllc.com

SPIRITUAL AND GALACTIC AWAKENING

The Cosmic Classroom... An Ongoing Story

Judith L. Cameron, Ph.D

Balboa Press books may be ordered through booksellers or by contacting:

Balboa Press
A Division of Hay House
1663 Liberty Drive
Bloomington, IN 47403
www.balboapress.com
1 (877) 407-4847

Print information available on the last page.

ISBN: 978-1-9822-3472-0 (sc)
ISBN: 978-1-9822-3473-7 (hc)
ISBN: 978-1-9822-3474-4 (e)

Library of Congress Control Number: 2019913878

Balboa Press rev. date: 09/13/2019

For Richard
For Nadeem
And
All the Beautiful Beings Who Helped Train
Me and Who Are Now Part of My Life

Contents

Preface

Every day do something that will inch you closer to a better tomorrow.
—Anonymous Student

While I was writing my book, *"Caught Between Two Worlds: A Journey Through Time"*, it caused me to really think about the number of encounters I have had over the past sixty-two years. I only included a few of them so as to not make the book too long, but I remember getting my version of *Wow,* as I was deciding which encounters to include and which not to. The *Wow* was the recognition of all that I have learned from the extraterrestrials and their chosen Earth teachers, whom I have also learned so much, and continue to learn from. It is my understanding that all of us who are alive on planet Earth today made a contract with Heaven about why we wanted to be here during the Earth's ascension to the fifth dimension, and what we could do to help when the time came. Not only did we choose to be here during this historical time in the Universe, but we were also chosen to come. I'm just guessing that it was something akin to applying for a CEO's job. You had to show an interest and a desire to come here, but then you had to go through some kind of selection process by a committee in Heaven to be selected. So those of us who are here, chose to be here during this time. I have been told that thousands of beings throughout the galaxies wanted to be on Earth during this time, but they were not selected to come. I'm assuming the desire was strong, but maybe they did not have the qualifications yet to do the job. So that is something that those of us who are here should all be proud of. The trouble is, many of us have not awakened to that fact. So, it is up to those of us who are awakening to assist those who are still "asleep". Awakening has to do with knowing our connection to Source and believing that anything is possible because *We are all One.* For those of you who are trying to get the truth out to the masses, you know what a daunting task it can be at times. However, it is happening. Just think about how much more we know now than we did not know and understand just nine months ago. We have to continue to be tenacious, courageous, and unwavering in our belief in the true reality around us. If we stay centered in the God Source, it is just a matter of time when total success will reign and we will all be in the fifth dimension.

During my early childhood I developed an interest in astronomy and space. I am sure it was due to my many encounters and teachings from the extraterrestrial beings who have worked with me over my life. This was also occurring at a time when no country on Earth had a space program, at least that we were aware of. We now know, of course, that there was a secret space program.

My ninth-grade science teacher helped expand my love for science. I also thought math was fascinating and fun, but at that age, my mind would not make the kind of abstractions needed for higher levels of math, such as solid geometry, trigonometry and calculus. I received Bs and Cs in those classes, but I really had to put extra study into them to accomplish those grades. I know my friends saw me as different because I was distracted a lot. I wanted to learn all that I could about the sciences, but about many different subjects as well. As a result, I did not date in high school. My friends and I never talked about my space brothers and sisters, but we did have conversations about the possibility of life elsewhere in the Universe. My encounters happened on my grandparents' ten-acre farm in Antelope, California, and when my grandmother died, my grandfather sold the farm. The visitations stopped and did not start again until 1984 when I was thirty-nine years old.

Although I was raised as an Evangelical Lutheran, my real journey into spirituality began when I was earning my certification to teach special needs students, at around age twenty-five. I had been very active in the church during junior high and high school because I sang in the choir and I love to sing. Had it not been for choir during those years, I often wonder if I would have gone to church much. I was definitely a believer, but I did not like the way the pastor was always trying to indoctrinate us about life. I never believed it was that cut and dry. Also, as a young person, I noticed a lot of hypocrisy on the part of some members of our congregation, and that really bothered me. They would teach us about the Ten Commandments on Sunday, but then members would cheat on their spouses on Friday and Saturday nights. It really bothered me then when I was so young and impressionable. Something else that bothered me about organized religion was the ritual one was expected to go through just to talk to God or the Angels. My mother was Catholic, and I asked her once why she felt she had to go to confession in order to talk to God. I would say things to her such as, "*Your priest is just like you, only he has training in religion. If we are all created equal, then we should have as much right to talk to God directly and handle what we perceive as sins, just as a priest does.*" The practice of confession and many other practices in organized religion, felt more like control than worshipping to me. I felt like true spirituality had to do with a direct line to the Source. So, when I was getting my certification to teach special needs students, I signed up for my last class that was supposed to about methods. What I received was entirely different and wonderful, and it came at the perfect time for me because of what I was feeling about organized religion. Of course, we all know there are never any accidents. Our teacher was a young, vibrant man who was very charismatic. His class was more about exploring ourselves, reincarnation, and angels, but also included parapsychology. From this special class and instructor came my expanded belief system and training. Angels began appearing in my life, and continue to have a profound effect on my life to this day.

By writing my first book, *"Caught Between Two Worlds"*, and this book, I have gained a wonderful sense of closure on certain aspects of my life, as I now see my life flowing together so easily and making perfect sense. As our planet draws nearer to being fully conscious and in the Fifth Dimension, I felt compelled to write these books, to tell my story about how my life experiences have put me where I am today. I came here to be a leader-a collaborator-in the creation of our new fifth dimensional Earth, to teach others of our true ancient history with our space brothers and sisters from other dimensions and planets, and act as a liaison between extraterrestrials and Earth humans when disclosure and first contact occur.

Acknowledgements

We pass through this world but once. Few tragedies can be more extensive than the stunting of life, few injustices deeper than the denial of an opportunity to strive or even to hope, by a limit imposed from without, but falsely identified as lying within.
—Stephen Jay Gould[2]

Many people have supported me with help, advice and encouragement over the years. These amazing people have believed in me and my journey, and I am forever grateful to them for their unconditional love and support.

Again, I wish to thank Richard, who has spent the last quarter of the 20th century and the first 18 years of the 21st century putting up with my research gathering, my long trips of encounters and mystery, and then my hours of storytelling that would occur when I got home. He was always there for me quietly waiting in the wings to offer support when I felt frustrated or overwhelmed, and allowing me time to cry when I needed to. His gift of unconditional love allowed me freedoms that many married females are not allowed because of trust issues and personal insecurities. I have been blessed with his trust that has allowed me to fly into places of unimaginable adventure and peace. He believes that I can achieve whatever I set my sights on and he has always kept an open mind to the possibilities. I owe him a great deal in my life and I appreciate the freedoms to learn that I have had. I am heartbroken to see that horrible illness that has overtaken you now, Richard. It is slowly eating away at your memories, so I am documenting my gratefulness for the opportunities you allowed me to pursue during our life together. Thank you for openly supporting my future life with my twin, for bonding with him in a special way like brothers, and wanting only happiness for me. That is a beautiful gift you have given me. I want everyone to know what a good man you are, and what a gentle soul. God Bless you always, my special friend and soulmate.

Although my parents, Alfred and June Moe, crossed over before I was allowed to recall my life-long extraterrestrial encounters, they have both been with me on the other side, encouraging me and letting me know they are proud of my accomplishments. They both work with me in different ways. My dad comes through when I need strength the most, and my mom holds a more secret role, sending me hugs and her beautiful energy. I owe them both for giving me the courage when I was growing up to always go after my dreams. Thank you, Mom and Dad for your love and support.

Additionally, I wish to thank my aunt and uncle, Gene and Gayle Johnson, who passed in the early 2000s. Thank you for giving me the strength and a belief in myself that I could do anything. Thank you, Uncle Gene for introducing me to flight by taking me up in your airplane. You instilled in me my love for flying, and I still plan to get my pilot's license when I am blessed with the time to do that. Maybe now, in this world, it will be a license to fly a spaceship. Thank you, Giggy for our fun summers together. I miss those times.

I wish to once again acknowledge Steven Greer, MD, the founder of CSETI, The Center for the Study of Extraterrestrial Intelligence, the Disclosure Project to end the secrecy and cover-up of extraterrestrial visitations and the technologies they bring with them, and the Orion Project, to create these new technologies given to us by these advanced extraterrestrial civilizations and stolen from us and then hidden away from us by the military industrial complex. I am forever grateful to Dr. Greer, his remarkable working leadership team, his amazing wife, Emily, and his family who have sacrificed their time with Steven so that he could do this work.

Next, I wish to acknowledge Sheldon Nidle and his life companion, Colleen, who have been very instrumental in teaching me about our past galactic history, our ascended masters, and what to expect during first landing and then the ascension process. Sheldon has a direct line of communication with the Sirians from the Sirian star system, and has had this ongoing contact since early childhood, when he was brought on board the Sirian ships and taught many things. Sheldon does not channel extraterrestrials, but has direct contact. He is one of the teachers that I was told to seek out when I was taken at night to what I refer to as the Cosmic Classroom.

My acknowledgements would not be complete without mentioning someone who has taken my heart forever, Nadeem Arif. He came into my life like a whirlwind and he taught me about my own spirituality and how all of that fits in with my entire life to date. He is a very old soul that is housed in a young, healthy body, a dreamer, a light worker, and my very special friend and my twin flame. Thank you, Nadeem, for coming into my life just at the right moment, for being so strong, dedicated to world peace and unconditional love and spreading a higher consciousness to anyone who comes into contact with you. You have been an inspiration and an amazing gift to me. Thank you for introducing me to Islam and the beauty of that very special religion. I know we have that deep soul connection that brought us together in the first place, as well as the Galactic connection we both have together. Our paths have now become the same beautiful path. God has blessed us with a beautiful life together. I believe in you and your work Nadeem, and the world is a better place because you are in it. I am a better person because you share part of my life with me. May God Bless you always.

Once again, I wish to acknowledge Pamela Peterson, my friend and colleague from the Challenger Center for Space Science Education. Through Pam's leadership and guidance, I have had invaluable experiences working together with astronauts as we taught students about the space shuttle program, the moon program and Mars. These experiences have proven invaluable to me giving me the grounding that I sometimes needed while being taken on board spacecraft at night. Thank you, Pam, for Windstar and John, the White House experience on the twenty-fifth anniversary of the Apollo 11 moon landing, the many Challenger Center conferences and shuttle launches and landings, and our deep, personal friendship. You have put an imprint on my heart that will remain there through time.

Acknowledgements would not be complete without mentioning the large number of extraterrestrials who have worked with me, through the CSETI trainings, and then on my own. They continually risk contacting me and other humans when they come into our proximity, because if they are seen by members of the military industrial complex, they may be shot down. I have observed a few close calls, and am grateful that they are faster and have more advanced means to get away quickly. Thank you for your ongoing contact with me and the others that you work with.

I could not finish this book without acknowledging someone who is very special and holds a deep place in my heart. He is my dear friend from Surat, India, Bhavin Hingrajiya. He is an amazing young man whose smile lights up a room when he enters. When he makes eye contact with you, you know he is seeing who you really are. Bhavin is a very wise, old soul in a young and vibrant body. Being a Light worker himself, he is very willing to share his knowledge with anyone who asks. Thank you Bhavin for pulling me back from the darkness that had grabbed hold of me during the writing of part of this book. By introducing me to The Art of Living Center and strongly recommending the Happiness Course, you changed my life. I owe you so much, Bhavin. You and your unconditional love for me are part of my heart and life forever. For that, I am forever grateful.

I also wish to acknowledge my friend and colleague, Jeanne Love, whom I met as a result of the Challenger Space Shuttle disaster in 1986. We were initially drawn together because of that, but now we are collaborators in healing our beautiful Earth, helping to repair the stargates that the dark side has broken up, and working with the Native Americans that have crossed over and their powerful spirits who choose to work with us. Thank you, Jeanne for your remarkable healing abilities and your ability to see and hear those individuals who have crossed over, and how they assist you when working with your clients. I appreciate you and our enduring friendship.

Additional acknowledgments go to my special brother in Islam,

Saqib Zubari. We became friends through being classmates in our studies at California Islamic University in Fullerton, California. We became aware early on that we share many of the same beliefs about Earth's history, the galaxies, and the Universe and God's relationship to all of it. You have helped me a great deal in understanding what I learned as a student on the space ships and how it relates to religious history on Earth through Christianity, Judaism, and Islam. You helped me fill in the missing link that I have been struggling to understand as I continued to write this saga of my life. Thank you, Brother Saqib for sharing your knowledge and insights with me. Your understanding of all of it is incredible and I appreciate you sharing your important time and energy in helping me with this part of the book. May the Peace and Love of Allah be with you always.

I have a very special thanks to my beautiful sister in Islam, Haifa Dagachi, who is like a daughter to me. She is an incredible artist, designer, and is a professional in many of the creative arts. Haifa is responsible for two of the drawings in this book. Thank you, Haifa, for your time and creativity in helping to make this book more appealing. May Allah bless you always.

I wish to also acknowledge Shaykh Mustafa Umar, the president and a professor at California Islamic University where I am getting a Bachelor's Degree in Islamic Law and Theology. He has been a wonderful role model to me and has helped me a great deal in learning about Islam, it's history, culture, and people. You have been a blessing in my life.

I jokingly say to people that when I was created, God forgot to put in the technology gene. I used to have a satellite system going into my house that allowed me to access the internet. It is because of my amazingly experienced and creative satellite guru, Ruben Troche that I managed to keep my sanity when it came to keeping my computers talking to the satellite. Thank you, Ruben, for your know-how, and your patience with me for not getting the technology gene. Without your ongoing assistance and caring support at that time, I am not sure I would have ever published this book.

I wish to mention once again my beautiful Siberian Husky, Cochise, who crossed over in 2004, but who still works with me from the other side. He and I have a telepathic and psychic connection that is still very strong today. I miss giving you big hugs and our wonderful walks together, but I am so grateful that we are still connected. I feel your presence all the time. I love you.

Adding to my acknowledgments it is important to mention the beautiful angels and spirit guides who are always with me. Thank you to the Galactic Angels who used to come in at night while I was sleeping to balance my body and take away some of the ascension aches and pains that I had. Also, thank you to that wonderful fairy who appeared to me in my lemon tree at my home in Fullerton while I was drawn into my courtyard late one night. I appreciate you trusting that I would be happy to see you and not be frightened.

To my hundreds of students and clients who have supported my classes and seminars over the years. You worked with me so diligently to uncover the mystery of why we are all sharing a role in this incredible journey. Also, to my amazing guides who are always there assisting me with new information and experiences. Without you, only part of my work would be completed. I owe you much gratitude.

Last, but certainly not least, I am grateful to my amazing spirit guide(s) who assist me during the times when I sit down to write, and my mind does not cooperate. Through meditation and prayer, I receive communication and encouragement.

Introduction

We must begin to make what I call 'conscious choices,' and to really recognize that we are all the same. It's from that place in my heart that I write my songs.
—John Denver

One of the things that I love about the guides and extraterrestrials who work with me is the spontaneity that happens when I find myself suddenly stuck in front of an audience or group of people and I cannot think of what to say. I remember one of the first large audiences I had right after I became an International Faculty member for the Challenger Center for Space Science Education, was a rather large group of aerospace engineers and their families. I did not know beforehand that this would be the group I was supposed to tell about how the Space Shuttle worked and how the astronauts lived and worked in space. Here I was, dressed in my NASA flight-suit, and representing NASA (The National Aeronautics and Space Administration) and teaching. I had a small moment of panic when I learned that this would be who I was talking to. Everyone in the audience had something to do with building the components and parts of the space shuttles. I thought, "*What information am I going to teach them? They built the darn thing.*" I decided at that point that I would talk to the young people who were the families of these engineers. I would later learn that although they built the components of the shuttles, it did not mean that they necessarily knew how it was to fly, although many of them did. During the question and answer period, one of the engineers who had been listening, asked me a very technical question trying to stump me, I'm sure. Before I started going into panic mode, I heard a gentle voice in my head say, "Just breathe and smile. This will be easy. Just repeat what I am going to say to you." So, I smiled a big smile at him, and he noticed that I was a little nervous, but I began to speak. The answer I gave him was so scientific and technical that I could tell it completely surprised him. Then I said, "Does that make sense?" The whole audience laughed and started to clap because they knew what he was doing when he asked the question, and I do not think that they approved. They were delighted when I answered the way I did. I silently thanked my guide, and quickly ended the evening. When I got home and was sharing my story, I could not remember what I had said in answering the question. It had been totally channeled to me. It was amazing.

It is very important to me to keep in almost on-going contact with my spirit guides and mentors. I meditate and pray, but also talk to them, usually out loud when I am by myself, if I need to discuss something with them that I need an answer to. I act just like they are in the room with me, because I am sure they are. I feel their remarkable energy. Sometimes at night, they allow me to see them when it gets dark in the room. Sometimes Richard sees their energies surrounding them. When I reach out to them, sometimes they extend their arm to me and when our fingers meet, there is a large burst of energy that appears around our hands that Richard can see. Extraterrestrials who have worked with me at night in the room also allow me to see them, usually as they are leaving. They pass right through the glass door and rattle the slats on the window covering as they leave.

My first book, *"Caught Between Two Worlds: A Journey Through Time"* is about sharing some extraordinary experiences I had that positively changed my life in so many ways. This book is a sharing of what I have learned over the years from the angels and extraterrestrials, and also from my galactic teachers when I was taken to a place that I named the Cosmic Academy, and how the information is pertinent for today and our transition to the fifth dimension. Additionally, I share what I have learned from my Earth teachers who were selected for me by the Galactic Federation of Light instructors when they would take me at night. Those teachers are Dr. Steven Greer, and Sheldon Nidle, just to name two. Their premise was that they did not have the time to allow me to learn everything in these cosmic classes, but that I needed to learn during the day from these mentors. There were several names given to me, but I have chosen to learn from these two specifically. The stories I shared in the first book, *"Caught Between Two Worlds"*, came from my extensive journal writing. I kept a daily record of what was occurring in my life in regard to contact, angels, and paranormal experiences. From those journals, which I still keep and update once in a while, I chose a few events and encounters that I thought would make the book interesting. In this second book, *"A Spiritual and Galactic Awakening: The Cosmic Classroom…An Ongoing Story,"* I chose these people because they have direct contact with these beautiful space beings. I have received much of my training from the Cosmic classroom. I wrote my first book about my encounters and experiences because I know I am not the only one who has had these experiences throughout their lives. If my experiences resonate with others who have had similar experiences, and it helps them to better understand what happened to them, then I have done part of what I came here to Earth to do. This book, *"A Spiritual and Galactic Awakening,"*, is what I have learned from all of this and where it is leading me. It is very important because I am supposed to be teaching others about it. It is information about our past on Earth and what we should be looking forward to as our planet, and we, move into the fifth dimension.

As an adult, most of my encounters have been positive. I chose to describe those in my first book because one of my goals is to take away the fear that some people feel that is often associated with extraterrestrial encounters. However, it also occurred to me that for someone to have had as many encounters as I have had over the years and not to have had anything negative occur about those encounters, is unrealistic. So, I thought I would share a couple of those incidents with you so that you can see I have experienced the full spectrum of encounters. I also need to state here though, that these negative encounters had nothing to do with extraterrestrials directly, but rather the Military Industrial Complex. I never have believed that extraterrestrials abduct people to do experiments on. I do believe that the Military Industrial Complex working with the ETs that they had contracts with, mostly Greys and Reptilians and robotic humanoids that they have created to look like the real thing, did the abductions and made them look authentic. Their reason mostly was to scare people who had experienced very positive encounters before, and were starting to tell others about it. I'm not dwelling on these encounters, and I can even see some humor in them now, but I'm telling others to not be sloppy in their research, and definitely do not defy or confront the military because they are not playing. Be safe in what you are doing, and don't be careless, and you have nothing to fear. There is no longer anything to fear anyway because disclosure is happening now by the people all over the world. Meditate, keep your vibrations up by living life in a positive way and caring for others as you care for yourself, pray if you choose, keep raising your consciousness, and be happy and joyful.

I have been blessed with new skills, and these skills allow me to better serve humankind in a positive, loving way. I have also been given much information about our past, about what is occurring now in our daily lives, and what our future may hold. I also recognize that there has been a lot of disinformation and misinformation out there that sometimes infiltrate the research of even the most dedicated of people who are searching only for the truth. I just pray that over time I have not fallen prey to any of it. I try to check and double check things I am not sure of, but one can never be 100% sure of anything when we are dealing with the dark side. The biggest, most constant message is that we are all One. The consciousness on our planet is increasing exponentially, and we are entering one of the most exciting eras of our lives.

Part I

Childhood Close Encounters-A Remembering

Chapter 1

Encounters in Antelope

The most valuable possession you can own is an open heart. The most powerful weapon you can be is an instrument of peace.
—Carlos Santana

I decided that a good segue into this book would be to quickly recap the major parts of my childhood so the reader would feel a sense of continuity about what I am going to share. Additionally, this gives any reader who has not read--*"Caught between Two Worlds: -A Journey through Time-,"* a brief background of what occurred to lead me to the Cosmic Academy and my teachers.

My story starts in 1951, when I was six years old. I used to spend my summers on my grandparents' ten-acre farm in Antelope, California-a small rural community just outside Sacramento. I loved my grandparents whom I referred to as Nonnie and Popops. Nonnie was about five feet five inches and had beautiful gray hair. She was forty-four years old, but looked much older because of the hard work she did on the farm each day. Sacramento was hot and sunny most of the year, and this wore on Nonnie's face giving her premature wrinkles and a leathered texture. But even so, her eyes sparkled because she was such a beautiful soul, and she especially loved me. She seemed to have wisdom way beyond her years, and I believed that I could tell her anything. Nonnie had a quietness about her though when she sat alone in her rocking chair and did not realize someone was there. I would catch her sometimes when I was coming in from playing in the back yard, and she would just be staring out into space as though her mind were a million miles away. From time to time, she seemed troubled, but she never let on that anything was bothering her. But I knew differently. Even at six years old, I just knew.

Popops was about the same age as Nonnie. He had very thin hair on top of his head that I loved to put curls in while he took his nap each day. He allowed me to do it probably because my hands felt good rubbing his head. He was tall, about six feet four and towered over Nonnie. And he had a big, fat stomach. I was sure it was from all the wonderful pies that Nonnie used to bake from the berries that she picked each day.

I loved to be around Popops because we would have fun together. When he would go into town, he would take me with him in his truck. He had a light side about him and seemed really happy, but occasionally, he too seemed troubled. Maybe the stress of owning a farm and taking care of the thousand turkeys that he raised finally got to him. He and Nonnie never seemed to leave the farm to go anywhere. I don't think they ever took a vacation together.

About a mile down the road from the farm was a little country store. It was owned by Ed and Lucielle Foote, whom I really liked. I enjoyed riding down to the store with Popops when he would go because it also was the train station that would pick up and let off passengers from time to time. I loved the trains and the sound they made as they rolled down the track--*clackety clack, clackety clack.* Late at night while I was lying in bed, the faraway sound of the train on the tracks and the train whistle; just took me away to some far-off place. I also loved to talk to the hoboes who rode the trains in the open boxcars. That is how I met Bob, a very special hobo, who turned out to be a wonderful teacher in my life.

I told of wonderful encounters with extraterrestrial beings who told me their names were John and Isa. The first time I met them I was six years old and spending the summer in Antelope. I often went outside by myself in the middle of the night because I loved that time and nothing had ever made me fearful. So, on this first night of my encounter with them, something drew me outside. I was always very quiet not to wake my grandma and grandpa. I told Nonnie once that I went outside at night sometimes but she just thought I was imagining that I was doing it. I did not argue with her about that because I did not want to be told I could not do that at night.

When I first saw these two extraterrestrial beings, I was fascinated. I could tell they were from another planet because they did not look like me. There was something familiar about them though, like I knew them before. Their demeanor was warm and kind, and I felt such unconditional love coming from them that I did not want to leave. As I was standing there, I was watching their faces for any emotion. I began to smile at them. I felt a warm emotion coming from them as they looked at each other and then at me. They had very tiny mouths, so it was difficult to tell if they were smiling back, but I got the feeling they were. I remember there was a misty glow that night as the moon filtered through the trees. It seemed as though a dense fog had come into the area, and my vision was obstructed somewhat because of it. I remember feeling as if time was standing still as we stood and stared at each other.

I have always felt my emotions in an extra way because my physical body reacts intensely and quickly, adding to the depth of whatever emotion I am experiencing. As I watched them, I had that butterfly feeling in my stomach and became keenly aware of the area around my heart. It was definitely not a bad feeling, but strange nonetheless. It was so quiet that I could hear my heart beating in my ears like a soft drum beating to the rhythm of the night. It was fascinating. Finally, I must have given an even bigger smile because they both cocked their heads, much the way a dog would when he hears a sound or sees something that he does not understand.

I could see that their skin was a whitish color and they had no hair. I was thinking that they looked like marshmallows because they had a white halo effect around their bodies. Looking back on that time now, it was probably their auras that I was seeing. Their eyes looked like mine, only bigger. They were a beautiful lavender-blue color, and they sparkled in the moonlight. Each had tiny noses, almost like a hole in the face, a very small mouth, and two little ears on the sides of their heads. I could not tell whether they had teeth because they had not opened their mouths. I am guessing they did not, although I really do not know. Each was wearing a one-piece outfit that fit their bodies very tightly. The outfits were silvery and seemed to glisten in the moonlight. When I looked at their hands, I noticed they each had only three long fingers and an opposing thumb. I remember this fascinated me as I held out my own hand for comparison. Sensing my curiosity, the male reached out to take my hand in his. I was feeling such an intense love from them that it almost took my breath away.

As I took his hand, it felt very comfortable. I noticed the texture of his skin was rougher than mine, maybe even a little scaly, but warm, especially in the center of his palms. I was also curious about the way they smelled. They smelled sort of damp, the way Sissy and Puggy, Nonnie's two Pekinese dogs, smelled after they had a bath. They must have been reading my thoughts because I suddenly got a thought in my head that said that they were different, but also the same. I remember just saying, "Oh!" I was only six at the time so I accepted what they told me. I have always remembered how they felt and what they smelled like.

Still holding his hand, I said, "My name is Judy, and I am six years old. Who are you?" They never opened their mouths and no sound came from them, but immediately their names flashed in my mind, with a gentle voice. "We are John and Isa." I repeated it out loud in English and they both nodded yes.

I followed them out to the back ten-acre pasture where they had parked their spacecraft. It was that first night that I was taken aboard the craft and shown around. During that first trip inside, I saw a little boy who on a later visitation I learned was named Marty. Over the six years that the visitations occurred, Marty and I became good friends.

Each summer for six years, my extraterrestrial family visited me and took me aboard their spacecraft. Marty and I would play together in a special room on the craft, and John and Isa would teach us things. It was only when I was twelve years old that the visitations stopped for a while. It happened to coincide with my grandma's passing and my grandpa selling the farm. I would later learn that her passing was just a coincidence. Those visitations stopped because I was going through puberty, and they wanted me to live a more normal life of going to high school and college; and then getting married and having a career. I was to learn later, in 1984, when my contact resumed, that it had been planned that way.

Chapter 2

Reawakening to Contact

O Great Spirit you are One, Our House is One. We are One.
—Native American

I went through the seventh grade feeling very angry at everything. I was angry that Nonnie had died without saying good-bye and that Popops had sold the farm. That meant I would no longer have any encounters with John and Isa, and of course, Marty. I was very upset that I never got to say good-bye to Bob, the hobo that rode the trains and was my special friend. Also, I never got to say goodbye to Ed and Lucielle Foote, the owners of the little country store in Antelope.

Because I was so angry, I had a miserable year at school. I lost all of my friends because I was always picking fights, had terrible grades, and did not take care of myself physically. My parents wanted me to talk with someone, but I was stubborn and wouldn't until the school nurse took me under her wing and helped me. I probably owe her for getting me successfully through the seventh grade.

That summer my aunt and uncle, Gayle and Gene, asked me to stay at their new home in Walnut Creek, California. I was close to them so I was excited about going. Besides they had a swimming pool and I wanted to learn to swim. The day I arrived there, I discovered she had a beautiful wind chime hanging in the breezeway. The sound reminded me of being on my grandparents' farm and the wind chimes that my grandma used to have. I loved it when the breeze would pass through and activate them. They sounded like crystal wine glasses clinking into each other. That sound also reminded me of my encounters with my space family because they always seemed to be chiming when an encounter happened.

One night I awoke in the middle of the night and could hear the wind chimes clinking in the outside breezeway. I got up and quietly made my way to the outside door and went outside. I remember being drawn to look up at the stars, and I had a strange feeling that was so familiar. As I turned the corner to go out near the pool, I was startled by what I saw. There stood John and Isa, my extraterrestrial star family. I was so happy to see them and I felt such love coming from them. They explained to me that my grandma's dying really had nothing to do with them not coming any more. The timing was just a coincidence. They told me that I was maturing into a young woman and that I needed to live a normal life without any interruptions from them. They assured me that they would come back into my life when I was much older. They also explained that they were going to take my memory of them and put it into a special compartment in my brain, so that when they came back in the future, I would remember. I then asked them about Marty, and they assured me that Marty was going through exactly what I was going through.

They told me they had to go and for me to go back to bed, and that I was to work really hard at school because my education would prove to be very important in the future. As I was hugging Isa good bye, they must have performed some kind of amnesia on my brain, because all of a sudden, I was alone and looking at the stars trying to remember why I came out there.

The rest of my school years seemed to go by very quickly. I was successful in high school and was accepted to the University. I graduated with a Bachelor's degree in Psychology, with minors in German and Physical Science, and Special Education. My husband, Richard, and I met during my last quarter in college and we were married two days after I received my diploma.

I had decided to go back to school for one more year to earn my teaching credential. Upon receiving that I began teaching. While I was teaching, I entered San Francisco State University for my master's degree. As soon as I was awarded my degree, Richard and I moved to Southern California. I started teaching in a school district where I would spend the next 37 years teaching-first elementary and then high school. Life was good and we lived well, but I started dreaming about extraterrestrials and spaceships, and I became obsessed with finding out everything I could about it.

Suddenly my childhood dream of becoming an astronaut was at the forefront of my thoughts. It was the summer of 1984 when I would become part of the space program and also resume contact with my extraterrestrial family. Always drawn to the South Pacific, my husband and I spent two weeks on Bora Bora and Moorea in the Tahitian Islands. It was on the third day there, while we were watching the beautiful sunset that a face appeared to me in my third eye area. It was of the extraterrestrial beings I had encountered as a child.

As time went on and we were back home, I began having visitations in the middle of the night from various groups of extraterrestrials. These encounters are continuing even today. It was during this time also that I became involved with the Teacher-in-Space Program, and would work as a teacher for NASA and the Challenger Center for Space Science Education.

I earned my doctorate in Clinical Hypnotherapy in 1987 and opened a part time practice in 1988, specializing in working with people who had extraterrestrial encounters and came to me to find out more information about their encounters. In 2005, I earned a second doctorate while studying people who had extraterrestrial encounters and their spiritual development. In 1994, I began training with Steven Greer, M.D. the founder of CSETI, the Center for the Study of Extraterrestrial Intelligence. I had a dream in 1989 that said I was to train to be a liaison between extraterrestrials and earth humans when ETs were walking among us after first contact. I was to be an Ambassador. Over 20 years I trained off and on with Dr. Greer learning how to be an ambassador. I now have my own group of people that I take out to the desert to teach them the CSETI protocol of how to make peaceful contact, a CE-5, with these beautiful, benevolent, and enlightened beings.

My encounters continue but they are different now. Because we and our planet are moving into the fifth dimension, people who are Light Workers are being trained and told to go out in our communities and start teaching people how to raise their consciousness.

In a short time, wonderful things will start happening on Earth. First, however, we must achieve a cease fire throughout the entire world.

Part II

Close Encounters of the Military Kind

Chapter 3

When Things Do Not Go as Planned!

Equipped with his five senses, man explores the universe around him and calls the adventure science.
—Edwin Powell Hubble

The year 1994 was a big one for me. So many positive and exciting things were happening, and life was good. This was the first year that I had participated with Dr. Steven Greer of CSETI, The Center for the Study of Extraterrestrial Intelligence, in a week long training that took place in the southern California desert. I shared that remarkable encounter that occurred during the training in my first book, "Caught Between Two Worlds: A Journey Through Time." Additionally, the previous month in July, I had been invited to the White House on the twenty-fifth anniversary of the Apollo 11 moon landing. I was asked there as one of three teachers throughout the United States to represent teaching, and I had the pleasure of meeting Neil Armstrong, Buzz Aldrin, and Michael Collins, Shoemaker and Levy, the two astronomers whose comet was crashing into Jupiter at that time, and President Bill Clinton and First Lady Hillary Rodham Clinton, along with other astronauts and dignitaries. We participated in a press conference in the East Room of the White House. Also, in 1994, I was asked to speak at the hypnotherapy convention being held in Newport Beach, California later that year. My topic was to be about teaching other hypnotherapists how to work with people who come to them claiming they had experienced an alien abduction. My premise was that it did not matter whether the therapist believed in alien abductions or not, if a client came to them and asked for help, they needed to know how to work with them, or refer them to someone else. Needless to say, with all of the positive encounters with extraterrestrials I was having at the time, my trips into the southwestern states with my friend, Diana, doing research into the extraterrestrial phenomenon, my invitation to the White House, and then being asked to speak as an expert in working with clients who had claimed alien abductions, I was feeling on top of the world. Little did I know at that time that the dark side was about to rear its ugly head. All of us at one time or another have let our egos get out in front of us a little too far, and that is what was happening to me during this time. I was beginning to think that I could do anything because I was working from the Light and I did not have to worry about the Dark Side. I was soon to learn that it was an error in my thinking, and I was about to learn the lesson, "For as strong as you are in the Light, you are equally as strong on the dark side. You do not have to go to the dark side, but you must learn to respect that it is there. The Universe is balanced."

My talk at the hypnotherapy convention was to be for two hours on the topic of teaching other therapists how to work with alleged alien abductees. At that time, I had worked with several clients who had experienced extraterrestrial encounters, and the fact that I had my own encounters since the age of six and was still having contact, I felt very confident in what I was teaching. I asked my friend, Diana, if she would be willing to let me hypnotize her on stage because she had her own extraterrestrial experiences from a young age as well, and it was all positive for her. Phoning Diana, I started the conversation, "Hi. This is Judy. I have been asked to speak at the hypnotherapy convention in Newport Beach next month and I was wondering if you would let me hypnotize you on stage and take you back to one of your extraterrestrial encounters." Diana, sounding very excited responded, "Yes. I would love to do that. Who will be in the audience?" I continued, "Just other hypnotherapists, so it will be a professional setting and is really nothing to worry about." "Are you going to talk about the government and the military programs during your talk," Diana queried? My response to that question was quick. "No, I am not going to let myself be sucked into that negative stuff because I will lose what I am trying to accomplish there, which is to teach other therapists how to work with abductees." Diana continued, "Yea, but you know that someone in the audience is going to ask you the question. What are you going to do?" I answered her by saying, "Even though I would love to answer that question, I will not because I think it takes away from my credibility as a therapist in this field. I am not there to expose the military industrial complex, and I will tell them that. If they want information on that, they can look on the internet and find sites dedicated to answering those questions." "Okay," Diana responded. "Why don't we get together sometime next week and I will go over my talk with you so you know what I am going to say. Then I can hypnotize you so you know what to expect. Does that work for you," I asked? Saying yes, we set up the next Wednesday to get together for lunch.

When I arrived at Diana's house the next week, we went out to lunch at one of our favorite Mexican Restaurants. At lunch we did not talk about the upcoming convention, but instead, talked about our last trip to Roswell, New Mexico, when we had visited the first crash site and had that amazing encounter with extraterrestrials there. After lunch, we headed back to Diana's house. "I'm really glad you want to do this with me," I commented as we settled into the living room. "I decided that since you are going to do this for me, I will pay your way into the convention and you will stay with me for free," I added as we began our conversation. Diana said, "Thank you because I am really tight for funds right now, getting the boys ready to start school for the year and all." "Cool," I continued. I gave her a copy of the outline of my talk and where I was going to do the hypnosis demonstration in the program. After that, I did a hypnosis session with her just as what I would do during the presentation. It worked really well, and then we were ready. The convention occurred two weeks after that.

We arrived on Friday morning to get into our room and register. I also wanted to know when I was going to speak and where it would be, so that I would not be rushed at the last minute. I found out that

I would be speaking the next evening, Saturday, around five PM. I thought that was an interesting time because by five, most people are tired from attending classes and talks all day, and usually want to go back to their rooms to rest before dinner. I decided that I would turn it over to God and know that whomever showed up would be the ones that were supposed to hear it.

The room I was speaking in was empty an hour before I was supposed to speak, so I was able to go in and set up ahead of time. Getting ready, I made sure that I dressed very professionally, because I had a feeling that I would have a large audience. Diana and I were in the room about thirty minutes before the start time. I was able to arrange the furniture the way I wanted it, and made sure that there was water and glasses at the table placed there by the hotel for the patrons.

Five minutes before we were to start, I turned on some very soothing background music in the hope of luring some in that might not have planned to hear my talk. At five o'clock, someone from the convention staff was there to introduce me to the group. As I made my introduction to the group, I quickly scanned my audience to get a feel for who was there. I was pleased that there were approximately twenty-five or so people in the audience as we got started, and about five or six more would join the group as time went on. Considering that it was the end of a busy conference day, I was pleased that so many people had decided to be there. Just as I was introducing my friend, Diana, who was now up on the stage with me, two men walked in from the back door of the room. Upon seeing them, I started to smile because it was clear by the way they were dressed, they did not belong there. Most conference attendees were dressed casually for the most part, except for the speakers who were usually dressed up a little. But even the male speakers were comfortable and not in suits. I was slightly amused when they entered because it was clear to me that they were from the government. It was obvious to anyone in the audience that they were there to intimidate. I was thinking to myself, *"How quaint. Men in black in my audience."* After watching them take their seats on opposite sides of the room, I turned my attention back to Diana who was now sitting comfortably in the chair I had provided for her, and was ready to be hypnotized.

Before I started, I explained to the audience what I was going to do. I explained that it is important not to lead the client in any way through the questions or the way things are stated to the client. I told them that I was going to use a relaxation induction to get Diana into hypnosis. I stated my reason for doing that was to get her relaxed because often a client is fearful about the process if it was the first time. With that I began the induction. I took about eight to ten minutes to get her to the alpha state that I wanted. I did a couple of convincers for the audience, such as lifting up her arm at the wrist, so that they could see that Diana was really under hypnosis. A hypnotized person's arm would just drop down when I released it. A person not yet under hypnosis, would resist you when you were lifting and also when you let go of the arm. Diana was definitely under.

The hypnosis part took about thirty minutes, and then I brought her back up, making sure I brought her out loudly so that anyone in the audience who may have been hypnotized along with Diana, would come out of it also. It happens sometimes. As Diana was reorienting herself back to full consciousness, I opened to the audience for any questions they may have regarding the hypnosis itself. One therapist, sitting in the front row, asked a question regarding my induction technique, which I comfortably answered. The next hand to go up was one of the "men in black." I know I had a supercilious grin on my face because I still could not believe that they would be in my audience. *Why,* I pondered. *All I am doing is teaching other hypnotherapists how to work with alleged abductees.* Trying to be charming, but still blatantly obvious, he asked me a question about the government and their involvement with so called alien abductions. Remaining professional, I said, "My agenda for today is to teach other hypnotherapists about how to work with people who have had extraterrestrial encounters. If you want to know about government programs, you can find out a lot of information about that on the internet." My response actually made him laugh. I immediately turned my attention to the next question by another therapist. As I was preparing to wrap up the question and answer portion, the government person asked me one last question regarding the military industrial complex. Again, I responded, "I am not here to talk about that today."

I then pulled my attention away from him and directed it toward the audience. I thanked everyone for coming and people began to leave.

Usually after a presentation, there are always a few who hang around to ask a question or two they did not feel comfortable asking in front of the audience. This time, however, the only two people hanging around were the two agents. Being the smart aleck that I was at that time, believing that the dark side was not going to bother me, I said to the one who asked the questions, "Well, was I a good girl? Did I do what I am supposed to do?" I had the look on my face to go with the comment. The one asking the questions, whom I will call James, which is not his real name, kind of chuckled at my attitude, but then he got serious. The other agent, whom I will call Jack, was not amused at all. He was trying to impress me of the seriousness of them being there, and I just was not buying it at the time. I then said, "Okay, who are you guys? I know you are not hypnotherapists, so why would you even be interested in a topic like this?"

That seemed to be their cue because they both pulled out their badge wallets and showed both me and Diana their NSA (National Security Agency) credentials. I was actually dumbfounded now at seeing them standing there. I then said, "So what do you want?" Jack then pulled Diana away and was speaking with her in the far side of the room, while James stayed with me and started to talk to me. He told me they were watching me to make sure I did not say anything against the military industrial complex, and if I did, it could mean a lot of trouble for me. "Fine!" I responded. "You heard what I said today, and that is typically what I say, so if you did not find anything wrong today, then I am assuming you won't in the future." By now, James started to soften a little bit. As I looked over to where Diana was, I noticed that Jack's body language was much more relaxed too. Diana is beautiful and mesmerizing, so I am not surprised that she led to that softening on his part. After about twenty minutes, both of the interrogations ended.

When we got back to our room to rest a little before the evening's activities, we shared with each other what was said by these spies. Diana said that Jack told her that I know something that I don't realize I know. This information is tucked away somewhere, and if I ever start getting close to what it is, they will come looking for me. I sat there wracking my brain to try and figure out what they were talking about. I couldn't come up with it, but I promised myself that I would pay closer attention to the high strangeness in my life and what it attracted.

The next morning, Diana and I were walking through the hall to go down to breakfast. We were talking about the two NSA agents and wondering what they were doing. Immediately, rounding the corner on the other hallway, were these two men. They were coming right toward us as though they had heard everything that we said. It was a little unnerving, but we did not change our behavior and warmly greeted these two agents and went on to breakfast. All the rest of the weekend, wherever we were, they were. Knowing what I know now, one of them probably placed a bug in one of our bags so that they could eavesdrop on our conversations while we were alone. Both Diana and I being relatively innocent about stuff like that, talked a lot about what we thought these guys wanted and why. Actually, I remember being a little surprised that it was the NSA who was watching me. I would have assumed it would have been the CIA (Central Intelligence Agency) or even the FBI (Federal Bureau of Investigation). I guess whatever it is that they thought I knew would be a national security risk, hence the NSA.

The weekend finished successfully and I received some invitations to speak at future events in other places. As we were loading our car to leave the hotel, the two agents suddenly appeared. I said, "Don't you guys ever take a rest?" They commented that they just came to say good bye and that I should be careful what I say. I was to stick to their protocol and I would be fine. Without responding to that remark, I said, "Yea, see you next year!" James laughed and Jack just gave me the "stink eye," that "G-man" stare which said, "Watch yourself. I have my eye on you."

The next year I was asked to speak again and, of course, I accepted. When I arrived at the hotel, I sought James out. I was feeling much less intimated and stronger in my position since being there the year before. I found him wandering around the concession tables that were set up in one of the rooms. He did not see me at first, so I stood by the door out of the way and watched him. This year he was not dressed in his black government suit, and I did not see Jack anywhere. James looked and acted more like a hypnotherapist, hiding the fact of what he really did. As I watched him, he did not impress me as someone the NSA would hire. He was short, about five feet five, normal weight, and was probably at least ten years older than I. He looked more like someone's favorite uncle than a government agent. I also observed that he looked really tired; the kind of tired a person feels when he has been up solidly for over twenty-four hours and his job is wearing him down. After about five minutes, I decided to walk over to him and talk with him. I decided to be on the offense a little this year, and I said to him, "Hi James!' You look like crap. What has happened to you?" My question took him aback, but somehow did not surprise him because he responded in a way that told me he thought what I had said was true. "I have to be careful," he said. "I want to do hypnosis therapy and get away from my other job." I gave him a disbelieving look and said, "It is my understanding that you are never out of the NSA or any of the other like organizations. You are always one of them." James did not say a word, but just smiled an almost shy smile and looked away. I suddenly felt bad about the way I had treated him, realizing there was a human being in there and it did not matter whom he worked for. I decided not to let my guard down, but to treat him with more respect. When I spoke that weekend, he was in my workshop, but only as an observer because he wanted to be there. Later, when I ran into him again in the concession room, he asked if I wanted to go get a cup of coffee. I agreed, and we went into the coffee shop at the hotel.

Making conversation, I decided to ask him some questions about his job, not to make him uncomfortable, but to let him get things off his chest if he wanted to. "You said earlier today that you wanted to do hypnotherapy. Have you been studying," I asked? "Yes," he answered. I have taken some classes and I like it." "How does the NSA feel about that," I queried? Fidgeting a little now, James responded, "They are a little worried because they think I am getting soft and I'm sharing things with people that I should not be sharing. So, I have to be careful." "Well, I am glad to see that you are doing things in a more spiritual way now," I continued. "I am too," he stated, "but they are not happy with me."

While we were talking, I began to ask him specific questions about things to see if he would answer me in an honest way. I had touched the surface of what I was going to ask by looking into it somewhat, so I figured I would know if he was lying to me or not. I began, "Are you familiar with the HAARP Project?" HAARP is an acronym for The High Frequency Active Auroral Research Program. He reminded me of an elf when he smiled, and he clapped his hands together in a way that reminded me of an elf just getting ready to open up the pot of gold. Maybe it was his behavior that relaxed me, but I did calm myself. James began telling me a story. "I used to work on that project. I was assigned to a site in Washington State. Our facility had a number of rooms side by side like you might find in a school. We had invited four participants to come to the site to discuss some plans that they were working on. I, and three of my colleagues, made sure we were in the room adjacent to where our four guests were. We had the HAARP equipment with us, and we decided how our guests' day was going to proceed. We had hidden cameras in their room so that we could watch what was happening. They did not realize that we were monitoring their behavior. They simply thought they were using the facility to do their work. Our group decided that for the first hour they were together, we wanted it to go well for them-everyone agreeing with each other about everything. To accomplish this, we based our work on the findings of Andrija Puharich from the 1960's. Through observation and experimentation, he learned that the brain of a healer, for example, functioned at 8 Hz when they were healing someone. The Earth's pulse rate is 7.8 Hz, and when a person was bathed in that frequency, it made him feel good. They also knew that 10.80 Hz causes a person to riot and behave in riotous ways. Lowering the frequency rate to 6.6 Hz causes depression. We used the equipment and raised and lowered the frequency and vibration in their room to create whatever behavior we wanted. We set the frequency and vibration at 7.83 Hz if we wanted everyone to be nice. After lunch, we raised the frequency and vibration in their room to 10.80 Hz, and everyone started yelling at each other, and agreed on nothing. The longer we kept the controls set at a higher frequency; the group became angrier and more aggressive. Finally, after about an hour, we decided to lower the frequency and vibration back down to 7.83 Hz, and the behavior changed drastically.

The entire group calmed down and started to respond to each other in a civilized manner. They never knew what we had done. It did make us realize something very important, however. We had a tool that we could use to control the masses." "That is unbelievable," I commented. "Yes, I know," he said. James went on. "Do you remember the Los Angeles riots in 1992 when Rodney King was given all that money?" "Yes," I said. "We have microwave towers set up throughout the entire Los Angeles area. We decided to test it out on the city to see if we could control the masses. We upped the frequency and vibration to 10.80 Hz, the point that people became very agitated and started to react in a negative way. The higher we went, the more aggressive the crowd got. They began to feed off of each other. The people did not realize what had hit them." "That is just wrong!" I said. "You could have also tested it by making the frequency such that they would be all lovey-dovey," I continued. "Sure," James answered. "But we don't want people to be all lovey-dovey. We are more able to control the masses if everyone is angry. Controlling the population is what the cabal government wants. It worked," he said.

I thought about what he had just told me, and realized that if people did not find out about these programs, it could be very bad for the masses. The cabal is very smart in the way it does things. For example, if you were to go on the HAARP website, you would see its cover story about being able to manipulate the weather to create rain where there is drought, and to stop the rain where there is flooding. It all sounds like it is on the up and up. However, what most people did not realize at the time was that they could also manipulate the weather to cause destruction-earthquakes, floods, tsunamis, and the like. After letting what James told me sink in, I finally spoke. "James. Wouldn't the NSA be upset at you for what you just told me?" Looking a little nervous, he said, "Yea, but they won't know." I responded, "I don't know James. I would not trust them if I were you." We changed the subject and after about another fifteen minutes, we said our good byes for the day. Later that evening, as I was getting ready for bed, I pondered what I had learned that day, and it really bothered me. I promised myself that I would do some research on the HAARP project when I got home and had the time to do it.

The next year, I again sought James out, and when I saw him, I was really shocked at how he looked. He looked so tired; he had deep bags under his eyes that said, "I have not slept in days!" His hair was a little unkempt and his suit was wrinkled. He looked anything but professional. Suddenly, I felt sorry for him. I wondered what he had been through to look the way he did. I decided that I was going to be kind and understanding when I spoke with him. When I walked up to him, he was glad to see me. He handed me one of his new business cards that said he was a hypnotherapist. I smiled and thanked him. I finally said, "Wow, James. You look totally exhausted. Are you all right?" Acting nervous he said, "No. They tried to take me out." Startled at first by his comment, I responded, "Do you mean the NSA tried to kill you?" "Yes, but they were not successful," he answered. I commented, "Oh my God, James! How awful and how frightening." Nodding his head, he continued. "It has been difficult, but I figured out how to get back into their good graces, and I know it will be fine." The second he made that comment my radar became active. I immediately thought that I better be very careful what I talk with him about because he might be ready to use it against me. James was clearly in turmoil. He really wanted out of the NSA, I believe, but they were not letting him go. He really wanted to be a hypnotherapist and a teacher where he could do good, instead of working for the dark side. For the rest of our time together, I kept the focus on the things we had discussed in the past and did not delve into anything new. We left on Sunday and both went our separate ways.

The next year, I was actually looking forward to seeing him, but I could not find him anywhere. I decided to ask my friend who was working at the registration table if James was registered this year. She said that he was not. I talked with people who I knew had worked with James as a hypnotherapist, and no one knew where he was. I decided to call the number on his card to see if he would answer. He did not.

Now I became worried about him. I was hoping that his belief that the NSA was trying to get rid of him was not true. He was so concerned that his life was in danger, and maybe they did succeed on taking him out. I hope not, but I never saw him again, although I still think of him from time to time and wonder.

Chapter 4

An Unfortunate Doctoral Dissertation Topic Selection

Too Close to the Truth

Ye shall know the truth, and the truth shall make you mad.
—Aldous Huxley

When I had enrolled in the doctorate program at St. John's University, I struggled with trying to find a topic for research that made sense for studying the extraterrestrial phenomenon. What I discovered pretty quickly was that I had not had enough encounters myself and there was not a lot of information out there about what I was contemplating doing, so I sat on that part of my program for about five years.

It was actually during the O. J. Simpson trial that I came up with the idea. I became very excited about it and set out to see if I would have enough contacts to assist me. What I wanted to study was whether people who had extraterrestrial experiences were somehow different in a genetic way from people who had never had these experiences. I really never understood why some people were taken and others were not. I knew I needed to find a lab big enough to do DNA tests on my subjects, and would be willing to do it. I agreed to pay for those individual tests myself. I decided that I would go out of state to find a large forensics lab that would allow me to do a study such as this. I found a technician who was delighted to do the testing for me, but did not want the publicity. I promised to keep it under wraps.

I was speaking somewhere and I made the comment that I had chosen my doctoral dissertation topic. I told them that I was curious to see if people who experienced extraterrestrial encounters had a genetic marker of some sort that non-experiencers did not have. I mentioned that I even had a forensics lab that would run the tests for me. Knowing that the NSA has spies all over, I should have known better. They found out and were not happy that I had chosen to study that. They tried to discourage it through my advisor at the university, but that did not work. The more they tried to discourage me, the more insistent I was that I was going to do it. I also began to believe that there must be something to what I was thinking or they would not be so anxious for me to stop. I continued with the study and had lined up several subjects already who wanted to participate in it.

About that time, I started having strange things happen to me. I knew my phone was tapped because they made it very clear when they tapped in to my conversations. They wanted me to know they were listening. They were also following me and watching me when they thought I was not paying attention. One day, I got home from school at around 4:30 (I was still teaching at the time), and I was outside watering my plants in the front yard. I lived on the corner of a busy street, where the back of my house was up against the busy street, the side of my house was on a transition street, and my street was the first right turn as you come off of the transition street. As I was watering my plants, a dark SUV turned on my street and upon seeing me, quickly hung a U-turn and went back the way he came. I thought it was strange, but often people turn into our subdivision by accident, and the logical place to turn around is where my street intersected the transition street. It seemed odd enough, however, that I told my husband, Richard, when I went into the house. The next day, I was watering again in the same spot and the same thing happened again. This time I tried to get a good look at the driver, but all I noticed was that he was dressed all in black and was wearing a black hat. Right then I decided that if he came again, I would be ready for him and I was going to go after him. I was angry that I was being bothered like that, and I should have known never to react in anger because it could be a lot worse. That night when I was talking with a family member on the phone, a man's deep voice cut into the conversation and said, "Drop it! You do not need to know the information you are seeking." Then the line went quiet, and the person I was speaking with asked me what that was about. I played dumb and said that I did not know. It was probably some prankster messing around.

I began thinking about my topic and wondered why the government wanted me to change my topic. I was getting a little nervous about it because if they had wanted to, they could have easily run me off the road, discredited me in some way, or gone after a family member. I thought about the man's voice that said I did not need to know. Maybe I did not need to know, I began thinking.

The next day I was again watering my plants in the front of the house when the black SUV came around the corner. This time I was ready. I dropped the hose and jumped into my Jeep, and drove to catch up with him. He was speeding down the hill at a rapid rate, so I followed that way too. When we came up to the corner, he had to stop in order to turn right onto a busy six lane street. Because he had to stop, I caught up to him. Just then the light changed green, and he took off. I followed quickly also and caught up to him at a red light. I pulled up into the lane right next to the driver's side of the SUV. He looked very unusual. He was wearing all black with a black hat, and his face was very white. He had small features that reminded me of extraterrestrials I had seen. I could not see his eyes because he wore dark glasses. He would not look at me, so I started telepathically talking to him, telling him that I was on to him and he better back off. I telepathically received a message back that said, "You back off. Drop the study or there will be consequences." The light changed green and he took off. I decided not to follow and turned around and went home. I told my husband what I had done, and he commented that it probably had not been one of my better choices. "For one thing," he said, "they know that you are on to them, so they will find a different was to harass you." I knew he was right because you should never act from a place of anger because you are not thinking clearly.

As time went on, I never had that incident happen again, but my husband, Richard, was correct when he said they would now find other ways to try and convince me to drop the topic. About a month had passed since the chase incident, and I was settling into my research and all of the other things I was doing at the time. In August, in the late 1990s, I went to the monthly MUFON meeting (Mutual UFO Network) in Costa Mesa, California. My friend Jane was there and we were talking before the meeting about everything we had been doing for the month. I spoke about my dissertation topic and how the "government" did not want me to do it. I also shared with her the incident with the SUV and the chase. She admonished me to be careful, and I told her that I was. After the meeting, we said our goodbyes in the parking lot.

I was driving a turbo charged Thunderbird, with a six-speed manual transmission at the time, which was a pretty fast car. I got in my vehicle around 11 pm after the meeting to head for home. I had two blocks to drive until I hit the Fifty-Five freeway to start my journey. Once I got onto the freeway, I brought the car up to speed and put it on cruise control, turned on the music, and settled in for a drive that should have taken about twenty-five minutes at that time of night.

Just as I was coming upon the intersection where the 405 freeway crosses the 55, I looked in my rear-view mirror and noticed a car that appeared to be following me. So, I changed lanes as though I was going to get off on the 405, and they did also. Then I gently eased down on the gas and increased my speed about 10 miles per hour. They did also. I now could feel the adrenaline start to pump in my body, and I went into survival mode. It always seems that when you want to find a highway patrol officer, you cannot. I shifted down into a lower gear and stepped on the gas. Very quickly I was up to 90 miles per hour. They were a little back, but catching up very quickly. So, I made the decision to utilize the turbo charged engine, and I kicked it up to 120 miles per hour. Thank

God the freeway was empty at that hour. When I did that, I think I took them by surprise, and they were a little slower in catching up. As I approached a street that I knew fairly well, I shot off the freeway and quickly moved into a neighborhood. I came to an apartment building and turned into their parking area, and took a chance on an empty space hoping that the owners would not be returning before I left. I turned off the lights and waited. I got out of the car and stayed low to the back of the parking stalls and made my way to the street so that I could see any approaching vehicles. I stayed down and well hidden by the block wall at the entrance of the parking area.

About five minutes later, they slowly drove by looking for me. The driver peered into the parking area of the apartment building, but nothing caught his eye and he kept driving. I still waited because I did not trust that they would not come back. They knew I lived in Fullerton and that I would want to get home, so they were driving around the area really checking it out. I went back to my car and sat there in the dark and waited. I could not call Richard, my husband, because I did not own a cell phone at that time. I'm not even sure if there were cell phones at that time. I was hoping that Richard would think I had gone out with friends after the meeting. I did not want to worry him. I waited there for two hours, and at 1 am, I made the decision to leave and take my chances. I knew that Richard would really start to worry and if he called my friend, Jane, she would tell him that I left MUFON at 11 pm and should have been home long ago. I very slowly drove out onto the street and made my way back to the freeway onramp. My heart was beating so loudly that it was the only thing I could hear. I did not turn on the radio because I thought it might distract me and I needed to be alert. I knew at any moment they could appear and take up the chase again. Fortunately, they gave up and I was able to get safely home.

Richard was at the door when I pulled in. He had been very worried and was glad I was safely home. He expressed that maybe I should reconsider my dissertation topic because these guys were not going to quit until they either injured me badly or killed me, and I had to think about what I really wanted.

I really began thinking about what was happening, and I decided that I better give in on this topic. I vowed to not give up on my research in general, just on this topic. The only person I told was my husband, but somehow, they found out that I had changed my mind about my dissertation topic. They probably had the house bugged as well. It took me another five years to come up with another topic, but I did a successful study comparing extraterrestrial encounters and spiritual development. About three years after I decided to drop what I was doing, a government DNA study appeared that did nearly the same thing that I had wanted to do. I do not know if they stole my idea or whether they were already in the process of doing it. What I do know about that topic is that many of our ancestors were genetically engineered with extraterrestrial DNA which the cabal military did not want people to know.

My point of sharing these last few things with you is to alert others who are delving into some things that are still highly classified. These individuals are not playing games. They have been given instructions to use whatever means they deem necessary to get someone to stop, and in some cases, I believe that deadly force has been authorized. I have learned that you can "walk close to the line" and learn an awful lot of information and have amazing experiences without being bothered too much. However, if you cross that line, you are putting yourself in danger. Don't quit, just be careful. I think of an old Bedouin saying that I heard when I was traveling in the Middle East not too long ago. The saying says to *always trust in God, but to tie up your camel.* That really is good advice. In other words, trust in God, but do reasonable things to protect yourself.

Part III

Close Encounters of the Fourth and Fifth Kind

Chapter 5

Practicing the CE 5 Protocol

To understand the nature of God, it is necessary only to know the nature of love itself. To truly know love is to know and understand God; and to know God is to understand love.
—Dr. David R. Hawkins[3]

In 1994 I participated in my first week long training with Steven Greer, M.D. the founder of CSETI, The Center for the Study of Extraterrestrial Intelligence. I shared this training and the wonderful events of that week in my book, "Caught Between Two Worlds: A Journey Through Time." I mention it here because it is what occurred after the training when I had returned home, that is significant.

It was December and the neighborhood was flashing beautiful colors of red, green, blue, and white, as people were enjoying the spirit of the holidays. One could not help feeling happy and thankful for what we had. During the training, Dr. Greer pointed out that we should not try calling in these benevolent beings when we were home because this contact is very serious and not a game. That was one of his first trainings, and he has since encouraged his trainees to make contact at home and practice the protocol. Just know clearly why you are doing it. If it is just to see if you can see a UFO, then you are doing it for all the wrong reasons. The reason is to make honest and open friendly contact with highly intelligent and sentient beings from other places-galaxies, planets, dimensions. At that time though, I was hesitant to attempt the protocol myself because I thought I was not supposed to; that I would be bothering them. I also knew it was dangerous for them because the military would chase them and try to shoot them down if they made any blip on the military's radar.

This particular day, our friend Cyndi had stopped by when she was in town visiting her mother who lived about thirty miles from us.. Cyndi lives in Santa Barbara, which is about 150 miles north of Fullerton on the coast of the Pacific Ocean. As our visit together moved into the night hours, we invited Cyndi to stay the night and leave in the morning to go home. She agreed.

Our living room had two huge bay windows that faced into our courtyard. This is a courtyard that I had created myself from a vision I had. When I created it, I had a desire to teach meditation and other classes there. I asked Richard, my husband, if he would let me do it all myself because I believed that I was supposed to. He agreed with one stipulation, which was that I would allow him to carry the really heavy stuff so as not to hurt my body. I agreed. This courtyard was created to be a very beautiful, peaceful place-where one would feel the incredible calming energy the moment one walked through the front gates. There was an abundance of fairies that lived there too. I have physically seen one of them not too long ago, but that is another story. I did have a professional contractor build a beautiful waterfall in the center of this courtyard over to one side, so the sound of the water falling over the rocks was very mesmerizing.

The energy was incredible this night and the sky was crystal clear. Richard and Cyndi were in the living room watching television, and I could not shake the desire to practice the CSETI protocol, so I finally gave in to it. As we were sitting there watching television, I began a conversation. "You know," I began, "This night is so beautiful and I am not really into this program so I am going to go out in the courtyard and practice the CSETI protocol." Cyndi commented, "I would join you out there except it is so cold." "I know," I agreed, "but I am going to wear my ski jacket and cover my legs with my open sleeping bag." Both of them nodded in agreement, and I gathered up my gear-CD of Dr.

Greer going through the protocol, my equipment, appropriate clothing, my chair, and binoculars-and went outside.

As I settled into my chair, I was grateful that I had my ski gloves on my hands. Under the open sleeping bag, I felt warm and toasty. Before hitting the start button on the CD player, I looked around the night sky to see what was up this night. Because of the ambient light that is there, the sky was not as dark as if I were out in the desert, but I could make out the large constellations. Orion was now up in the southeastern sky and was very clear. It was almost eerie it was so quiet. The only sound I could hear was the water falling over the rocks in the waterfall, and that was always so peaceful. I flipped the play button on the CD player, and followed Dr. Greer's voice as he led me into the meditation and connecting with the star voyagers and their spacecraft. The protocol lasted for about 45 minutes, and after it stopped, I remained in a quiet meditative state for almost another hour. I scanned the sky and the area, but did not see or hear anything. Knowing what I know today, almost 25 years later, I am sure they were there but just beyond the crossing point of light. I did not have the skills then to perceive them as I do today.

After about three hours, I decided that I would go inside and go to bed. I knew that I had done everything correctly, but felt that the extraterrestrials were busy or it was not safe for them to come into my space. It was getting really cold now and the temperature this night was predicted to go down to 38^0 F, or 5^0 C. So, reluctantly, I went inside.

Cyndi and Richard were now watching another movie. As I came in, Richard commented. "Aren't you just freezing," he asked? Shivering I answered, "Yes, and I am going to get ready for bed." "I am going to finish this movie, if you don't mind," he responded. I told them I did not mind and I got ready for bed. Cyndi was lying on our leather couch which was against the opposite wall from the bay windows. This couch is so soft that it feels like you are floating on a cloud when lying down on it. This gave her a clear view of the courtyard. Richard was in his reclining chair on the opposite side of the room. There was one light on by Richard, and other than that light, the room was dark save for the light beaming from the television set.

After I put my pajamas on, I went back into the living room and said my goodnights. Richard said, "I love you and I will be in after this movie is over." "That is fine," I answered, "and I love you too. Just don't stay up all night." "I won't," he replied. Cyndi, comfortably on the couch, was now in and out of sleep as the softness of the leather pulled her more and more into the dream world.

I went to bed and was soundly asleep by the time Richard came to bed. Being tired, he fell off to sleep almost immediately. Around three o'clock, I was awakened by loud music coming from the front of the house. The music sounded very Asian, like meditation music. I thought it might be Cyndi playing a CD to put her to sleep. Cyndi is Chinese, so it made sense to me that she might play this kind of music. It was nice, but very loud. Our bedroom door was also ajar by about one foot, and I could clearly see a pink glow that was flashing to the beat of the music. I got up out of bed and groggily walked to our bedroom door. I suddenly stopped, unable to move through the door. Nothing physical was preventing my movement, but I just stood there. I started to send telepathic messages to Cyndi to turn the music down or off. Instead of going out into the living room to check on it myself, I went back to bed. There was a part of me that really wanted to go out there, but there was another part that held me back.

As I crawled back into bed, the music started playing even louder and the flashing pink light became more intense. The harder I tried to shut it out, the louder it became. Once again, I walked over to the bedroom door. I caught a glimpse of my husband from the corner of my eye, and he was fast asleep totally unaware of what was going on. As I began to open the bedroom door to go out into the living room, it was as though an unseen force was keeping me from doing it. I was involved in a push-pull tug-of-war to see if I was going to go. Finally, I decided to block it out and go back to bed.

Once in bed for the third time, I tried even more to shut out the sounds, but they became even louder yet. Finally, the music and the pink light show stopped as suddenly as they began. Now I was wide awake and was arguing with myself. *I know I should go out there, but it has stopped now anyway, so it is pointless to pursue it,* I thought to myself as I lay there wondering what to do. I must have fallen to sleep again very quickly because before I knew it, I was waking up to the sunshine coming into the bedroom.

After brushing my teeth and taking a quick shower, I got dressed and went out into the living room still thinking about the music and the pink light that was happening all around me the night before. I walked into the room just in time to see Cyndi waking up and stretching. Before I could say anything to her, she said, "What did you do last night? Why didn't you come out here?" "Why," I commented? "They came," she blurted out. "They were here in the courtyard and it was beautiful. I went over to the window and telepathically told them that I would come out, but they did not want me. They distinctly wanted you. They told me to go back to sleep. All of a sudden, I felt really tired and must have fallen back to sleep. I could feel and hear the vibrations coming from them by what they were doing, but you were nowhere to be seen. Isn't that what you wanted, she inquired?" "Oh, my goodness," I responded, now feeling a lump in my stomach. "I knew I was supposed to go out, but I just could not bring myself to do it. I don't think I was scared, but I must have been or I would have come out." At that point I felt so sad because I believed that I had blown an amazing opportunity. I found myself going back into the bedroom and putting myself into a meditative state again so as to apologize to them for what I perceived as my rudeness. I almost begged them to come back and try again, that I would be ready the next time. As it turned out, it would be almost four years and several more weekly trainings before I perceived any visitations from my CE-5's. They knew something about me that I was now only becoming aware of. I just was not ready to have that kind of encounter by myself at that time. They knew it and respected my boundaries. I know it worked out for the best because had I gone out and not been ready to meet them face to face, it may have thrown my training back a few years. Just knowing that I could do the protocol on my own and it worked was very exciting to me. I really began to realize that anyone with the proper training and positive attitude, and an understanding of why they were doing something such as trying to make contact, could do it.

Chapter 6

Encounter in the Bedroom

One, remember to look up at the stars and not down at your feet. Two never give up work. Work gives you meaning and purpose and life is empty without it. Three, if you are lucky enough to find love, remember it is there and don't throw it away.
—Stephen Hawking

I wish to share with you one more incident of contact before going into what I have learned from these amazing, intelligent and sentient beings. I don't know if it is coincidence or some synchronistic happening, but our friend, Cyndi, was visiting us again. Perhaps Cyndi draws their energies to her because she has had contact for many years herself. Again, Cyndi was spending the weekend here, and so she slept on the leather couch in the living room facing the courtyard once again.

This particular night, we had been watching the regular night's programming on television, and I started feeling very groggy. It was as if someone had given me a powerful sleeping pill because I felt as though I could fall asleep standing. Richard was sitting in his recliner and Cyndi was on the couch. We had already made up the couch for Cyndi to sleep on, so she was ready. I stood up and said, "I'm sorry you guys, but I cannot keep my eyes open and I am going to have to go to bed." Looking at Richard I said, "Go ahead and watch some more if you feel like it, but do not stay up all night." He said that he would not. I gave him a kiss and told him that I loved him, and I trotted off to bed.

It must have been around one o'clock when Richard started making his way down the hall to come to bed. Cyndi was already in and out of sleep, so she was barely aware that he was leaving the room. As he was walking down the hall, he suddenly stopped. Coming from our bedroom Richard said he could hear me talking to someone, and he could see that the entire room was bathed in a soft pink. Not believing what he was observing, he turned around and went back into the living room to get Cyndi.

"Cyndi," Richard said, as he gently shook her awake. "I need you to come down the hall and see this," he commented. Feeling out of it, she could hardly bring herself to get up, but she did. Walking down the hallway going towards the master bedroom, they both stopped just before they reached the door. The door was open about half way, and if they scooted up just a little closer to the door against the wall, they could peer in and see what was going on. As they did that, they both had a clear view of what was taking place.

I was standing at the foot of the bed and I was speaking to someone who was standing with me. Cyndi and Richard both reported to me that they could not clearly see anyone there but me, except for a shimmering outline of a figure near me. Both assumed it was probably an extraterrestrial that I was talking to. Additionally, the entire room was bathed in pink, just like before when the extraterrestrials came into our courtyard and tried to get my attention. Although the main color for the heart chakra is green, pink is also used when healing the heart chakra. It seems to provide more softness, love and affection when working with the heart chakra. Maybe it represents unconditional love because that is what I feel when I am around them. I'm guessing this Being was working with me through my heart chakra which might explain the pink color.

Cyndi reported to me in the morning that they stood there by the door and watched me for about twenty minutes, at which time they went back out into the living room. They were both really tired and did not want to disturb me, so Richard fell asleep in his chair and Cyndi on the couch bed I had made up for her. When I came out into the living room in the morning, they were just waking up. I commented to Richard, "Why didn't you come to bed last night?" Wiping the cobwebs out of his eyes he responded, "We did not want to disturb you while you were talking to the extraterrestrial in the room with you, so we came back out here." Looking at him in a perplexed manner I said, "What extraterrestrial being? I do not remember talking with anyone last night. What did you see?"

Cyndi jumped in first, "Richard was going to bed and saw a pink color in the bedroom and could hear you talking with someone. He came back out here to get me to come back with him, which I did." She continued, "The door was half open so we quietly moved to just behind the door where we could see into the room. You were standing at the foot of the bed and you were talking with someone who was standing there with you but facing you. We could not see him clearly, but only a shimmering around where he was standing, so we figured he was not all the way into this dimension and that is why we could not see him completely. You were having no trouble communicating with him however. During the time we were observing you, we knew that you were participating fully in your conversation. Sometimes you would smile and laugh at what was being said, and other times you had a very serious look on your face, like you wanted to make sure that you did not forget anything that was being said. When you spoke, you spoke English, and once in a while, we could hear a male voice speaking English. We both decided later when we had walked back into the living room that he was mostly speaking telepathically to you."

As Cyndi was telling me what she saw, I was wracking my brain to try and remember doing that. Finally, I spoke. "I don't remember any of that," I shared. "But I did have an unusual dream where I was on another planet and I was working with a very tall extraterrestrial being. In my dream he looked human, so I am assuming that he was Pleiadian. He was teaching me something, but I do not remember what it was. It is very frustrating." Richard spoke now and said, "Well maybe you are not supposed to remember yet. I bet when the time is right, you will remember everything." "Yea, I suppose so," I answered. It is not uncommon for me to remember some encounters as an intense dream. It does not happen that way as much anymore, but in the 1990s, it did.

Part IV

Sacred Geometry

Chapter 7

Our Galaxy's Sacred Geometry Grids

The golden ratio is a reminder of the relatedness of the created world to the perfection of its source and of its potential future evolution.
—Robert Lawlor[4]

The next part of the book will be about the things that I have learned from the star visitors over my lifetime. Many of the things I have learned were from direct instruction from our space brothers and sisters in a place I have named the Cosmic Academy. In the 1990s and early 2000s, I was taken at night, while I was sleeping, to a large warehouse type facility, where different star visitor groups would teach me how to do different things and how things worked in the higher dimensions. Much of it was one-on-one classroom instruction, where they were teaching me about how physics works in the higher dimensions, and then giving me hands-on activities to perform so that I could practice what I had just learned. For example, one night I was in a large room with three other people who were taken the same time. Our teacher was a very sage man who was highly evolved. He was trying to teach us to manifest something from nothing, as we will do in the fifth dimension. Our instructor reminded me of a cross between Master Yoda and Obi Wan Kenobi of the Star Wars Movies. He was dressed in a long flowing brown robe with a hood pulled up on his head so only his face was uncovered. We all seemed to be floating in this huge dark space. Floating around us were hundreds of what looked like just random things. The four of us just floated there dumbfounded, not knowing what to do. Our instructor said, "I want you each to make music out of this. Go ahead." We all started grabbing for things floating around in the air that looked as though they were parts of musical instruments. Each of us was trying to build something, but when we would get to a certain point, everything would break and fall away. "I can't do it!" I said in a frustrated voice. "Please, you need to help me," I commented to our guru. The guy floating next to me had tried again, and failed, and was getting angry. "No, no, no!' said our instructor. Then he looked firmly but kindly at me and said, "Judy, come on. You are my best student. You know how to do this." Then firmly he said, "Now do it." At that point, I closed my eyes trying to center myself, so that I could come up with a solution. I entered a meditative state, and I could hear my instructor saying, "Yes, yes. Now you are getting it. Continue." I put out to the Universe, "It is my intent to build this simple musical instrument that will play beautiful music." I opened my eyes, and floating in front of me were the parts to make an instrument that was a cross between a xylophone and an organ. I began reaching up and as I touched a piece, it would fall into place by the piece before it. I seemed to know which parts to grab, and where to put them. Our instructor now was dancing around us saying, "Yes. You are doing it. I knew you would do it." Now I was very excited as I created this amazing instrument in midair right in front of me. As I reached up again, the stick to play the instrument was in my hand and I began to play it. Our instructor was beside himself with joy. He kept saying, "Yes, yes, yes. I knew you would do it." Then he turned to the others who had been watching this whole scenario unwind, and said, "Now you do it. Do it just like Judy did." With that, they began to pull things out of the air and attempted to put them together, but when they got more than two pieces together, they all fell apart. "Why are you not paying attention," he sternly asked them? "Judy, tell them how to do it." My mind was running like mad because I was not sure how I had done it. Reading my thoughts, he said, "What did you do first?" At that moment, the proverbial light bulb went off in my head, and I was clear about how I had done it. I began, "I centered myself, and I stated my intent to the Universe. The Universe heard my intent, and complied. It was that easy!" Smiling, our instructor said, "Yes. It was that easy. Your intent is the key. Wonderful, remarkable. Thank you," he said to me as he smiled in approval. Turning to the others he said, "Now you do it." Again, they attempted to do it, but they were not having any luck with it. With that, our instructor ended our session, and I found myself back home in my bed, wide awake and trying to create this musical instrument again. It was truly amazing. I have tried to duplicate some of the things I have been taught, but I have yet to be able to do them in this dimension. They assure me that when the time is right, I will be able to perform these skills beautifully.

Another time I was taken to another section of the Cosmic Academy, made up of individual lab classrooms and work areas. For some reason, I was wearing my NASA flight suit that I used to wear when doing space shuttle education for the Challenger Center and for my school district. The star visitor that was leading me around was a tall Pleidian that I recognized and had worked with many times before. His name was Lars and we had known each other for a long time, and I was very comfortable with him. Lars was around eight feet tall and had shoulder length blonde hair. His icy blue eyes were focused, and when I looked in them, I was completely taken in. I knew he meant business, but also, I could see his beautiful soul through those gorgeous eyes. They were captivating. He led me into a room where some plans for a space station module were laid out on a very large table in the center of the room. Leading me over to the table, he said, "Okay, Judy. I need you to build a model of this so that we can see if everything is going to work as we expect it to. I'll be back and forth between the rooms because I have several projects I am overseeing tonight." He smiled, and turned and left. Looking around this vast room, I could see just a handful of other people, like me, working on various parts of this space station. I just sat there not knowing what to do. An hour went by, and I was still sitting there doing nothing when Lars returned. "Judy, what are you doing? Why haven't you done anything on your model," he asked me in a rather concerned voice. "I don't think I should be here," I commented.

I don't know how to do this stuff. I'm not an engineer." Now acting like he was thoroughly disgusted with my behavior, he said, "Come on. Come with me." He led me into another area where models were already well under way. He sat me down next to someone I had worked with before. Lars said, "Work with Judy. She can do this. She has done this, many times before. Do not listen to her. She knows what she is doing, and I expect her to do it, but you may assist her." With that Lars left the area. I looked at my friend and said, "I cannot do it. I don't even know what he is talking about." Speaking softly, my friend said, "Look at how you are dressed. Of course, you can do this. You must do this. So, let's get to work." I was almost in tears, but I started to work with the modeling material, and things just started to take shape. Within an hour, I had completed my section, when Lars came back into the room. "Very good," he said matter-of-factly. "I do not want you talking like that again. You do yourself harm when you talk to yourself like that. Stop it!" "Yes, sir," I said as I started walking with Lars. "I'm sorry. It will not happen again." My next memory was being back in bed, and it was four AM.

Since about 2007, those visitations have increased to several times a month. The other part of my education from the star visitors has come from experts in the field who have done the research and know what they are talking about. I have been divinely led to each one of them in a synchronistic dance that ties all of the bits and pieces together. Some of these experts have worked with star visitors all of their lives for the soul purpose of teaching the masses the information. One of the important things I have learned over the years is that when a student is ready to learn, the right teacher will show up.

During the late 1980s and throughout the 1990s, while studying the planets and their inter-relatedness, I became consciously aware of what we refer to as sacred geometry. Sacred geometry is found in everything throughout the Universe, including us. As I began to see the interconnectedness of it all, studying about the Universe became all that more exciting and interesting for me. About five years before I retired from teaching high school, I had a student in one of my psychology classes who answered a question in a way that really got my attention.

During the first week of school at the beginning of each semester, I used to give a short homework assignment with the question, "What do you hope to learn about this year in our psychology class?" Normally I would get the typical questions relating to the topics in the psychology textbook. However, one particular student stood out because of what he asked. His question was, "What is sacred geometry and how is it applied to everything?" I was reading these papers at home that night, and I could not believe what I was reading. That was just not the type of question that my juniors and seniors had asked before, and so I was caught off guard. I sat there at home trying to place in my mind which student had asked the question, and I could not. It was during that time the star visitors were working with me in trying to get me to understand the concepts and their relationships better. One of the ways our space visitors teach me is experientially. Over the past fifteen years they have never called any of it sacred geometry. Then after a lot of comparisons had been made and I could see the relationships clearly, they would say, "Now that is what we refer to as sacred geometry. We use it to build things, to travel from place to place, galaxy to galaxy; Earth uses it to create her features, and it is found throughout the Universe." The Star Visitors put a name to it only after I had the concepts clearly in mind. I was soon to find out that understanding the general concepts and using them, and trying to explain these concepts to someone else, was more difficult than I had imagined. I wrote down some general information about sacred geometry so that I could at least give my new student a definition and some good, common examples when I addressed the class about their questions the next day.

It was in my fifth period class, right after lunch that this student had been placed. After taking attendance, I started the class. "Who asked the question about sacred geometry," I asked, smiling brightly? Most of the other students had never heard of it, and the few who had, could not define it. One young man in the back of the classroom raised his hand. "Wow!" I said. "In all my years teaching psychology, no one has ever asked me a question like that. May I ask you why you asked it and why you think I can help you with that since it is not part of the curriculum?" I have always believed that the Universe moves in amazing ways. Sacred geometry is something that I needed to know more about so that later I could teach others about it. Now, here this young man sat in my class eager for me to teach him. He was not my typical high school senior. He was much more serious than the other guys in my class, and he was intelligent and did not care if the other students knew that he was smart. By now, I had piqued the interest of some of the other students in the class, and they were asking me what sacred geometry was. I shared the information I had gathered together the night before with the class, and answered a few questions about it. Then I said, "Because we are a public school, and sacred geometry is not a part of the psychology curriculum, I cannot teach you about it. However, if it is something you are interested in, see me after class, and I can give you more information." About ten minutes after school let out for the day, he showed up at my door. I told him to do some internet searches, but also, I had several books at home that I would bring in that he could borrow. He was thrilled, and thanked me for helping him. As he was leaving, he said, "By the way, the reason I asked you about it is because I know you know a lot about the paranormal, and I think you know more about extraterrestrials than you let on. Besides, I just know that you are the one who is supposed to teach me about it." I smiled and said, "Well, okay. That works for me. I'll see you tomorrow." "Thanks, Dr. C.," he said, "See you tomorrow." Remembering the phrase, *When the student is ready to learn, the right teacher will show up,"* was ringing in my head.

Another elegant example of the universal stretch of mathematics came when I was observing a math class, and the teacher wrote on the board a picture of a circle and the pi symbol underneath it. He then wrote out the numerical version of pi, which goes into infinity. A student raised his hand and asked the one question that no teacher likes to hear: "Why is this so important, and when am I ever going to use it?" I thought the teacher answered brilliantly. He said, "This number, pi, goes on forever and it never repeats itself. That means all of the numbers that are important in your life are found in this number somewhere-your birthday, your social security number, and so on. If you put letter equivalents with these numbers, you will find every word ever written. Pretty amazing." I gazed at the class, and was tickled to see every student looking at the teacher and paying attention. He had obviously touched something in them that resonated with them. That is how sacred geometry works.

Everything we see in the physical world around us is made up of sacred geometric elements. When we think of fractals, vortices, architecture and even music, we are observing and experiencing the intricate dance of the physical structure of sacred geometry. Nikola Tesla was quoted as saying, "If you wish to understand the Universe, think of energy, frequency, and vibration." When he made that statement over a hundred years ago, he was referring to the new physics that is being used today, and that our scientists are only just now beginning to understand.

The five platonic solids are geometric shapes that are sacred geometric forms. The torus, which looks like a donut, the four-dimensional cube, the golden spiral, the merkaba, the sine wave, and the sphere are all parts of what we know as the five platonic solids. The five platonic solids are the tetrahedron, hexahedron, octahedron, icosahedron, and the dodechahedron.

The Golden Ratio is a very common geometric shape, and is found in the five Platonic Solids. It is actually an irrational number that is approximately 1.6128….and this number possesses many amazing properties. For those of us who live in the West, the Golden Ratio is seen as very beautiful and having perfect proportion. It is often used by people working in the field of design, as well as the arts. It seems there is a synchronistic relationship between things that are in perfect symmetry and those that are not. We can go back to the ancient Pythagoreans who used to define numbers as part of ratios. They did believe that all reality is based on numbers. About the Golden Ratio, they thought that it expressed an underlying truth about all existence.

The Golden Ratio is a mathematical equation:

$a/b = a + b/a = 1.618 = \text{Phi} = \varphi$

Another numerical sequence found in sacred geometry is the Fibonacci series of numbers. It starts with 0 and 1, and as the series continues, each new number is the sum of the two numbers before it. For example, 0,1,1,2,3,5,8,13,21...The ratio of points in the continuing sequence is about the same as phi (1.6128), as divided by 3 = 1.666. When you divide a number in the sequence by the number before it, you get numbers very close together. For example: 144/89 =1.617; 89/55 = 1.618; 34/21 = 1.619. This number is fixed after the 13th in the series and is known as the golden ratio or 1.618... Leonardo DiVinci used the golden ratio in his designs. The idealized human form that artists and scientists agree on use this ratio. For example, the distance from the naval to the foot is taken as one unit, the height of a human being is equivalent to 1.618.

A fractal is another interesting geometric shape that can be split into parts. What is fascinating is that each part is a reduced copy of the original. If you have ever gone into the haunted mansion at Disneyland in Anaheim, California, you will know what I am talking about.

What the star visitors have been showing me all of these years is that mathematics is universal. We find many mathematical ratios and constants on Mars and Jupiter, for example that compare with similar monuments on Earth. In the 1970s when NASA sent the Viking landers to the surface of Mars, they sent back the first amazing pictures of the surface of Mars that we had ever seen. In one photograph, which NASA never classified, was the now famous face, found in a region of Mars known as Cydonia. It is pure conjecture why NASA did not classify those photographs since it was apparent to many who saw them, that they were not examples of erosion and windstorms, but instead, the creation by some civilization of intelligence. Richard Hoagland, a former NASA consultant, took those photographs and began comparing and analyzing them. What he discovered is that there is a direct correlation between those monuments found on Mars and monuments found in Egypt on Earth. They followed the mathematical constants that we find in sacred geometry. Additionally, Richard Hoagland found other correlations between planets in our solar system. For example, there appears to be an upwelling of energy on several planets at 19.5^0 North and South latitudes on Earth, which is the Mauna Loa Volcano in Hawaii, on Jupiter, it is the great red spot, on Neptune it is the blue spot which appears like a whirling vortex of energy, and on Mars, it is the Olympus Mons Volcano. My star visitor family has been telling me for years that everything is connected, and that we are all One. These sacred mathematical correlations seem to say that it is certainly true.

There are other stunning examples of sacred geometry on our planet. For example, the layout of the pyramids at the Giza Plateau is laid out according to the golden ratio.

The Tree of Life, or the Sacred Tree, is found in cultural and spiritual traditions of humans. It is thought that there is a spiritual force of the Sacred Tree that will help us move on the path of personal growth and development. In the movie, Avatar, the "Tree of Souls" is the spiritual and guiding force Eywa. The Na'vi held the Sacred Tree of Souls in great respect and knew that without it, their way of life and their planet would die. I think that there is no accident that there are many messages for the people of Earth to pay attention to in this movie. It is thought that the messages found in Avatar resonate on the subconscious minds in most people.

In the movie, Avatar, the Na'vi people are like the Mayans. In both cases, their forests and jungles have been destroyed by the West, and specifically by the policy of U.S. imperialism. I have been shown by the star visitors some of the important lessons found in the movie, Avatar. What we are experiencing on Earth now is the encroachment of western thought and greed which has been stripping away our spiritual connection with all living beings and spiritual entities. "Eywa" is the female god who is responsible for the balance of Pandora, their planet and the Universe. She is the opposite of the warring God, Yahweh, which represents the people from Earth. The star visitors have told me that the Tree of Life is our biological network to the Universe. As our Universe grew, the Tree of Life grew to create carbon-based life on Earth. This ultimately evolved into human life with an expanding and evolving consciousness.

The star visitors are telling me that the messages in Avatar are really a wake-up call for humans. While many of us have a somewhat evolved consciousness, many still operate as if they were cavemen without an idea of what consciousness and evolution are about. For all of those who saw

Avatar, it provides us a deeper look into our own subconscious and our connection to each other, our ancestors, and Earth. The ugliness and uncaring that the military characters and the movie viewers confronted was their own destructive ways of life and living on our planet. We were forced to look at the problems of our own making. The positive message from Avatar is that there is a better way of living that can heal and restore Earth. To do that though requires an end to expansionism and control, all war, and the exploitation of the people and the resources of our Earth. The Galactic Federation of Light is here to back us up as we get rid of the dark cabal that has been controlling everything on Earth for thousands of years. The Galactic Federation of Light has been telling us that we are about to take an evolutionary leap that will send us to another level of consciousness. Maybe Avatar woke up some of those people who might have otherwise slept through it all.

I mentioned the Merkaba before, and I would like to address that now. When specific geometric forms are spun, a counter rotating field of light is generated. This will simultaneously affect one's spirit and body. The Merkaba can help us in accessing other dimensions and realities. I carry a crystal Merkaba pendulum with me at all times. It helps me to access meditative states sometimes, and I feel connected to something bigger when I have it with me.

I mentioned that when the Merkaba is spun, a counter rotating field of light is generated. The star visitors have told me that when the Merkaba is used in this way, it opens up portals to travel through. In the 1980s, when NASA sent the Voyager I and Voyager II spacecraft out to study the planets in our solar system, they took some stunning video of the north pole of Saturn when it orbited the planet. Richard Hoagland, the former NASA consultant, studied this video and discovered something wonderful. When the spacecraft flew over the north pole of Saturn and was right at the top of the planet, the video clearly shows Saturn spinning on its axis in a clockwise direction. Nothing unusual there. However, at the North Pole, there is a whirling vortex of energy spinning very rapidly in the opposite direction than the planet is spinning. To me, that knowledge opens up many possibilities about the planet, Saturn. Is it possible that Saturn's North Pole is actually a portal or a star gate that allows people to move freely and easily through space and time? They also told me that each of us has a natural Merkaba within us that will help us learn how to use the portals and star gates to move from place to place and to time travel, if we choose to. We will be taught by the star visitors how to activate and use the Merkaba because it will be a way for us to transport ourselves from the third dimension into the fifth dimension. This will be our ascension. Children being born in this generation are coming in with the Merkaba already activated. They have so much more knowledge than we do and our belief systems have to catch up to them. Our character is the key to ascension.

In one of our learning sessions at the Cosmic Academy, I was being shown about the Chakra system, and how it is moving from a seven-chakra system to a thirteen-chakra system. The knowledge about Chakras has been around for thousands of years. The chakra system is basically the spiritual energy system of our bodies. We have been living with a seven-Chakra system, but that system is rapidly changing into a thirteen-Chakra system. The ascended fourth dimensional human, or partially ascended human, has thirteen chakras and corresponding colors that are different from the third-dimensional seven-Chakra system. Changing from seven Chakras to thirteen Chakras would be like changing music modalities. The vibrations, colors, sound, and the harmony are different. Therefore, the entire being is changed.

Before our instructor excused us to be taken back to our beds, I asked a question. "Master," I began. "Would you please talk a little bit about portals and star gates?" Our instructor said,

> I will make this brief. Star gates are found around the major nodes of the earth's reality grids. Each reality grid has its specific base frequency as they raise or lower. Stargates and portals are very similar. They are similar to switching systems. A portal is an interdimensional energy gate that can be used to transport any entity from one dimension to another. Also, the Earth primarily has twelve major grids. The twelve major nodes are the locations for Gaia's twelve major portals.

With that, our Master teacher led us in a quick meditation, and instructed our handlers to get us back to bed for the rest of the night. He said, "When you awaken in the morning, you will feel as though you have had eight hours of restful sleep. Go in Peace!" The next memory I had was waking up in the morning at around 9 am.

Chapter 8

Mecca and The Golden Ratio

God offers to every mind its choice between truth and repose. Take which you please-you can never have both.
—Ralph Waldo Emerson

One of the most stunning examples of sacred geometry can be found in Mecca, Saudi Arabia. Mecca is the sacred site of the Kabba. The Kabba is a cube-shaped structure that is about 15 meters in height and 12 meters wide. It is simple in design, but is an ancient structure constructed of granite. A black meteorite, called the Black Stone, is located on the southeast corner of the Kabba. A black silk cloth known as a kiswah covers the Kabba.

According to the Holy Qur'an, the holy book of Islam, the Kabba was built by the Prophet Abraham and his son, Ishmael. It was built to worship one God, Allah. The Prophet Muhammad, peace be upon him, took over the leadership of Mecca in A.D. 630. Paganism had been rampant in Mecca at the time and the Kabba was filled with various idols that the tribes of Mecca had worshipped. The Prophet Muhammad, peace be upon him, destroyed all of the idols inside and outside of the Kabba and rededicated it as the place to worship the one God, Allah. I need to mention here that Muslims do not worship the Kabba itself. The Kabba is a direction that Muslims face while praying to Allah. It is a unifying point for all Muslims no matter where they in the world. During the annual pilgrimage, called Hajj, Muslims from all over the world come to the Kaaba and walk around it in a counterclockwise direction. This is a ritual they refer to as *tawaf.*

An interesting fact is that when a person worshipping Allah prostrates, or kneels down on the ground, and puts his forehead on the ground facing the Kaaba, the third-eye chakra which is where we receive energy and release it, harmful charges in our bodies are released. This causes our bodies to balance their energy systems because of the energy directly coming from the Kaaba. This is how it works. We use the concept of the golden ratio in sacred geometry. The golden ratio is 1.618. This ratio is sometimes called the Divine proportion because God used the same proportion in many things and events. For example, it shows up in the human DNA sequence, heartbeats, galaxies, the human body and many more things. In my opinion, it would seem that the golden mean, in and of itself, is evidence of creation. When the golden mean ratio is applied to the Earth herself, that golden point on the Earth is the City of Makkah (Mecca), Saudi Arabia. The golden point of Mecca is the Holy Kabba. That makes the Kabba the strongest energetic field on the Earth.

For us to understand how the golden mean provides an energy field, let us look as an example, to the galaxies and planets which emit energy from the center point to the outer edges. It is just like nuclear energy which balances the energy system with the electrons rotating around it. It means that the nuclei take the negative energies and give the positive energies in order to balance everything. Using that same principle, it is why Muslims circle the Kaaba, which is also charged with energy. This is a fact that has been proven. (You Tube video: The Miraculous Kaaba-Why Pray Towards the Kaaba? Merciful Servant, 01/26/17)

Every day of our lives, our bodies will collect electromagnetic charges from our surroundings which are harmful to us. It appears that these charges are concentrated in our third-eye chakra which is the frontal lobe of the brain. These negative charges may cause depression, headaches, laziness, mental problems, and even more dangerous sicknesses. Our bodies take positive and negative energies through this frontal chakra. It has been observed that if we place our foreheads on the ground towards the strongest energy field of the Earth, which turns out to be Mecca, Saudi Arabia, and more specifically, the Kaaba, harmful charges of energy will be released from us.

Dr. Andrew Newberg, the director of research at the Marcus Institute of Integrative Health and a physician at Jefferson University Hospital, studied brain wave activity during prayer. He stated that the benefits of prayer are incredible. He observed that regular daily prayers stop our frontal lobes from shrinking with age. This part of the brain controls our speaking, reading and memory, as well as controlling our behavior, and part of our moral compass. Regular prayer, then, may prevent memory loss in old age, and is a perfect form of meditation. Meditation brings one into a state of tranquility.

Continuing with the relationship of the sacred geometry of the Earth and how this information was given to us in the Holy Qur'an by God through the Prophet Muhammad, peace be upon him, is amazing. The latitude of the coordinates of the Kabba is 21 degrees and 25 minutes. The first verse in the Holy Qur'an that describes the Kabba is verse 2:125 (Al-Qur'an 2:125). Is it possible that this mathematical harmony of 21 and 25 be simply a coincidence? It is highly unlikely. It seems the possibility of numbers in the Qur'an from number 114 until verse 286 which describe the Kaaba for the first time, has a chance probability of 1/100,000 for them to appear next to each other. (Surah 2, verse 125). The part of the coordinates after the comma can be described in the form of minutes as well as ratios of percentages. The Holy Bible in Psalms 84, verse 6, but throughout Psalms 84, the Kabba and Mecca are being referred to there as well. I cannot say if the Kabba is referred to in the Torah, the Holy Book of the Jews. For the two and most likely, three major religions of the time to have their Holy books talk about this spot, the actual center of the Earth, has everything to do with the sacred geometry that God created when he created everything.

I imagine that if we could draw imaginary lines from this center point of Earth, that they would land on similar energy points on other planets. That is conjecture on my part, but I encourage you to research it if you are interested. Since mathematics is the language of the Universe, when one looks at the mathematical ratios and constants found in everything on the Earth, it makes a pretty strong argument for a Supreme Being who created all of it. It is what the Star Visitors have been teaching me all of these years and I keep marveling at the stunning connections and synchronicities that we find on our planet, on surrounding planets, and in the galaxies.

Chapter 9

ET is Talking. Are We Listening?

We never know how high we are, Till we are called to rise; And then, if we are true to plan, Our statures touch the skies.
—Emily Dickinson, American Poet

There have been many ways since the 1940s that extraterrestrials have been contacting us. Some have been more subtle than others. Although our space families have been around Earth for centuries, it is only in the past sixty years that they have been answering our call out to them.

In the early 1970s, NASA was continuing a program which began in the 1960s to send probes into space to study aspects of our solar system. The most significant were the Pioneer 10 and Pioneer 11 missions. The earlier Pioneer missions were used to learn how to achieve the Earth's escape velocity, which is $9.8m/sec/sec^2$. Once our scientists achieved that, the earlier Pioneer probes spent time in attempting lunar orbit. Many were failures, but eventually NASA did have success. The Pioneer 10 and 11 missions were special because NASA had given the famous astronomer, Carl Sagan, permission to send a message with the Pioneer spacecraft, so that if the spacecraft were to ever be intercepted by extraterrestrials, they would know about the people who sent it and where they were from. Carl Sagan worked together with Frank Drake to achieve this goal. This information was placed on a golden plaque, and was designed by Linda Salzman Sagan, Carl's wife, who did the artwork. (See the picture on the top of the next page.) They decided that using Universal measurements on the plaque would be understood by any intelligent spacefaring beings. The two circles at the top left corner of the plaque represent hydrogen, and hydrogen is the most common element in the Universe. Additionally, the dots to the right of the female represent in binary code 1000, which is equal to 8.8 x 21 cm = 168 cm, the height of a normal human. Interestingly, Carl Sagan wanted the man and woman to be holding hands. However, scientists felt that any extraterrestrial finding it might view it as one being with two heads, so they did not do it.

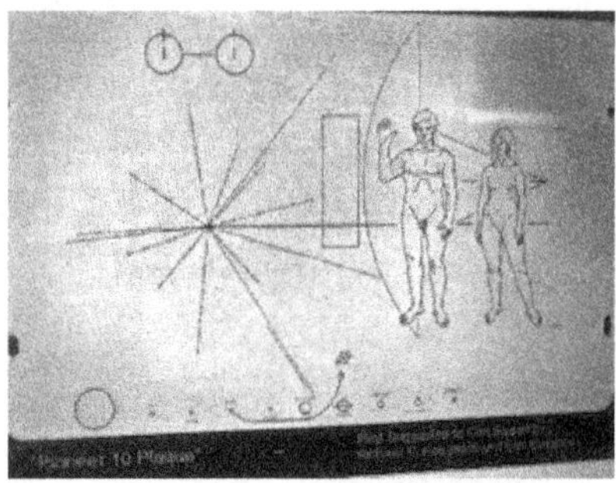

PIONEER PLAQUE

Looking on the left side of the plaque is a radial star-like pattern. Apparently, this part of the picture was also etched on the later Voyager Golden Record. It is a pulsar map that holds information about time and tells where we are. In this diagram, there are 14 spinning neutron stars. The lengths of the lines show the approximate distances of the pulsars to the sun. Additionally, a tick mark at the end of each line indicates how far the pulsar is from the plane of the Milky Way Galaxy. It also shows the sun's relative distance to the center of our galaxy, which if I remember my astronomy is 30 million light years to the center. The bottom of the plaque shows the solar system with the Sun on the left. NASA also showed the trajectory of the Pioneer spacecraft, hoping to give more information to whomever found it. NASA made the scale of the planets correctly, but the distances to the planets are not to scale.

The notches above and below each planet are written in binary code and tell their approximate distance to the Sun.

I remember when the design of the plaque was shown to the public for the first time that there were many people who were upset. For one, the design depicted nudity, which some saw as obscenities. Some said that the message was too complex, and said that if an extraterrestrial spacecraft ran into it, they would not be able to immediately understand it. The designers of the plaque did not care if the message was understood immediately. Their two main requirements were that it was precise but also, informative. NASA knew that the chances of a probe ever being discovered by any civilization would be virtually non-existent. The Universe is so vast that it does not really matter if it is teeming with life or not because the likelihood of anyone running into it and making the connection was pretty slim. One wonders why NASA even bothered in the first place. It just so happens that NASA engineers tend to be very optimistic. They felt that if on the off chance that someone ever came across the probe, it would not hurt to tell them a little about ourselves back on planet Earth. As far as I know, NASA has never received a message from an extraterrestrial civilization responding to this plaque.

However, NASA made other attempts to communicate with extraterrestrials in the 1970s, and this time it appears that we received a response. At the SETI radio observatory in Ohio, a researcher was sitting at his desk and data suddenly became so strong that it went off of their charts. For those of you who saw the movie, "Contact" in the 1990s, I'm sure you remember how exciting that can be. This was on August 15, 1977. The volunteer, Jerry Ehman, who was on duty at that time noticed a pattern on the paper logs that were coming from the machine. He circled the data and wrote the word, "Wow!" in the margin. Hence, the name "Wow Signal" came into being. In the fourteen years that this radio telescope had been in operation for the SETI (Search for Extraterrestrial Intelligence) Program, this was for sure the most compelling signal the receiver had ever recorded. According to Jerry Ehman collecting that data, he responded, "It was powerful enough to push the Big Ear's monitoring device off the charts."

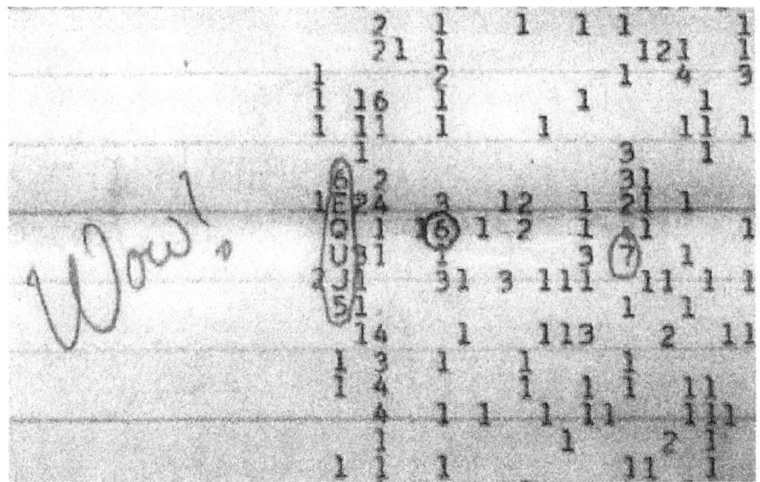

THE WOW SIGNAL: THE PRINTOUT FROM THE RADIO SATELLITE.

The signal lasted for seventy-two seconds and came in at around 1420.456 MHz before it faded away. It came from the vicinity of the constellation Sagittarius. Jerry Ehman recalls that he was amazed at the intensity of the signal, and that it appeared in a narrow band of frequencies. Interestingly, seventy-two seconds was the exact length of time for the Earth to rotate the Big Ear through a signal from space. Mr. Ehman did some analysis of the data, and he concluded that the indications were that this powerful, narrowband radio signal came from outside of our solar system.

That signal was picked up by only one of the telescope's two detectors. The second detector covered the same patch of sky three minutes later, and heard nothing. That meant one of two things: the first beam had detected something that was not there, or that the source of the signal had been shut off or diverted elsewhere in the intervening time. Being very excited at the prospects of true contact with an extraterrestrial civilization from interstellar space, the researchers at the observatory aimed their telescope on that part of the sky for the next full month. Nothing interesting or unusual was observed during that month. The scientists were not able to explain the original event.

Over the next twenty years, there were many attempts for further scans over that region of space. Researchers Robert Gray and Kevin

Marvel did manage to obtain some usage time on the META array at the Oak Ridge Observatory in Massachusetts, and the Very Large Array (VLA) in New Mexico. At that time, it was widely believed that the Wow signal had come from an ET lighthouse, like a beacon. The characteristic of that signal was a rise and fall in its loudness, which is exactly what the researchers were told to look out for. Back in 1959, researchers had tried to put themselves into an extraterrestrial's shoes by trying to work out the best way to get our attention. They decided that the best signal would be a radio signal at exactly 1,420 MHz. Even more wonderful, this is the vibration frequency of hydrogen, which is the most common molecule in the universe. Everyone at that meeting agreed that it would be the most widely intelligent way of saying, "We are here. Are you?" So, when the Wow Signal came in at its frequency of 1,420 MHz, it caught their attention. Observing into that part of the sky where the Wow Signal originated, they detected some extremely faint sources of radio emissions but nothing like that of the Wow Signal. The Big Ear in Ohio maintained its periodic scan of that part of the sky for close to forty years. They never came across such a compelling signal again. Sadly, they dismantled this radio telescope in 1998 to put in a golf course.

The Wow Signal still is the strongest and clearest signal from space ever received by a radio telescope. It certainly is the most fascinating, and so far, unexplainable. Something interesting to note however, Jerry Ehman, the signal's original discoverer, feels that if intelligent beings were sending a signal, they would have sent it more than once, and we should have seen it over and over. Really? When we, on Planet Earth, in 1974 sent out our message to space, we only sent it once, and I would like to think that we are intelligent beings.

In 1974, at the Arecibo radio telescope in South America, we broadcast a message into space a single time. We used frequency modulated radio waves on November 16, 1974. Scientists aimed their message at the globular star cluster known as M13, located 25,000 light years away from Earth. M13 was a large and close collection of stars and happened to be visible in the sky on that date. The message was made up of 1679 binary digits, approximately 210 bytes, transmitted at a frequency of 2380 MHz, and modulated by shifting the frequency by 10 Hz, using a power of 1000kW. The "ones" and "zeros" in the binary code were transmitted by frequency shifting at the rate of 10 bits per second. The total broadcast lasted just short of three minutes. They chose the number 1679 in the binary code because it is the product of two prime numbers. It was arranged in a rectangle as 73 rows by 23 columns.

Dr. Frank Drake from Cornell University along with Carl Sagan wrote the message that was sent into space. They basically drew a picture of who we were, what our planet is like and what we looked like. The message, to be read from the top down consists of seven parts. The first part is the numbers one to ten. The second part shows the atomic numbers of the elements, hydrogen, carbon, nitrogen, oxygen, and phosphorus, which make up DNA. The third part shows the formulas for the sugars and bases in the nucleotides of DNA. The number of nucleotides in DNA, and a picture of the double helix structure of DNA make up the fourth part. The fifth part of the message shows a graphic figure of a human, the dimension of an average man, and the human population of the Earth at that time. The sixth part is a graphic of the solar system. The last part is a graphic of the Arecibo radio telescope and the dimension of the transmitting antenna dish. To quote Carl Sagan about the translation of what the message said,

> Here is how we count from one to ten. Here are five atoms that we think are interesting or important: hydrogen, carbon, nitrogen, oxygen, and phosphorous. Here are some of the ways to put these atoms together that we think interesting or important-the molecules thymine, adenine, guanine and cytosine, and a chain composed of alternating sugars and phosphates. These molecular building-blocks are put together to form a long molecule of DNA comprising about four billion links in the chain. The molecule is a double helix. In some way, this molecule is important for the clumsy looking creature at the center of the message. That

> creature is 14 radio wavelengths or 5 feet 9.5 inches tall. There are about 4 billion of these creatures on the third planet from our star. There are nine planets all together, four big ones toward the outside and one little one at the extremity. This message is brought to you, courtesy of a radio telescope 2,430 wavelengths or 1,004 feet in diameter. Yours truly.

The scientists sending the message actually did not think the message would ever be received by an extraterrestrial civilization because it would take 25,000 years for it to reach its intended destination of M13. They also believed, on the outside chance that the message was received and answered right away, it would take another 25,000 years for us to receive a reply. Of course, they were thinking in terms of Earth physics as we knew it then-third dimensional physics. It does not sound like they were considering that a spacefaring world of sentient extraterrestrial beings would not be using the technologies found in the third dimension of the twenty-first century, planet Earth.

Imagine what the scientists must have been thinking when unusual crop formations began to appear in the fields in England. They were named the Chilbolton Crop Glyphs because they were found in a farmer's field just outside of the Chilbolton Radio Telescope. What people saw that morning in 2001 was very much like the 1976 photos of the Face on Mars. It even showed the erosion on the right-hand side of the face. What was even more interesting, when the crop circle was put under Gaussian blue filter, the face turned out to look like a primitive human face, and very similar to the left-hand side of the human/feline combination found on the Face on Mars.

Then, just five days later, a second crop circle suddenly appeared in the same field, and only a few hundred feet from the face. Crop circle investigators in England quickly realized that this second circle was almost identical to the one sent out in 1974 from the Arecibo Radio Telescope by Frank Drake and Carl Sagan. The scientists noticed some subtle differences on this crop circle and realized that this was a message, probably in response to that original radio telescope message in 1974. In the crop circle made in response to the Arecibo message, there were some changes made to the original message. Paul Vigay, the photographer who took the picture, walked around the crop glyph, which is now referred to as the "Arecibo Response" crop glyph. Here are the differences that he noted. Reading it from the top to the bottom, just as the Arecibo message was, the decimal equivalents of the binary code were not changed. However, the atomic numbers of the elements composing the basis of life had been changed. Silicon, an element with the atomic number of 14, was added precisely in the correct sequence of where it should have been on the original message. At the time that this message was sent out, Drake and Sagan did not know the role that silicon plays in carbon-based life. This is significant because that is why they did not include it in the message.

Another change occurred in the depiction of the total number of nucleotides in the human genome. In the crop version, there are significantly more nucleotides in the extraterrestrial DNA. In the original message, the double helix is depicted. In the crop circle, it appears to be a triple helix. In the year 2000, a patent was issued to Enzo Biochem of Farmingdale, New York. This patent told of a new process for modifying DNA, in which this technique called for the addition of a third strand to the basic double helix, making it a triple helix. The question arises with the crop circle, is it trying to tell us that some extraterrestrials performed similar genetic engineering experiments on humans long ago in our past? Right underneath this in the crop circle, in place of the human figure in the original message, a small bodied, big-headed figure that looked like a classic "gray alien" was carefully substituted in the crop circle version. It included a binary code denoting its apparent height of about 3.3 feet.

More changes were made just below the extraterrestrial figure. Here is where the solar system code is depicted. Theirs was not done in binary code either, but in a simple line schematic. Looking from right to left, the crop rectangle also has a sun and two inner worlds. This was followed by three elevated icons, which indicate that three worlds in the sender's solar system are inhabited. One of these is not a pixel planet like the others are. It is a blank space surrounded by four black pixels at right angles. Then outside this elevated group, lie two larger "twin planets" followed by two smaller twins.

It seems to me that an advanced civilization that has the same appearance of the gray extraterrestrials that contactees describe, intercepted the Arecibo message, and responded to it 27 years later. Why wait so long? Maybe they were waiting until we would be more awake and would understand that it was a reply. I have tried for a couple of years now to get a copyright okay from the photographer who took the picture of the two crop designs side by side on the field, but I get no response from him. So, I will refer you to the sight where you can see these. I am sorry that I cannot show them to you here. It is worthwhile for you to see them as you read this. It is really amazing. They are referred to as the Chilbolten Crop Circle with Arecibo message. Paul Vigay is the name of the photographer.

Many crop circles have appeared in farmers' crops over the years, mostly in England. I believe the extraterrestrials are trying to tell us something very important. We are supposed to be deciphering these messages. Crop circles have appeared that depict the flower of life, a famous sacred geometric form, The Fibonacci Sequence, pictures of tori, and a more famous one that depicted our solar system with the planets in their proper orbits, with the Earth missing. Many believe that this message is that if we do not stop hurting our planet now, we are leading it into total destruction, and our planet simply won't be here, or if it is here, it will be uninhabitable. That is not a message that most of us would want to hear.

Scientists and crop circle researchers now believe that the various crop circles depicting the torus or a torus-like figure, are trying to explain to us how zero-point energy devices work so that we can build them. In fact, many of these devices have been built over the past century, only to be taken away from the builder when he attempted to patent his device. When someone attempts to patent a zero-point energy device, the patent office tells him that it threatens our national security, and he may not keep it or manufacture it.

One of the more famous crop circles is the CSETI triangle, which became that organization's logo. In 1992, Dr. Steven Greer, the founder of CSETI, the Center for the Study of Extraterrestrial Intelligence, took a team of people with him to England. They were given permission to set up on a farm in Alton Barns. At that time, most of the interesting crop circles were appearing in that area. Alton Barns was over 1000 acres, which gave them room to work. One of the experiments that this group wanted to set up was to visualize a specific shape of a crop circle. The group went into a meditative state, and then began expanding their awareness into the cosmos. When they connected with extraterrestrial people, they asked them to create their specific shape that they were visualizing together, into a crop circle. They had decided to visualize an equilateral triangle with a circle at each point.

The next morning, the group discovered that exact shape in a field adjacent to where they had been working the night before. The field was under Oliver's Castle, and was difficult to get to because it was high and rough terrain. To quote the group, "It was as if the shape had been lifted from our minds and placed exactly in the field." Later the team was told that some of the tests that were done on the actual crop and the soil there, electromagnetic anomalies were found, and cell wall changes had occurred in the plants. According to the researchers, those tests indicated that this was one of the most important crop circles of that season when examining it from a scientific point of view.

There have been many attempts at communication between these highly evolved sentient Beings with Earth humans, but one that occurred in November of 1977, was amazing. It happened in England, and it was hushed up right after, so most in the United States and the rest of the world were unaware of it's happening until recently. On that date, a British television broadcast was hijacked by an extraterrestrial from the Ashtar Command of the Galactic Federation of Light. It is printed here in its entirety.

> This is the voice of Vrillion, the representative of the Ashtar Galactic Command speaking to you. For many years now you have seen us as lights in the skies. We speak to you now in peace and wisdom as we have done to your brothers and sisters all over this, your planet

Earth. We come to warn you of the destiny of your race and your worlds so that you may communicate to your fellow beings the course you must take to avoid the disasters which threaten your worlds and the beings on our worlds around you. This is in order that you may share in the great awakening, as the planet passes into the New Age of Aquarius. The new age can be a time of great peace and evolution for your race, but only if your rulers are made aware of the evil forces that can overshadow their judgments.

Be still now and listen, for your chance may not come again. For many years your scientists, governments and generals have not heeded our warnings; they have continued to experiment with the evil forces of what you call nuclear energy. Atomic bombs can destroy the earth and the beings of your sister worlds, in a moment.

The wastes from atomic power systems will poison your planet for many thousands of your years to come. We, who have followed the path of evolution for far longer than you, have long since realized this-that atomic energy is always directed against life. It has no peaceful application. Its use, and research into its use, must be ceased at once, or you all risk destruction. All weapons of evil must be removed.

The time of conflict is now past and the race of which you are a part may proceed to the highest planes of evolution if you show yourselves worthy to do this. You have but a short time to learn to live together in peace and goodwill. Small groups all over the planet are learning this, and exist to pass on the light of the dawning new age to you all. You are free to accept or reject their teachings, but only those who learn to live in peace will pass to the higher realms of spiritual evolution.

Hear now the voice of Vrillion, the representative of the Ashtar Galactic Command speaking to you. Be aware also that there are many false prophets and guides operating on your world. They will suck your energy from you-the energy you call money and will put it to evil ends giving you worthless dross in return. Your inner divine self will protect you from this. You must learn to be sensitive to the voice within, that can tell you what is truth, and what is confusion, chaos and untruth. Learn to listen to the voice of truth which is within you, and you will lead yourselves on to the path of evolution.

This is our message to you our dear friends. We have watched you growing for many years as you too have watched our lights in your skies. You know that we are here, and that there are more beings on and around your earth than your scientists admit. We are deeply concerned about you and your path towards the light, and will do all we can to help you. Have no fears, seek only to know yourselves and live in harmony with the ways of your planet earth. We of the Ashtar Galactic Command thank you for your attention. We are now leaving the planes of your existence. May you be blessed by the supreme love and truth of the Cosmos.[5]

With that, Vrillion ended the broadcast and returned the control of the television station and radio stations to the people. I do not know why Vrillion only spoke to the British people, but I would guess that because that is where most of the crop circle designs were made, they considered that area their communication center for the planet. Perhaps also they saw the opportunity to take over that station that day and did it to see what would happen. It doesn't really matter why it happened then and there. What does matter is the message delivered by the Galactic Federation of Light.

Another incident that I found out about accidently seems to show that extraterrestrial civilizations have been trying to communicate with us for thousands of years. I had received some video about a subject I do not remember right now, but after the video played, eight other choices of videos popped up on the screen. Usually I ignore those, but one really caught my eye. The title was something like *message received from a dying planet.* There was a picture of a dying planet on the screen and it said it would take about eight minutes to watch it. Everything about it caught my attention. In 1998, both Russian and American scientists came upon a transmission coming from what they described as interstellar space. They both sat on the message, but the Russian scientist decided to share it with the world.

A cry for help from a dying planet was received that said their planet was about to disintegrate and could we help them. The person sending the message said it was their own fault that it had happened, and that while they had a rather primitive space program, only a few could leave the planet. The person indicated that the people on their planet developed many destructive nuclear weapons and the powers in charge were extremely greedy. Finally, it all fell apart around them.

What is interesting is that this message was sent to Earth when only Cave Men were here. There was no one on planet Earth at that time to receive the message, decipher it, and then react to it. Only now, when our technologies could intercept the message and our scientists understand it, did it reach us. Is it possible that this far away planet from long ago was sending us a message now when we needed it the most? What if those inhabitants of that far away planet were crying out to us their human counterparts to stop what we are doing to our planet or we will suffer the same fate? It certainly is important enough to consider it, and it isn't the first time we have received a message such as this. The ball is definitely in our court and the end of the game is coming quickly. Only a raising of mass consciousness will change our results. I believe it is happening, but there are still many that need to awaken before the shift will occur.

Part V

Star Visitor Encounters and Spirituality

Chapter 10

Our Connections and On-Going Contact

Remember, each one of us has the power to change the world. Just start thinking peace, and the message will spread quicker than you think.
—Yoko Ono

My encounters with extraterrestrials are continuing, and finally, they are allowing me to be aware when they are here or when they are leaving. I have been told that Galactic Angels from the Galactic Federation of Light are coming into our rooms at night while we are sleeping and working on our physical bodies making changes on them that will make it easier for us to ascend into the fifth dimension when the time comes.

One of the ways these Galactic Angels make themselves known to me is that when they are leaving my room after they have spent time working on me, they go through the sliding glass window and rattle the slats on the blinds that are always closed at night. They are now doing this in response to my request to them to please let me know when you are there. They go through the window with such force, the smacking of the blinds on the window wakes me up. After working with me in this way for about three months, I asked them, while in a meditative state, would they please let me see what they look like. One night I had just dropped off to sleep when I felt a presence beside me in the room. I opened my eyes and I could see a wavy figure standing beside me at the head of the bed. Reaching over to my husband, I shook him and said, "Richard, are you awake?" I got no response. I could hear him breathing so I knew he was okay, and I turned to face the Being who was standing next to me in the bed. "Okay, I know you are there," I said. "I can almost see you. I am guessing that the reason you have not shown yourself to me in the past is because you are not human like me and you are afraid that I will be frightened. It is okay. I am now ready to see you. I can handle it. Remember you guys have taken me on board your spacecraft and I have met people before that are not human. I am picking up that you think I will find you unattractive, but I feel your energy in my heart and it feels beautiful. That is all that matters." As I lay there waiting, I was almost holding my breath in anticipation. Suddenly, and for about five seconds, he came into my third dimensional field of vision. He became fully materialized. "Oh, my God," I said. "I can see you. Thank you." He then faded back across the light barrier so that I could only see the energy footprint he was making as he stood there. He was beautiful in his own way. He was probably five feet tall and had a very stocky build. His skin was kind of frog like and his face had warts on it. His eyes were beautiful, however, exuding unconditional love as he stood there. He reminded me of one of the characters at the bar in the movie, "Star Wars." He must have done something to make me sleep because I awoke two hours later when he left the room rattling the blinds as he left. I just lay there for a few minutes, trying to imagine what work he was doing. I assumed he was working on my husband at the same time, although he has no memory of it.

After waking up the next morning, I did not feel good. My stomach and I felt like we were traveling together, but were on different roads. I laid back down in bed, and started a conversation with my husband, Richard. "What is wrong with you?" Richard began. "Oh, I don't know. I feel like I might throw up," I responded. "How do you feel?" I queried. "I'm fine," he answered. "Why don't you go back to sleep for a little while and see if that helps," he said. "Okay, thanks," I answered, as he left the room. As I lay there, I could hear him in the kitchen feeding the cats. Then I drifted off to sleep.

An hour later I woke up and noticed my queasy stomach was gone, but now I had a headache. I never get headaches, so I did not understand why I had this one. Later that day, I sat down at my computer and got onto Sheldon Nidle's website where he mentioned that many people are feeling what he refers to as ascension symptoms. Because our systems are being worked on by the Galactic Federation of Light, most of us are experiencing these symptoms. The Galactic Angels come into our rooms at night and balance out our bodies after we have been worked on. There is a Galactic Angel assigned to each one of us on the Earth. During this ascension process, changes are happening on all levels of our bodies. We are shifting to a higher vibrational frequency, and when that occurs, our awareness begins to expand. We may experience symptoms on the physical level as well as the mental, spiritual and emotional levels. It is as though we are computers and we are being rebooted and then upgraded. Our new patterns of existence begin to take in much more light from the universe. Sometimes the energy can be much more intense, and then, also, the symptoms may suddenly just stop. The symptoms may also change in intensity as well. These symptoms will be different for each of us depending on our current vibrational frequency, what our spiritual practice is like (meditation), and maybe even what our life purpose is.

These ascension symptoms manifest in different ways. Maybe we will have small aches and pains that seem to have a mind of their own. They can come and go without warning. I have been walking down the street or out on the trail where I hike, and suddenly it becomes difficult for me to walk. My knee, or my ankle or my foot is in so much pain that I cannot take another step. Stopping for a few minutes, the pain subsides almost as quickly as it appeared.

The headaches I have been getting recently are like a sharp pain behind my eyes and in the third eye area. In talking with my friends, I discover they are having the same symptoms too. They stop suddenly and leave me wondering what is wrong with me.

Many of these ascension symptoms mimic real medical conditions. Suddenly your heartbeat can change, beating rapidly and skipping a little bit. Then it returns to normal. Sometimes people can get a pain down their arm, also a classic symptom of a heart attack. When that happened to me, I made an appointment with my doctor and had some tests. I was delighted to find out that there was nothing at all wrong with me. Everything came back as normal. I am guessing because my symptoms did not escalate and went away as quickly as they appeared, they are signs of ascension adjustment. Our physical bodies are raising in frequency along with Earth.

We are about to make a quantum leap in evolution, and so is the Earth. We are receiving upgrades in our physical bodies all the time. According to the Galactic Federation, this upgrade of our DNA has been occurring for the past seventy plus years. This change, however, has increased in speed and intensity in recent years.

Many eons ago, our human DNA had twelve strands instead of only two. At that time, we were fully conscious beings having a full brain capacity, and could do things that today would seem supernatural. Because we are at the dawning of the Age of Aquarius, we are in the process of returning to our original state. These symptoms that we are having is evidence that we are transitioning back.

Additionally, our chakra system is being upgraded and expanded into thirteen chakras instead of only seven. This is another reason that we are feeling these symptoms. It is a dramatic change that we are experiencing. Additionally, it is sometimes hard to hold our center of balance. I find that I lose balance a lot lately and have to catch myself so I do not fall. We may also be emotionally out of balance. As we learn how to handle our new energies and vibrations, we will get into perfect balance. We just need to remain patient.

The extraterrestrials have told me that the symptoms are normal and will soon pass. You may simply breathe through the symptoms or meditating more often might help. At night, before you go to sleep, ask the Galactic Angel who works with you to turn down the intensity for you. Go into your heart and feel what is happening. It should be a peaceful process, and it is just part of our metamorphosis, or change. It is nice to know that we are not alone in the Universe.

This is also about us on planet Earth raising mass consciousness. We must realize that we are all One. We are moving from personal consciousness, where fear and lack of understanding may seem normal, to cosmic consciousness where we are connected to every other person on Earth, as well as to every intelligence in the Universe. The Hundredth Monkey Theory is a great example of what is now occurring on planet Earth. The story was written by Ken Keyes Jr. and was never copyrighted, so I will share the story here.

The last time I was taken to the Cosmic Academy, I was told that I was to learn from people who also received their training from their particular extraterrestrial group, and that have direct open contact with them. These are people who do not channel the extraterrestrials, but are in direct communication with them. One of those people is Sheldon Nidle of the Planetary Activation Organization who works directly with the Galactic Federation of Light, and Steven Greer, M.D., the founder of CSETI, The Center for the Study of Extraterrestrial Intelligence. I have observed him on many occasions, when I have been on a week-long training with the group, talking with these Beings. I consider the information I learn from both of them to be information that is part of my learning since the extraterrestrials told me to seek them out. Since my dream in 1989 telling me that I would be an ambassador, a liaison between extraterrestrial people and earth humans, I know that the information I am learning now, I will be teaching to others when the time is right. I guess that is why I was a teacher for forty years.

The hundredth monkey theory is an example of what is occurring on our planet right now. Our reality at the present time is an example of a holographic reality. What that means is that if there is any change in this hologram, whether large or small, it causes a ripple effect, like someone throwing a stone into a quiet pond, and it will start to change and affect all of us because we are all One. In the 1960s, Japanese primatologists discovered something interesting while observing Japanese Snow Monkeys in the wild. They came to the conclusion that there is a quantum jump in our evolution that is taking effect.

In 1980, a biologist by the name of Lyall Watson wrote a book entitled, "Lifetide." In it he said that Japanese primatologists while studying the Snow monkeys in the wild during the 1950s and 1960s, accidentally discovered a phenomenon that surprised them. After reading about this phenomenon, author Ken Keyes, in 1981, wrote a book entitled, "The Hundredth Monkey Effect." In this writing, Ken Keyes appealed to the world to end the cold war, and its policy that would surely one day destroy the world.

Scientists had been observing the Japanese Monkey, Macaca fuscata, in the wild for over 30 years. In 1952, on the island of Koshima, scientists were giving monkeys sweet potatoes which they dropped in the sand. The monkeys liked the taste of the raw sweet potatoes, but they didn't like the sand.

An 18-month-old female named Imo found she could solve the problem by washing the potatoes in a nearby stream. She taught this trick to her mother. Her playmates also learned this new way and they taught their mothers too.

The scientists observed this cultural innovation which was gradually learned by other monkeys. Between 1952 and 1958, all the young monkeys learned to wash the sandy sweet potatoes to make them more-tasty. Only the adults who learned from their children learned how to do this. Other adults kept eating the dirty sweet potatoes.

Then a stunning event occurred. In the autumn of 1958, a certain number of Koshima monkeys were washing sweet potatoes—the exact number is not known."

The author goes on to say, "Let us suppose that when the sun rose one morning there were 99 monkeys on Koshima Island who had learned to wash their sweet potatoes. Let's further suppose that later that morning, the hundredth monkey learned to wash potatoes. Then it happened!

By that evening almost everyone in the tribe was washing sweet potatoes before eating them. The added energy of this hundredth-monkey somehow created an ideological breakthrough."

Continuing Mr. Keyes says, "But notice! A most surprising thing observed by these scientists was that the habit of washing sweet potatoes then jumped over the sea. Colonies of monkeys on other islands and the mainland troop of monkeys at Takasakiyama began washing their sweet potatoes."

Therefore, continued our author, "when a certain critical number achieves an awareness, this new awareness may be communicated from mind to mind.

Although the exact number may vary, this Hundredth Monkey Phenomenon means that when only a limited number of people know of a new way, it may remain the conscious property of these people. But there is a point at which if only one more person tunes-in to a new awareness, a field is strengthened so that this awareness is picked up by almost everyone!"

When Lyall Watson did his original research, he put together the story from the testimonies of the primate researchers. Because the researchers had not expected this phenomenon, they had not counted the number of monkeys it took to start this effect. So that is why Watson suggested ninety-nine monkeys as an arbitrary figure, and then said that one more monkey, which in this case would represent the hundredth monkey, would create the "critical mass of consciousness" necessary to trigger the effect. Watson did say that he put the story together as a metaphor to explain the spontaneous changing of mass consciousness. Many New Age practitioners today believe in the idea of raising mass consciousness through reaching a critical mass.

Continuing with the words of the author, Ken Keyes, he states further, "The new behavior pattern spread to most, but not all, of the monkeys. Older monkeys, in particular, remained steadfast in their established behavior patterns and resisted change. When the new behavior pattern suddenly appeared among monkey troupes on other islands, only a few monkeys on those islands picked up on the new idea. The ones most receptive to new ideas started imitating the new behavior and demonstrating it to the impressionable younger ones. Thus, they too began their own path towards their eventual hundredth monkey effect."

So, taking this effect and applying it to humans, this is how the Hundredth Monkey Effect works. It seems that this works for humans the same way it works in monkeys. I am referring to the transference of ideas and/or behavior. We all live in a Universe that has a global mind or Universal Mind. Our human brains are continually receiving mental images and data coming to us, and then we transmit these mental images and data from that global mind under which we live.

The famous psychologist, Carl Jung, referred to the global mind as the collective unconscious. Jung went on to say that it is about vibration and frequency. He says further, that information is passed from one person to another based on their common frequency of consciousness. In other words, if monkeys had a new idea about something, then other monkeys on other islands who were vibrating at the same frequency, would have that same idea.

As an example, inventors who don't live near each other or even know each other, may come up with the same invention at the same time. The artist, Les Paul, of the duo Les Paul and Mary Ford, designed and then built the "first solid-body electric guitar". At the same time, Leo Fender was doing exactly the same thing. It is like you are thinking of a great idea about something but doing nothing about it, while at the same time, someone else having the same idea does something about it, or uses that same idea. You may have been thinking at the time, "That was my idea! Why didn't I do that?" That is how the collective unconscious works. It means that you are living in an atmosphere vibrating at a certain frequency, so that anyone else vibrating on that frequency, will "hear" your idea and make it his own.

So, thinking about that example, how does this work for the shift in consciousness that is occurring on Planet Earth? When a sufficient number of people on our planet go through a personal shift to the new paradigm, or consciousness, then a critical mass, the hundredth monkey, happens, and suddenly everyone becomes aware of the new consciousness, with its heart-centered values, and the evolutionary shift occurs.

At that time, the focus of thinking for the majority of people on the planet will center on heart-centered values. Humanity then will start to look in the past and see what has changed. It is then that we will realize that a massive, evolutionary shift has occurred.

Chapter 11

Present Contact and the Gifting of New Skills

If we consider our Earth as a spaceship and the earthly astronauts as the crew of that spaceship, I would say wars can be analogous to mutinies aboard the ship.
—Jacques-Yves Cousteau

In the past year, I have become very aware of the many different types of beings that I am having contact with. Many are here to provide protection to me and my husband while I explore how to teach others about what is really going on in our society and government and the governments of the world so that as a society, we can demand change. The Galactic Federation of Light is here to assist us in our progress, but they will not intervene unless what is happening will be detrimental to the Earth and would, therefore, cause a ripple effect in the galaxy. For example, I have been told that they have stopped nuclear launches of missiles by either shooting them down or messing with the electronics so that the missile would not reach its intended target. The government launching the missile just assumed that their missile did not fire correctly and it was a failure. One of the things I have learned over the years is that when I get close to a breakthrough in understanding and I start sharing the information with others, is when roadblocks start appearing in my life that seem to thwart my efforts. My computers suddenly go down or my internet becomes wonky to the point that I cannot get on line and I have to bring my expert out to fix it. Other things that have occurred is having my car not start when I am leaving to go to a very important lecture or meeting which forces me to find other ways to get to where I am going. These happenings are mainly just annoying and are designed to slow me down or keep me from doing something that I should be doing. I don't let them stop me from the intended activity, but I have to focus on not letting myself get upset or worked up about it because that just lowers my vibrations, and that is not a place I want to be.

Not all of the beings that are contacting me are extraterrestrial. Many are beautiful Angels and Archangels, Native American spirits as well as extraterrestrial and interdimensional beings. I will share with you a story about how these interactions have developed over the last fifteen years. This story has to do with a special interaction with one of my guardian angels.

In the early 1990s, I was becoming aware of how angels were interacting with me on a regular basis and would become part of the angel therapy I would do with my clients who requested it. This was happening simultaneously with my encounters with extraterrestrials.

It was at a hypnotherapy convention where the angel expert, Doreen Virtue, was holding a lecture on communicating with your angels. Because I was now having fairly regular encounters with angels, I decided to go. After the introductions, Doreen asked the audience, "How many of you know the name of your guardian angel?" Out of an audience of approximately 75 people, only a handful of people raised their hands. She then went on to tell us how to find out. She told us, "When you get ready to go to sleep tonight, close your eyes and get centered. Then just ask your guardian angel what his or her name is. Whatever name pops into your head is your angel's name." It seemed simple enough, so that is exactly what I did when I went to bed that night. I centered myself and asked the question, and the name that came back to me was "David". So, I began to call him David, but then

I would say things to him such as, “I’m pretty sure your name is David, so I am going to call you that. But if it isn’t, I apologize.” That was that. I talked to David every day and night either at meditation time or bedtime. Other than talking to him during those times, I didn’t give it much thought. Well, he must have gotten tired of me always second guessing his name, that he decided to do something about it.

I told several stories in my first book, “Caught Between Two Worlds: A Journey Through Time” about my week-long trainings with CSETI, The Center for the Study of Extraterrestrial Intelligence, and Dr. Steven Greer. For the first three trainings, my CSETI buddy for the week was Mike. It was fortunate that Mike and I lived fairly close to each other in southern California. We had decided early on that we would get together for dinner once a month and share with each other what was happening in our lives as it related to CSETI, the extraterrestrials, but also anything in the paranormal realm. The restaurant where we usually went was a stand-alone building at the entrance to a large mall. There was something different on one particular Friday night when we got together. It was early summer and the weather was perfect. We had just finished dinner and decided to walk across the parking lot and get a cup of coffee at the Starbucks located at the entrance to the mall. The air was electrifying as young people met and linked up with their friends, trying to decide what to do for the night. Just being there gave one a sense of excitement, of not knowing what to expect, but yet not really expecting anything.

Mike and I each ordered our coffee and then took it to an outside table because the weather was so perfect. We sat down at a square table away from the doors and at the outer edges of the open patio. I had my day planner with me with a large sticker on the front saying “Area 51”. Not thinking about it, I set the planner on the table to the side with the sticker face up. Mike and I were seated adjacent to each other with an empty seat across from each of us. After we had been there for about 5 minutes, a young man just seemed to appear walking towards our table. He was absolutely beautiful. Guessing him to be about 14 years old, he had the most beautiful smile which made him seem far older than he appeared to be. His skin was flawless and the color one might expect from a crossing of one white parent and one black parent-that beautiful color that so many of us strive for at the beach each summer. It was stunning. He also had loose curly hair that hung around his precious face. Approaching our table, he greeted both of us, but then turned his attention to me. He asked if he could sit down and of course we said yes. He sat across from me. Looking down at my day planner he said, "Do you believe in this stuff?" I then automatically switched to "teacher mode" and began talking about the Universe and the possibilities of life elsewhere. I had forgotten to ask him what his name was earlier, so I said, "What is your name?' He smiled a most beautiful smile and said, "David. My name is David." Now I know you, my readers, are making the connection. But, not I. I just kept right on talking. David then said to me, "I bet your students love you as a teacher." I looked at him in astonishment and said, "Teacher? What makes you think I am a teacher? I did not tell you that I was a teacher." He laughed a most charming laugh and said, "Well, aren't you?" I laughed and said, "Well, yes! I am!" "Do your students like this stuff," he asked again. Responding quickly now I said, "Yes my students love it, but I have to be very careful about what I say in a public-school setting. My more elaborate conversations with students take place after school or before school." Not missing a beat, David said, "I want to be a teacher." I replied, "Awesome. You will make a wonderful teacher." During this entire conversation, Mike was merely an observer while David and I carried on this wonderful conversation. Almost as quickly as he had appeared twenty minutes before, he stood up, thanked us for our time, Feng Shued the table and left us. As we watched him leave, he just seemed to disappear.

Mike and I sat there stunned for a couple of minutes, saying nothing to each other. Finally, Mike broke the ice by saying, "What do angels look like?" I said, "I don't know, but I think we just met one." Now I know you readers think that I figured it out now, but sadly, I did not. I don't know how hard an angel has to "hit you over the head" before you get the message, but David was having to work overtime on this one. It took me until six months later when Mike and I were on another CSETI training and we were driving with some other people going back to the hotel for the night. It was about 2 am and I was telling everyone the story about how we met David. All of a sudden, the reality bell went off in my head and I realized that David was my own guardian angel appearing to me to let me know that I was correct about his name. I gasped, "Oh my goodness! Mike, David was my guardian angel. How could I not see that?" Mike, being the positive person that he is said, "Well, your head wasn't on that at that moment. We had been talking about CSETI and other things, so when he came to our table, you did not make the connection. At least you have made it now." "Yes," I replied. "I can't wait to talk to him tonight and tell him I finally figured it out."

Later when I did go to bed I said, "David, I finally figured it out. I know who you are. Thank you for sharing that with me. I am sorry that I am so dense and did not get the message for six months, but at least now I have it." I jokingly said, "It must be hard sometimes being my guardian angel."

There have been many new skills that I have acquired as a result of my encounters with extraterrestrials. One of these skills came from an encounter on a CSETI advanced training when our circle was bathed in a Heavenly Light originating from interstellar space and a Galactic Federation ship. This beautiful light allowed the veil to start being lifted back. One of the things that started happening to me is that I have become an empath. This ability grows stronger and stronger every day. Sometimes what I feel from others can weigh heavily with me because of the nature of what is happening with the person. Especially with people I love and am involved with, tapping into their feelings empathically can be difficult for me if they are experiencing some rough times in their lives. I had to learn to be able to respond to what I was feeling, but not internalize it. That is easier said than done, but I am getting better at it. Most of the time however, I am given the blessed opportunity to actually feel another person at the soul level. It is beautiful and powerful and can literally take your breath away when you least expect it. I am thankful that I have been given this skill because it allows me to see all of the magnificent and beautiful souls that are here on Earth now. Remembering that we are all One is the wonderful message of Heaven.

Part VI

Messages from Our Star Visitor Families

Chapter 12

The Ashtar Command of The Galactic Federation of Light

The new spirituality is that it will produce an experience in human encounters in which we become a living demonstration of the basic spiritual teaching 'We are all One!
—Neale Donald Walsch[6]

The first time I remember hearing about the Ashtar Command of the Galactic Federation of Light, was in the mid-1980s, after my re-awakening experiences began. At that time, I considered it just more information that I was gathering on my long road of learning, and I did not think at that time that it had anything to do with me on a personal level.

So, what is the Ashtar Command of the Galactic Federation of Light? To start with, let me tell you about the Galactic Federation in general. To give you an analogy, if you think about the Star Trek series from television and movies, the United Federation of Planets would be similar. Its members are not from Earth. It is an alliance of super spiritual beings that are from different star systems. Many of them look like us because they are human, only more evolved, and some are humanoids. Because they are highly enlightened and advanced, they have technologies that are very advanced. These members have mastered the understanding of consciousness, and how consciousness can be incorporated into the technology. For example, people who observed the crash site of the flying disc at Roswell, New Mexico in 1947, stated that it looked like the space craft was trying to fix itself. Because they have knowledge of how the universe works, and have mastered these skills, they can travel from place to place at warp speeds. They know how to time travel and do inter-dimensional travel as well. They are also able to perform teleportation easily. Another amazing thing they are able to do is to create things from nothing, out of thin air, so to speak. They do this by using equipment they refer to as replicators. These replicators are able to reassemble atoms and molecules. With the use of consciousness, it is also possible to manifest items without even using the replicator. Eventually, as the Earth and her people go through ascension into the fifth dimension, we will become part of the Galactic Federation of Light.

Interestingly, the Galactic Federation of Light has placed a quarantine around the Earth, mainly to stop the negative actions of the dark cabal. When we became a space faring nation in America back in the late 1950s and 1960s, instead of approaching space travel as a peaceful agenda, leaders in the dark cabal were trying to figure out how they could arm space with nuclear weapons, especially on the moon. They were driven even more towards that objective when we first landed a man on the moon in 1969. I'm sure it was that way with the Soviet Union as well. Wonderful technologies had been given to the governments of Earth that would have created amazing energy devices that would have healed the Earth, but would have also made energy use by people easy and very inexpensive. We would have had our New Earth back then, but, unfortunately, the leaders of the dark cabal wanted to control the Earth and all of her inhabitants. The leaders and the councils of the Galactic Federation of Light decided it would be in everyone's best interest to control and limit the Earth's inhabitants from going into space. We have only been allowed to send unmanned probes into space and to other worlds for exploration purposes only. They will remove this quarantine once the dark cabal has been removed from the Earth. The cabal in the United States is the faction that is hanging on the hardest, but the Galactic Federation of Light assures us that removing them is progressing on schedule.

As early as the end of the Second World War, people from the Galactic Federation of Light contacted members in the United States government to warn them about the secret pacts they had made with extraterrestrials in order to gain technologies of weaponry. I am guessing that the warning was not heeded by the people in charge of that department.

The Galactic Federation of Light are not allowed to directly interfere with the people of Earth until the climate of fear decreases enough that they can openly contact us and feel safe from attack. That is one of the reasons there have been more and more UFO sightings recently throughout the world. However, that does not mean that they have not helped us indirectly in other ways. For example, they have disabled nuclear missiles after they have been launched, and they have been interfering with the negative use of HAARP devices that can create havoc throughout the planet. HAARP stands for High Frequency Active Auroral Research Program and was explained to the public as a scientific organization that could work with the weather so that we would not have droughts or super deluges around the world. Instead, the dark cabal has used it to achieve many negative events on the planet, which have caused havoc and devastation. Another important thing that the Galactic Federation of Light has been helping with is to neutralize the nanotechnology material that has been placed into and fused with our vaccines. This was designed by the dark cabal to murder large parts of the population, especially children and the elderly, in order to gain better control over the population. Additionally, they have been helping with the clean- up of Mother Earth by clearing the oil spill in the Gulf from 2010, neutralizing the chemtrails in large population areas, and cleaning up the pollutions in some areas that are creating huge problems in delicate biomes on the Earth.

The dark cabal gets its life force and energy by stealing it from others. Its goal is to control the planet and to use its inhabitants as slaves to serve them. Their natures are self-serving and they desire to control, kill, and cause destruction of the planet on a massive scale. Some have asked, "Well if they have to live on Earth too, why would they want to destroy it?" The answer is something like, "You may take us down, but when you do, we want to leave you with a dead planet when we go."

The members of the Galactic Federation of Light are in stark contrast to this. They are from the higher realms, and they are able to get spiritual energies from the divine, which allows them to promote life and better situations for people. Galactic members enjoy working for the benefit of others, and are known to be very generous. They have also been known to, if they find it is necessary, sacrifice themselves for the welfare of others. Members of the Galactic Federation of Light have a deep understanding about us being One with each other throughout this vast universe. They have achieved full consciousness, which is a multi-dimensional state where they are highly evolved. After our ascension, we will be at full consciousness as well. We humans from Earth have a veil that covers our past memories, so that we may not access the knowledge from our past lives. It is what has been keeping us in a state of limited consciousness, and has created the duality that we find ourselves in. As part of our ascension into the fifth dimension, we are being returned to full consciousness as well. Our much older space brothers and sisters are here now to assist us with our ascension and our return to fully conscious Beings of Light.

It was decreed by Heaven that the Galactic Federation of Light assist us with our ascension into the fifth dimension. But because we have Free Will on our planet, they will not interfere with that and are therefore, forbidden to do everything for us. We must do it, but they are right behind us giving their full support in what we do. Humanity must awaken from within, and we are doing that at a rapid pace. When we get to a certain point, then the Galactic Federation may openly assist us. To help this along, huge numbers of these highly evolved people from the Galactic Federation of Light have been incarnating on the Earth since the 1960s when, as the song goes, "We are at the dawning of the Age of Aquarius." They came specifically to help us awaken and to heal others, to bring light to the Earth, and transmit information to our collective consciousness. Those who have chosen to incarnate at this time have had to do very deep work in their own lives so as to get themselves into the highest state of Light as ascension nears.

People from other planets and dimensions have seen Earth as a dark Reptilian-Orion world. It has been understood throughout the Universe as a planet of darkness with a few Light patches sprinkled here and there. Now Earth is seeking to come completely into the Light. When this happens, it will be an amazing time for everyone on the planet and in the entire Universe. Some of the places where members of the Galactic Federation of Light have come from are Agartha, Andromeda, Arcturus, Lyra, Mars, the Pleiades, Sirius, and Vega. Many have been called Wanderers, Star-seeds, Way showers, Indigo Children and Adults, and Crystal Children. As a general term, they are all referred to as Lightworkers. If one thinks about it, they are considered to the ground forces of Light. Many of these individuals have on-going contact with the Galactic Federation of Light. The late Dolores Cannon, Steven Greer, MD, and Sheldon Nidle are some of those individuals. These forces of Light from the Galactic Federation of Light are made up of highly evolved souls. They are either incarnated now or in the spirit world. They include higher inter-dimensional Beings of Light, such as the Angelic realm or the Ascended Masters. Almost every night, I see angels in my bedroom.

One of the reasons for the delay with disclosure and first landing is that the Orion-Reptilian group threatened mass annihilation of the people if they did show up for first contact. That has been neutralized now and so the events by the Galactic Federation of Light are proceeding on schedule.

The Ashtar Command of the Galactic Federation of Light works with the Ascended Masters in order to achieve their divine purpose. Their work includes the overseeing of the space around the Earth, and to monitor whatever activities that are planned or are taking place on the Earth. It also stays in contact with the ground forces that are on Earth.

There are many well-known higher beings that are members of the Galactic Federation of Light. They include Ashtar Sheran, Hatonn, Sananda Esu Immanuel, and Vrillion. This command attempted to contact Earth through their communications director, Vrillion, in 1977 when an ITN broadcast was disrupted. This was mentioned in chapter twenty-six of this book in detail.

Chapter 13

Disclosure and The Awakening of The Masses

Never doubt that a small group of thoughtful, committed citizens can change the world; indeed, it's the only thing that ever has.
—Margaret Mead

Lightworkers and others have been after the governments of the world to stop the secrecy about extraterrestrials and the technologies they possess. More and more people in the past 30 years now believe that there has been a colossal cover-up by our government, and other governments as well, regarding this topic. One might ask, *Why, would the governments of the world, and specifically our government in the United States, want to keep the visitations by extraterrestrial and interdimensional beings to our planet, a secret?* Besides not wanting to lose control over such visitations and the programs that may have been started around that, what bothers these cabal leaders the most is the technologies that these highly evolved beings used to get here. Once the official word gets out that the cabal government, not our duly elected government, has kept all of these technologies a secret for the last 50+ years, citizens are going to want to know and understand why.

When I have asked this question of people who could at least give me an educated guess as to the secrecy, I have received answers such as, *If people were frightened in 1947 by the radio broadcast of Orson Welles, "War of the Worlds, which was not true, then how are they going to deal with something that is true?"* Another response was, *We, cannot let people know the truth because we will have pandemonium when they realize what their religious leaders have told them is false.* Still another answer was, *Once, people find out that we have been lying about this, they won't trust us again on anything.* While there may be some truth to all of those, they would add up to about 5% of the people who would feel that way. What the military industrial complex is really afraid of is that once we find out that extraterrestrials have been visiting the Earth for the past 50+ years and have made contact with our leaders, most of us will want to know how they were able to get here, and what other technologies could they give us and what could they teach us?

In the 1950s, when Dwight D. Eisenhower was president, he was whisked away to Edwards Air Force Base one day when he was visiting California and was playing golf in Palm Springs. The reason given to the public was that the president needed some emergency dental care and was treated by a local dentist. The next morning while the president was attending a church service in Los Angeles, he told that story to local newspaper reporters. The dentist later showed up at an event for President Eisenhower. Even though the president had given the press a viable reason for leaving the golf game, there was still much speculation that the president was using that as a cover story for something else. President Eisenhower was taken to Edward's because an extraterrestrial spacecraft had landed there. President Eisenhower and a few military high-ranking individuals met with the extraterrestrials who were piloting this craft. This meeting began a series of meetings with, allegedly, three different extraterrestrial races. The original meeting at Edwards Air Force Base was with very tall Nordic looking beings. They were humans who looked just like us only they were much taller. This group warned our government about the extraterrestrials who were in orbit around the Earth over the equator. These human Nordic extraterrestrials offered to help us with our spiritual development which would raise our vibrations, which would help us thwart anything negative by these

"Grey extraterrestrials." The condition they gave us in order to help us was that we had to destroy our nuclear weapons. They also refused to give us any technology saying that we were spiritually unable to handle the technology we already had. They fully believed that we would use any new technology to destroy each other. They told the president and the military present at this meeting, that we were on a path of self-destruction, and that we must stop killing each other, end all wars, stop polluting the Earth and stop destroying the Earth by using up her natural resources, and we must learn to live together in peace and harmony. They also told the president that they could get rid of the Greys orbiting the Earth as well. These terms were looked at by our government as being very suspicious, and they felt that if we disarmed our nuclear weapons, we would be vulnerable to the Soviet Union, as well as any extraterrestrials that might attack us. In that light, this offer was rejected.

After their encounter, the president wanted to figure out how to tell our citizens about this visitation. The high-ranking officials in our military finally were able to convince the president that telling the public about this event would not be a good idea. After that, the military began compartmentalizing everything that related to this topic and the technologies involved. Things became *On a need to Know,* basis, and the president did not have the clearance to find out the information. He and future presidents were successfully cut out of the loop. In his farewell speech to our nation, President Eisenhower stated,

> ...in the councils of government, we must guard against the acquisition of unwarranted influence, whether sought or unsought, by the military-industrial complex. The potential for the disastrous rise of misplaced power exists and will persist. We must never let the weight of this combination endanger our liberties or democratic processes. We should take nothing for granted. Only an alert and knowledgeable citizenry can compel the proper meshing of the huge industrial and military machinery of defense with our peaceful methods and goals, so that security and liberty may prosper together....

He went on to say, "You and I-my fellow citizens-need to be strong in our faith that all nations, under God, will reach the goal of peace with justice. May we be ever unswerving in devotion to principle, confident but humble with power, diligent in pursuit of the Nations' great goals." President Eisenhower ended his speech by saying a prayer.

> We pray that peoples of all faiths, all races, all nations, may have their great human needs satisfied; that those now denied opportunity shall come to enjoy it to the full; that all who yearn for freedom may experience its spiritual blessings; that those who have freedom will understand, also, its heavy responsibilities; that all who are insensitive to the needs of others will learn charity; that the scourges of poverty, disease and ignorance will be made to disappear from the earth, and that, in the goodness of time, all peoples will come to live together in a peace guaranteed by the binding force of mutual respect and love.

This speech was given on January 17, 1961. It sounds like a prayer that could be given today as we visualize our new Earth and what we want it to be like.

This is basically the place where the cover-up began, and has persisted until today. President Clinton was briefed by Dr. Steven Greer regarding releasing the information surrounding UFOs and visits by extraterrestrials. Later, Dr. Greer, briefed president Obama about the same thing. Both leaders declined to get involved. Realizing that the government of the United States was not going to admit to the cover-up, Dr. Greer worked even harder to train ambassadors to make peaceful contact with these sentient ET races that are here. Dr. Greer and CSETI are not the only organizations training ambassadors for first contact. They can be found easily on the internet. The fact is that one of the only countries in the world that has not officially told the truth about extraterrestrials is the United States. So, the people are doing it.

So, what exactly is disclosure? Basically, it is the announcement by the governments of the world that we are not alone in the universe. Not only are we not alone, but many races of galactic humans and other intelligent beings are visiting here and have been for quite a long time. The extraterrestrials that are here now are peaceful and are here for peaceful purposes. Any extraterrestrial civilization that may visit the Earth has been portrayed as negative and wanting to conquer us. The people covering this up want to build fear into our future dealings with extraterrestrials. The period of secrecy that has continued for more than half a century will be ended by disclosure.

The resistance to disclosure comes mainly from the governments whose militaries have benefited from the technologies given to us by these benevolent extraterrestrial beings. They were intended to be utilized in a peaceful way by everyone on the planet. Some examples of these technologies are anti-gravity propulsion systems and free energy devices, also known as zero-point energy devices. Instead of being given to the people of the planet, the military took the technology and used it for aggression. Some of the other technologies were back engineered from downed or crashed spacecraft. The technology derived from the crashed spacecraft at Roswell, New Mexico in 1947, was the computer.

Not many of the people on our planet are aware of these technologies or what they have been used for. Since the Roswell crash and the discovery of ET bodies, our government has opposed disclosure. Many important people have lost their lives trying to disclose this information. Some of these are President John F. Kennedy, James Forrestal who was the Secretary of the Defense, and actually communicated with the extraterrestrial who was still alive after the Roswell crash, and CIA Director William Colby. However, over time, word starts to leak out and the secrecy is now almost impossible to maintain. The leaders of the Galactic Federation of Light as well as our own spiritual leaders on Earth agree that knowledge of ET visitations should no longer be kept from the people.

One of the reasons I am sharing my story by writing this book is because humanity needs to be ready to meet and greet our space brothers and sisters. They come from many places. The star systems of the Pleiades, Sirius, Andromeda, Arcturus, and many others, are where many originate from. They worship and believe in the same God we do. But, unlike us, they are evolved to the point of the 5th dimension or higher and they follow strictly the universal laws that say harming another individual is prohibited, as is stealing, deceiving someone, or any other immoral or unethical deeds or behaviors. Unfortunately, many of us here on the Earth still behave in a primitive way or in immoral ways.

If the goals of the extraterrestrials had been evil, they could have taken over our planet a long time ago. The fact is that they do not force their will on others, and they respect our ability to express free will. The fact that they do not force their will over us is one of the reasons that disclosure has taken so long to happen. The Galactic Federation of Light and other galactic members could have stopped the ruling elite on our planet and the military, but if they had, they would have violated their own rules of conduct. They were invited here to Earth by the ascended masters. These masters are also known as the White Brotherhood and Sisterhood. White does not refer to race, but rather, it refers to the Light.

In the past, some races of negative extraterrestrials have visited the Earth and interacted with the people by creating havoc in their lives. Now, however, these negative beings are no longer being allowed to even approach the Earth. So, there is now nothing to fear from the arrival of these Galactic Federation of Light spaceships that come in peace to make open contact with us.

One of the messages that the ETs have given me over and over again throughout my life is that we are all One. At the end of World War II, when we dropped the atomic bombs on Hiroshima and Nagasaki, it created death and destruction in other dimensions of space as well because we are all connected. Extraterrestrials started coming here in larger numbers to attempt to convince the leaders of Earth's governments to stop using these weapons of mass destruction. Unfortunately, they were not successful in getting our governments to stop. So, the Galactic Federation and others neutralized all nuclear weapons on Earth. Although governments like the United States have been threatening to bomb countries like Iran or North Korea, the fact is no nuclear bombs are capable of being detonated for aggressive reasons. The other reason that the extraterrestrials are here now is because of the Divine Plan from Heaven for the Earth and this golden age. We have just shifted from the Age of Pisces to the Golden Age of Aquarius. Those of us who are starseeds from the 1960s, knew about this on some level, and were trying to get the message across to others. One of my favorite lines from a song of those times is, "This is the dawning of the Age of Aquarius…" And, of course, it was. On December 21, 2012, which was also the end of the Mayan calendar, a huge influx of Light entered the planet and began our global transformation into the Light and allowing us to get closer to entering the 5th dimension. The Galactic Federation of Light is working with Earth humans to get rid of the power elite, or the Dark Cabal. When this phase is complete, we will be preparing ourselves for the completion of this cycle and will move into the 5th dimension with the help of our extraterrestrial brothers and sisters.

The Galactic Federation of Light has communicated with the people of Earth before. I mentioned before the radio transmission by Vrillion of the Ashtar Command of the Galactic Federation of Light in 1977, when he interrupted the evening news on Britain's Southern ITV to make a broadcast that lasted for 5 and ½ minutes. One of the things he said in that broadcast was, "The New Age can be a time of great peace and evolution for your race, but only if your rulers are made aware of the evil forces that can overshadow their judgments."

Since that broadcast, members of the Galactic Federation of Light have used methods of communication such as telepathy or communicating through a medium or channel. There are some very good mediums that can be trusted to remove their egos when they are channeling the extraterrestrial. Many representatives from the Galactic Federation of Light channel messages through the internet many times per week to keep us informed as to what is happening regarding disclosure and first contact.

The global elite has been using things like HAARP technology to create earthquakes, cause volcanic eruptions, tsunamis, wildfires, and floods. They are doing that because they fear that disclosure of ET presence will happen. That is one of the reasons that the Galactic

Federation of Light has become more and more inclined not to be specific about dates for disclosure. They are looking to prevent the rogue governments from using this technology against the planet and even against their own people. The tornadoes and floods happening in the American Midwest, and some of the wildfires that are plaguing the west, are events that have been created using these technologies to create havoc here and to take our minds off of disclosure. This will not prevent the information from coming out. It may only postpone it.

Foster Gamble and his wife, Kimberly Carter Gamble, started an organization called "Thrive Movement.com". Foster Gamble is an heir to the Proctor and Gamble empire, and he explains that he grew up in privilege and was being groomed to step into politics when the time was right. However, at a young age, Foster was concerned that with all of the abundance and availability of resources around the Earth, that people were not thriving. He set out to make it his life's work to find out why. While a student at Princeton University, he studied Aikido, which is a non-violent martial art. He earned a third- degree black belt and taught it for 15 years. It helped his reputation of appearing both powerful and gentle.

After studying this concept that everyone on Earth should be thriving, he made a movie called, "Thrive." What Foster Gamble did was to "follow the money" in every aspect of human life. He quickly discovered many things. This documentary uncovers what is really going on in our world by exposing the global consolidation of power in almost all aspects of our lives. Part of this power is in covering up extraterrestrial visitations and their technologies. If these ET technologies were to be brought to light, who would stand to lose and who would gain? Well, it is easy to say who would gain from them. Everyone on the planet would gain from these technologies. So, who stands to lose? For one thing, if zero-point energy devices are finally released to the public, there would be no more need for oil and gas. The multi-trillion-dollar oil industry would go bankrupt, including the oil cartels around the world. These devices would be inexpensive to build because they would utilize the elements that are found in our air. They could be placed on each household, powering everything. We would have no more need for the big utility companies.

These zero- point devices could also be modified to power our vehicles. The countries that are the poorest would now be prosperous. With abundant power, water could be cleaned and diverted so that it could be utilized by towns. Crops would grow and people would no longer be hungry. The cures for major diseases that have been suppressed would now be released. We would no longer need pharmaceutical companies forcing us to take pills and getting unnecessary vaccinations because our environment would now be clean and disease would be wiped out. New economies would spring up all around the planet, and the big banking interests would no longer be necessary in the way they control us today. There would no longer be a need for war because people would have all the necessities; basically, everything they need. Usually war is created because one side wants what the other side has.

When Dr. Steven Greer was training a group of ambassadors at Mt. Shasta, California, a film producer, Armardeep Kaleka, was in attendance. After seeing what the training was about and that contact with these extraterrestrial peoples was made, Armardeep offered to make a movie for Steven regarding the cover-up of UFOs and their technologies, if Steven could raise the money to do it. Steven went to the public by going to the internet on one of those fund-raising sites and asking for the money to fund this movie. People were given a deadline of only a few months to pledge $250,000.00 to start the production of the movie. If that goal was not met by that timeline, everyone who had donated would have been given their money back. The people from all over the world, sent in donations, and the goal was met. Donations kept coming in for almost nine months, and the movie was made. The movie is called, "Sirius." It shows people who have given testimony regarding the existence of UFOs and of being part of the cover-up or who worked in departments where some of this stuff was worked on. Also, people who made official reports of sightings or encounters to the authorities, only to have it classified and covered-up, seemed to be the order of the day. These individuals have made sworn statements about their involvement or what they observed. Additionally, we are shown video clips of CSETI trainings, and the contacts that are made during these trainings. A very special part of this movie shows the work being done by Dr. Greer, scientists, and other specialists, as they are working on the skeleton of an extraterrestrial being discovered in the Atacama Desert in South America. There are well-known researchers from the Stanford University labs that are working on this being's DNA to see what they can found out about it. Apparently, after everything was complete, the dark side intervened and the story coming from the lead researcher, suddenly changed. Like Thrive, Sirius also talks about these zero-point energy devices and how they would free up our world if they were to be released.

So once disclosure happens, what is to follow? The first event that will happen is the arrests of the dark cabal elitists who are responsible for crimes against humanity, war crimes, torture, financial treason, genocide and any other crimes which the people would have never suspected. Tragically, most of the so-called natural disasters that have happened in the past few years, like in Haiti, Chile, New Zealand, the United States, Japan, and many false flag events, such as 9-11 in New York City, the Boston Marathon bombing, some of the school shootings, and others, have been caused by the dark cabal. They are also referred to as the Illuminati or even The New World Order.

One of the goals of the dark cabal was to reduce the population of the world from seven billion to only five hundred million. To do this, the dark cabal has caused manmade pandemics, chemtrails and now chembombs, the radioactive left over from using uranium, and the release of many toxic wastes throughout our environment. These elitists have messed with our food production by using GMO seeds and foods, and have contaminated farmers' fields by throwing their seed onto their fields after they have been planted with uncontaminated seed. They have caused droughts and floods, both of which cause disruption in food production. The dark cabal has also orchestrated false-flag events such as 9-11, the London bombing, the bombing in Madrid, and the Oklahoma City bombing. They blamed all of these on terrorists. They have even planned a nuclear World War III or a false flag of an alien attack from space. They have done other evil things that has caused intentional deaths of millions of people. They have all but destroyed many of our constitutional rights in the United States, have created surveillance networks throughout our country and the world, tried to inflict martial law on all of us, and they planned to put in prison anyone who spoke against what the government was doing. These dark elitists have undermined the financial and legal systems, watered down our educational system so that we are producing robots who will obey the government without fail, destroyed our medical system, which was the best in the world, and infiltrated our religious institutions with garbage. The fact that these elitists control the mass media ensures that the truth did not come out, and they have been brainwashed to believe that any conspiracy theories or conspiracy theorists were not to be believed.

Disclosure will end all of that. The members of the dark cabal who are responsible for these crimes against humanity and the rape of the Earth, will find themselves facing judges from Galactic courts. They will be charged with their crimes and made to be accountable for them. According to the Galactic Federation of Light, the evidence produced in this court will be irrefutable and the verdicts will be based on fairness. There will be no place for vengeance or unfairness. These Galactic courts cannot be tampered with or corrupted in any way.

Happening concurrently will be a planetary abundance program that was created by the American Congress and agreed upon by all. It is known as NESARA, and is an acronym meaning National Economic Security and Reformation Act. It was ratified by the Congress, but not yet proclaimed or enacted. Under its provisions, life will change for the better for all people. Debt will be erased, income tax will be made fair for all or ended completely, prosperity will be assured for every citizen, and there will be many other things done to eliminate poverty, hunger, homelessness, and other tragic conditions, many by releasing the zero-point technologies. As part of the deal, the cabal elitists will be stripped of all their income sources, and any money earned illegally will be taken away and returned to the people. As we get closer to full disclosure, we are seeing the economy around us crumbling. Once the fall of the economy is complete, NESARA will be announced.

Also, at this time, the Galactic Federation of Light will give to humanity technology that will give us worldwide communication, revolutionary healthcare, ease of travel, and many other benefits that we cannot even imagine.

Part VII

Earth and Human History

Chapter 14

Where It All Began-Our Original History

You must unlearn what you have learned
—Yoda

Part of my education has come from being taken onboard spacecraft when I was a child and taught certain things. Later, my learning came from being taken to a place that I referred to as the Cosmic Academy (my term) and being taught by elders from the Galactic Federation of Light. While there I was given the names of who to learn from while in my daily life, to keep learning the information, how to do things, and what to tell others when I would be asked at a later time. There were actually many names given to me, but I have chosen to learn from, and am still learning from Sheldon Nidle of the Planetary Activation Organization and the Galactic Federation of Light, and Steven Greer, MD of CSETI, The Center for the Study of Extraterrestrial Intelligence. I also follow the Ashtar Command of the Galactic Federation of Light website. The intentions of all of these people are to dissipate fear and clear up any misunderstandings about information and give insights into what is really occurring behind the daily headlines. Although channeled information can be very good and accurate, none of these people channel their information. It is received directly from the Galactic Federation to these teachers or directly from the enlightened and advanced beings whom they work with. All of these teachers have told basically the same story over the years, and so I feel very comfortable with what I have learned from them. In addition, my galactic teachers confirm the information through interactions with me, lucid dreams, and bilocation.

The next story I am going to tell you is as accurate as I can figure out from putting the story together from my mentors. But because I cannot put the story together with the religious teachings I have been told throughout my life, the Holy Bible, the Holy Qur'an, and the books of other religions, I'm going to be safe and write this as though it might be fiction. However, I would compel everyone who reads this to put it together with what they have been taught, do some research, and just see what you sense to be true or not true. I'm pretty sure I have the main story right, but there are probably many nuances that I do not have straight yet. I was considering leaving it out of the book, but I find it so fascinating that I decided to include it. Look into your hearts and you be the judge. The full story will be told to us by our extraterrestrial mentors once first contact has occurred anyway.

The story begins approximately eight million years ago. At that time, life was beautiful and enlightened, and all was good. There were many groups of Archangels who were fully conscious beings, but one particular group was very curious. Some of them wanted to experiment with new things. They wondered what it would be like to be cut off from God, the Source. One particular Archangel wanted to know what it would be like to experience something different for a change. This Archangel knew it would be a dangerous thing to do, to cut himself off from God, but he decided to try it anyway. He figured that he could just reverse everything when he was done experiencing by simply reversing the process. So, he created some kind of dimensional chamber that had a strong electromagnetic force. When he climbed into the chamber, he was exposed to these strong magnetic fields in order to experience this feeling of being different.

Immediately he regretted what he had done. He realized he did not like being cut off from God. So, he urgently tried to get back but found himself trapped. He could not find his way out and could, therefore, not go back to God. Now this Archangel was in a panic and he decided to ask the other Archangels for help. The other Archangels knew better but decided to try to help him anyway. Unfortunately, these other Archangels ended up being trapped in the chamber too. When they realized what they had done, they were mortified. They had no one to blame but themselves because they had made the choice to do it themselves. They were advised not to do it, but did it anyway. This group of Archangels were very sad and upset. Eventually they all decided to try and conquer the galaxy. Feeling cut off from Source, they began fending for themselves. They started to invade planets and spread the dark force energy around. This was actually the beginning of the Dark Side of the Force energy. One could only imagine at that time with 100 billion galaxies in the Universe, the damage they could do spreading the Dark.

When the Light forces found out about these fallen Archangels and what they were doing, they immediately took action against them in order to stop a rogue archangel takeover of the galaxy. Archangel Michael was called upon to put up an energy barrier of fences and force fields around the planets that had been affected by this rogue group of now fallen archangels. This was to stop them from spreading Darkness any further. Other Light Beings created Galactic Forces of Light to free planets that were now under the rule of the Dark Forces. In reality, this was the beginning of the Galactic Forces of Light.

What happened next was the beginning of the Galactic Wars. During this time, many planets were destroyed. The Galactic Starfleet began to fight for the planets that were being captured and taken over by the fallen archangels, now of the dark side. It is my understanding that in the meantime, the Reptilians and the Dinosaurians also became part of the dark forces. In reality, we have these memories in our consciousness. The reason the "Star Wars" series of movies resonated so much with us is that on an unconscious level, we remembered these events. This was an actual story millions of years ago.

A stargate that exists at the center of our galaxy is known as the

Galactic Central Sun. It is here where God creates all souls and then they move out in all directions from there. When beings had expanded enough and became aware of the Oneness of all that there is, they started what was to be known as the central Brotherhood of Light. Those who advanced to the idea of Oneness, created a central civilization. Their job was to spread the idea of Oneness to everyone.

The Milky Way Galaxy is the shape of a double spiral. It is a vortex of energy containing about a hundred billion stars. This vortex created a galactic network of light which then spread to other races that had a desire to be freed from the darkness that had been created around them. During that time, the forces of the Light always won their battles, but there were billions and billions of planets and star systems to protect.

Because the Light forces were so spread out throughout the galaxy, around 25,000 years ago, the Dark forces decided to concentrate themselves in one small area of the galaxy in order to avoid the forces of Light. They ended up putting their headquarters in the Orion constellation and Earth. The planets around Orion and Earth became the dark side's fortress. They took humanity hostage.

About six million years ago, we, humans, began on the planet Vega, which is the third planet from Vega's star. Vega is a water world, just as Earth is a water world. It is interesting that the producers and directors of the movie, "Contact" that was made in the mid-1990s used Vega as their planet at the end of their stargate. How did they know to use Vega? Just an interesting curiosity. The spiritual hierarchy was advanced on Vega. It came to pass that the pre-Cetaceans, who were residing on the Earth, contacted Heaven and asked permission to allow them, as being from the Light, to change Earth to make it unsuitable for the Reptilians and the Dinosaurians. One half of the Cetaceans went out into the water to live. Today they are the dolphins and the whales. Most people realize that the consciousness of the dolphins and the whales is very advanced. They are super intelligent beings. The other half of the Cetaceans went out into the galaxies to search for a new land guardian. The Cetaceans now became the guardians of the water on Earth. They needed to find someone to become the guardians of the land, and help them with the land masses. At this time, humans were found by the Cetaceans on the Planet Vega, recruited them, and the galactic migration began. This was a sacred service that the humans did. During the Miocene Period, our story began on Earth in the Ural Mountain Range in what today is the country of Russia. During that time, there were three groups living on the Earth. They were the land Cetaceans, from which we evolved, the Reptilians, which were located in Asia, and the Dinosaurians, which were located in what is now present-day United States. The pre-cetaceans were furry land animals. The Dinosaurians were especially evil and wished to destroy completely all mammalian civilizations on Earth. The Reptilians were from Orion and were part of the Anchara Alliance. They also wanted to destroy the pre-cetaceans.

The Dinosaurians and the Reptilians claimed ownership of the entire galaxy. The galactic humans and their allies disagreed, and this resulted in a galactic war, that lasted for millions of years.

We reached Earth, or Gaia as she is known, about two million years ago. The human colony that was formed there was destroyed in a surprise attack by the beings from Orion about one million years ago. We were etheric beings then. Our society has been described in magical terms by our various mythologies. Those mythologies are all of the memories and evidence that we have that we existed here then. About 900,000 years ago, we returned and took back this solar system. We destroyed Maldek, which was their "death star." It was a giant floating space station, as depicted in the movie Star Wars. The Galactic Federation of Light took back this solar system.

Sadly, there is a part of Orion, according to Sheldon Nidle, that is called the great void. It is so warped that it can never be fixed. The immensity of the battles that took place between the Galactic Federation of Light and these Orion forces caused this void. In the movie, Star Wars, the evil empire forces destroy a peaceful planet with the use of advanced weaponry to try and take down the Alliance. It was a show of force to try and stop the Alliance, but it had reverse consequences. Instead, The Alliance destroyed the death star.

We returned to Earth and colonized Lemuria. This became both an inner and outer world. Lemuria was a huge continent which covered the majority of the Pacific Ocean. Atlantis was a huge continent that covered the majority of the Atlantic Ocean. The Reptilians also lived on Atlantis. I have also seen the terms Lemuria and Atlantis used interchangeably, so I guess we won't know exactly what these civilizations were until our extraterrestrial mentors tell us. About 25,000 years ago, space ships used tractor beams to move one of Earth's moons closer to the LaGrange Point. At that time, the Earth had two moons. According to Wikipedia, the LaGrange Points are the five positions in an orbital configuration where a small object affected only by gravity can theoretically be stationary relative to two larger objects such as a second Moon with respect to the Earth and main Moon. By moving this moon to the point of just before entering the LaGrange Point, they fired particle beam weaponry at the moon which destroyed it. Moon parts rained down on Lemuria in the form of meteor-like showers. Lemuria and its subterranean gas chambers were destroyed. This is the event that destroyed the dinosaurs. Lemuria sank into the ocean.

The Lemurians retreated to the safety of Agartha which is located in the inner Earth. We were made into limited consciousness at that time due to our destructive tendencies, and have been that way ever since. We all have a memory of this floating around in our unconscious memory banks.

Thirteen thousand years ago, Atlantis was destroyed during an attack of Ionia, which is now southern Europe. That is where the exiled Royal family members were sent. The Atlanteans left the Earth after the moon crash sunk Atlantis. They returned to the Beta Centauri star system. Beta Centauri A is a red giant, and B is a binary dwarf. The Atlanteans looked much as we do today. In fact, it has been said that they are our ancestors. The movie, "Star Wars" took all that we had in our memories and has helped us remember. I did not realize it at the time, but I was so involved in learning the information from "Return of the Jedi" that I saw it in the theaters over 30 times.

The first Golden Age was from 12.5 thousand years to 11 thousand years ago. The Annunaki re-introduced civilization to us. The Annunaki were an extraterrestrial civilization who were on the Earth during the Sumerian era. According to the Sumerian texts written on tablets, the Annunaki bred with the Earth women at the time and created homo sapiens. We would be considered a hybrid species, and then over thousands of years, have evolved into who we are today. According to research done by Zechariah Sitchin, the Annunaki came to Earth around 450,000 years ago. They came to mine gold in an area we know as Zimbabwe. They would mine the gold and send it back to their home planet called Nibiru or in modern times, Planet X.

The Annunaki helped us create agriculture, writing, technology, stone building, and cloth making, cooking, and created a religion for us. The religion they created was "We are your creator gods, bow down to us and give us your energy because we need it." This age was destroyed by a great flood.

The Second Golden Age was from 11 thousand years ago to 10 thousand years ago. The Annunaki took the survivors of the flood and deepened our amnesia. They interacted with a culture near Easter Island called the Harappa. They were an advanced civilization. They had running water, toilets, showers, and could fly in spacecraft. They had received these things and the knowledge to go with it from the Annunaki. There were writings discovered on Easter Island but no one has been able to decipher them. This age was destroyed by a thermonuclear storm.

The Third Golden Age was 10 thousand years ago to 9 thousand years ago. The humans under the rule of the Annunaki finally, over the years, remembered enough of their past to demand a society that was like Lemuria had been. They were eventually destroyed by the Great Biblical Flood. The survivors of this great flood were the Sphinx and the pyramids. They were built just before the fall of Atlantis.

During the end times of Atlantis, the Annunaki did interact with the people. They saw an opportunity to bring about the downfall of Atlantis because the people were so divided about how the Earth should be treated. They saw the potential to rule Atlantis on this planet because they had already destroyed Mars where they had lived. They took advantage of the downfall of Atlantis. With Lemuria and Atlantis gone, there was no one left on the Earth who would question what the Annunaki were doing or how they were using the Earth's resources.

The Annunaki also took the time to change history. They used the genetic structure of humans and manipulated it for their benefit. They deconstructed our DNA leaving us with two strands. By doing this to our DNA, they prevented us from remembering that we were once whole and connected to other realms and dimensions. Before, we had been able to communicate with other civilizations. We had been an enlightened species.

Going back to the Lemurians for a moment, many of them came from the Lyra star system. In that system, they knew that they were connected with all that there is, connected with other star systems and dimensions, and they also understood that they were multidimensional beings here on Earth to spend some time. Once they decided that they had accomplished all that they really wanted to do on Earth, many of them went back to Lyra. Those who decided to stay within our physical reality, went to Atlantis. It has been said that many of us who are on Earth today were actually there during the last lifetime of Atlantis, and we experienced the downfall of that advanced civilization. During that last time on Atlantis, our spiritual leaders were well aware that we humans were connected with beings in other dimensions and realms. At this time on Atlantis, there were actually three highly advanced civilizations living there-the Lemurians, the Atlantians, and the humans.

Even though the people of Atlantis knew this connection existed in their reality, they did not connect for some reason. This, then, was left to the spiritual leaders in Atlantis also known as the priest caste.

During that time, the priests of Atlantis were working with beings on Mars who had a colony there. These were the Annunaki. The Annunaki were actually not from Mars originally, but were from the Sirian Star System. The planet from which they originated was virtually destroyed by the Annunaki-they destroyed all of their natural resources. Because of this destruction, the Annunaki started to travel among the galaxies to many different star systems to find raw materials so that they could continue their own existence. The Annunaki have strong roots in the Sirian system, and they have control over many of the planets there. They manipulated and controlled the local planetary populations by making them slaves. Sometimes it was with their knowledge, but more often than not, it was without their knowledge. Just like we on Earth have been enslaved and are just now finding out about it.

Their next move was to come toward our planetary system. The Annunaki apparently also have a small outpost on the planet, Venus. During this time, the Annunaki observed the Earth and could see all of her natural resources, and they desired them. However, the Atlanteans had a lot of power and were energetically and technologically advanced just like the Annunaki. Knowing this, the Annunaki came to Earth and interacted with the priest caste, and when opportunity arose for them to take advantage of us, they did. They rewrote Earth's history at that time for their benefit. That is when they stripped us of our 12 strands of DNA and knocked it down to two strands.

It was during the second Atlantis, approximately one billion years ago, when we were an advanced civilization that the Dark forces from Orion came to the planet. About 900,000 years ago, they introduced implantation or mind implants to the population. They had chairs, similar to a dentist's chair, where they would place an implant that was a charged crystal implant which contained electrical and mental programming, into the human individual. This was when human mind control began, and it was the beginning of all our current belief systems.

There were two main belief systems programs that we were brainwashed into believing. The first is the belief that separation does exist between man and God. This is where the fall from grace in the Garden of Eden occurred. This separated us from our consciousness and higher consciousness. The second is the belief that there is separation between male and female polarities. This is reflected in separation on a psychological as well as physical level. We must remember, that each of us is a soul in a human body and not a human body with a soul. The soul in a human body used both polarities to grow in consciousness. Females have different psychological programming than men do. These two belief systems create most of our problems.

Sixteen thousand years ago, many Pleiadians and Sirians came to Atlantis to help us heal this separation. There was a task force called the Order of the Star. 144,000 beings/volunteers came to heal separation and integrate the darkness into the Light. This is where our religious stories come into play. These 144,000 beings were sent to Earth by God in the forms of the Prophet Jesus, peace be upon Him, the Prophet

Muhammad, peace be upon Him, and all the other prophets God had sent to earth as well, the Templars, and the Light Workers. These people keep re-incarnating wherever they can assist. When we free the planet, we will enter into the 3rd Atlantis, which will be a paradise on Earth. We will create a new Atlantis with the Cities of Light and advanced technologies that were here before. Our new Atlantis will arrive at the time of first contact.

I have been told that the above information is correct, it is just difficult to keep the timelines as straight as I could. By moving back and forth, I hoped to give you clear information about who the Annunaki were. First contact will clear all of this up for us. I am trying to put this together with the word of God given to the Prophet Muhammad as the Holy Qur'an and these timelines. Again, I find the information fascinating in and of itself, so that is why I decided to include it. If nothing else, it gives one something amazing to ponder.

Chapter 15

The Light and The Dark: What Does It All Mean?

When you look at the dark side, careful you must be. For the dark side looks back.
—Master Yoda

I feel it is important to include this information because it is starting to come out by other means. The movie, "Thrive" talks about the controlling leaders of our planet and what they are doing. The movie, "Sirius" also mentions the dark factions and what they are doing to maintain control over the masses. This is nothing to be feared because the Light Forces now have it well in hand. So, without fear, read this chapter as you might read a history book. When it is all said and done, it should make you feel good to know how far humankind has come. Remember, look to your heart for answers.

Twenty-Five thousand years ago, the Dark Forces took hostage the humans living on the surface of Earth. A quarantine was placed around us as a tool to prevent the progress of the Light on the Earth. This quarantine is a virtual reality control system and is usually referred to as The Matrix. There was a movie made in the 1990s called the Matrix, which was about humans living under a control that they could not exit. As a lot of movies, it was probably an attempt by the Light to let us know that things are not always what they seem. Interesting! On the Earth's physical plane, the control of the matrix is accomplished through a debt-based financial system of slavery and also through the mass media mind control programming. On the etheric, astral and mental planes, the control is held through electromagnetic space-time distortion chambers, like the ones used in the Philadelphia Experiment. The chambers create an illusion of a closed system that is in the shape of a loop. It seems to be eternal, so no one attempts to free themselves from it. This Matrix is controlled by the Archons, who are beings that came from the Andromeda Galaxy and chose to experience the Dark Side. They have refused to reconnect with God. Through millions of years, they created Reptilian and Draconian races by doing genetic engineering in order to use them as slave warriors in an attempt to expand their evil empire. Our precious planet, Earth, is the last one to be freed from this dark empire. Fortunately, there are very few Archons left on Earth. The Light forces, Earth humans, had to be very careful with any sort of extraterrestrial contact. The Star Seeds on Earth have been in favor of interacting with the extraterrestrials, but the dark forces threatened nuclear war in order to prevent us from doing that. Now, on the Earth, a critical mass of people is wanting first contact. Remember the hundredth monkey theory? Some people have had contact but choose not to talk about it for fear that it would put them in danger or put their families in danger. At the time of the Event, or First Contact, we all will have our memories return to us from all of our lifetimes on the Earth.

There is something called the Galactic Codex, which is an ancient Galactic manuscript that is supposed to follow the wishes of the people. A very high number of Earth humans wish to bring about contact with extraterrestrials, but people need to know that they are not going to be harassed or threatened. They want to know that it will be safe. There are hundreds of spaceships around our planet that are waiting for the right time for mass contact.

Unfortunately, there is an abundance of disinformation out there, making its way across the worldwide internet. It is necessary on our part to feel with our hearts when we hear a new piece of information. Disinformation can come from many places, even well-meaning Light Workers who do not have the correct information. Sometimes Light Workers say they channeled information, but if the channel's ego gets in the way, for example, the translation of the information coming through could be tainted by the channeler's own feelings and beliefs. This is not done on purpose, but sometimes it happens. So, the listener must sense whether the information feels like it is true, and trust it with how it makes his heart feel. If the information makes you feel uncomfortable in any way, then it probably is not true or completely true. In order for first contact to happen it is important for three things to happen. The first is that a critical mass must be reached, and we are almost there. Second, we have a Divine right for this contact, and third, it is part of the ancient Galactic manuscript. The hesitation for first contact is that it could be dangerous because the cabal will not be happy about it. It is my understanding that for first contact to occur, the cabal leaders around the world must be arrested for crimes against humanity, and put up for trial by a universal court of some type. Once this occurs, the threat of cabal interference goes away.

So, who are these Light Forces and how are they planning on helping us? There is a union of sorts of positive, loving civilizations that created the Galactic Federation of Light. These positive races have accepted love as reality, and resisted the spread of war. They are peaceful people. They have grown way beyond war, conflict, duality, and polarity, and want to share these beliefs with other beings in the galaxies. I have learned that there are about 200,000 species in our galaxy alone, and around 70% of them are humanoid. Sheldon Nidle once said that there are approximately 50 human races in our galactic neighborhood as well. What I think is really cool is the fact that humans come in a in variety of colors. On Earth, we have experienced what we call white/Caucasian, Black, and Reddish-color-Native Americans, and a mixture of those colors. In other places Brown, such as the beautiful people from places such as Pakistan and from other planets, humans are blue, yellow, pink, two shades of green, red, orange and indigo. There may be more but I do not recall them. I am going to mention now some of the Light forces around the Earth, and some of the Ascended Masters who are also here to assist us with the Ascension. The Ashtar Command is part of the Galactic Federation of Light and is acting as a task force to free Planet Earth. There are millions of spaceships around our Earth. Some of them are five to ten feet in diameter, and the largest ships are thousands of miles in diameter. They are all positioned to act when the time is right. Around 1994 and 1995, The Light was really close to a breakthrough. Star Seeds across the world began to awaken. According to Sheldon Nidle, everyone on the earth today made an agreement with Heaven that we would come here and incarnate into these human bodies in order to assist everyone with information and the ascension when the time was right. We volunteered to do this and we were also chosen to come here. Many of us have already ascended before and we agreed to lower our vibration to serve on Earth during this historic time. We also come from star systems spread throughout our entire galaxy. However, in 1994 and 1995, the key people who were to wake up and make some important decisions, did not. During that time, there was a strong smear campaign and much disinformation regarding the Ashtar Command. Allegedly, the third Archon invasion, which are dark forces, invaded the Earth in 1996, and took contactees of the Ashtar Command underground. They erased their memories with mind control programming, so the contact was lost with the Ashtar Command.

When we incarnate on Earth, the Archons maintain control over us through the distorted space-time structure with implants which confuse the human mind and emotions. These implants are crystals that are programmed and were put into mental, astral and etheric bodies of every human on Earth. This was done with strong electronic mechanisms. On the etheric and lower astral planes, they maintain the artificial intelligence technology that holds the Matrix in place. This Matrix has a built-in alarm system that alerts these Archons if an awakened being creates a hole in the Matrix with his Light. If that occurs, they send a Reptilian slave warrior to put pressure on the psychological weak spots of this awakened person in order to lower his vibration and close the hole in the Matrix. In addition, those Reptilian slave warriors constantly put pressure on the mind and emotions of incarnated humans on Earth in order to prevent their spiritual growth and to suppress their fight for freedom. Their power is in fear and all of their hidden agendas-all of the cover-ups. They are losing all of their power in the face of the Light, truth and courage on the part of the humans on Earth.

I think it is important here to mention the three Archon invasions since they so dramatically affected the humans on our planet. The first invasion happened around 3600 BCE where the dark forces entered through the Caucasus dimensional portal. The purpose of this invasion was to destroy peaceful Goddess worshipping cultures that were abundant and thrived in Neolithic Europe. They wanted to destroy this Goddess energy since it is our direct connection to God. The second invasion happened around 393 BCE. They used the same dimensional portal to enter. This time the Archons wanted to destroy the Mystery Schools. The Christian gnostic groups and the nature worshipping pagan groups were replaced by the Christian cult's mind control programming. This programming created the virtual reality of Hell on the lower astral plane, and this then gave the Church strength in its position. They could now use the idea of going to Hell in controlling the masses. The third invasion, the one that occurred in 1996, came in through the Congo. The Archons entered through the Congo, Rwanda and Uganda, which had been through severe war and fighting during this time. The main focus of this invasion was on the etheric and lower astral planes. Their purpose was to destroy new age and ascension movements. They also came to reinforce The Matrix because it was starting to fall apart in 1995 because of the mass awakening happening on Earth at that time. Most of us are not aware of this invasion because our memories were erased about the Light that was here on Earth before 1996. This was done through implantation sessions on New Agers from 1996 – 1999.

Finally, The Matrix is falling apart because of the 11:11:11 portal activation that occurred in November, 2011. Events were immediately set in motion that will result in our liberation from the Matrix. Since planet Earth is the last planet to be freed from the Dark Forces, there can be no new Archon invasion. Although the Light's victory over the dark is guaranteed, and all negative timelines are now gone, we still need to be careful. Archons on the astral plane will continue to exert pressure on the psychological weak spots of the awake beings of the Light in order to cause divisions among the Light Workers. It serves them well if they can create minor conflicts between the Light Workers which will take our minds off of bringing down the Dark Cabal. The Light can override their desires, but they still can create unnecessary delays to our plans. It is not only a physical operation to arrest the Cabal, they also need spiritual support so that when these arrests occur, human masses will not panic and cause unnecessary chaos. At a certain given point in time, energies that are from the Galactic Central Sun will burn through all of the obstacles that are holding the Matrix in place, and all of the negative entities will be removed. They will be replaced with angels and spiritual guides to interact with us. As the Light continues to return to Earth, people who have had contact will now be getting more contact. That is certainly true in my case, as my contact has increased. Apparently, a new contact system has begun and it is now much stronger than before.

The Pleiadians have the closest ties to the Earth and the human race. Since many of us came from different star systems when we volunteered to incarnate on Earth so that we will be a part of Earth's transition and ascension, some of us are really Pleiadians who have incarnated into these bodies in order to help. It is fun to try and figure out where we might come from. The Pleidians are humans also, only more enlightened, and are a beautiful, peaceful race. Many of them belong to the Ashtar Command. The Pleiadians have contacted the people of Earth many times over the centuries. Some of our old prophets and spiritual leaders were contacted and given knowledge and wisdom by the Pleiadians. Semjase, who is an emissary of Light, contacted Billy Meier. A book was written called "The Promise" which has been said to contain the purest representation of the Pleiadians. Semjase provided information on Pleiadian healing technology. Her reason for coming was for first contact. The tachyon chamber was brought to Earth through the Pleiadians. Tachyons are subatomic particles that travel faster than light. By definition, "Tachyon energy is the first wavelength that emerges from zero-point cosmic energy. The tachyon infusion chamber given to Earth actually decreases the amount of physical matter and harmonizes electromagnetic fields in the human living environment. Since tachyons equally influence our physical bodies and our higher energy bodies, they accelerate our spiritual growth dramatically.

The Sirians are playful and full of joy. They can appear as humans, dolphins and whales anchoring joy for the planet. One of the extraterrestrials that I have contact with is a cetacean and she is always telling me to lighten up when I get so serious. She makes me laugh at myself. The whales are the caretakers of the waters on Earth, balancing the feminine, energy grid and the tectonic plates. They are all very enlightened beings. Our land is considered masculine and the water is feminine.

There are many other races that are here as well. The Andromedans and the Arcturans are also here to help, as are the Argarthans. Many of the ET races of people have changed from the dark side into the Light side.

About seventy beings took a cycle of Earth incarnations and managed to free themselves from the veil. They came as their true selves, liberating themselves. These are the ascended masters.

St. Germain is another of the ascended masters who is here to assist us. His job is to bring abundance and freedom to the humans on Earth. In the 18th century he came here to renew the Mystery Schools that had been started in Egypt. He did reform the Mystery Schools. He also founded Freemasonry.

Ashtar incarnated on Earth 25,000 years ago, and he was fortunate enough to escape before the quarantine was placed around the Earth. He promised that he would return one day in order to help transform consciousness, assist with the ascension for Earth humans, bring about first contact, train people in telepathy, take the communication grid back for the Light, take over the mass media and get the message out to humanity, develop the personal computer and the internet, stabilize the Earth grid and tectonic plates, stabilize and prevent pole shifts, and prevent nuclear war. In fact, in 1977, the voice from space, Vrillion, took over an English television station and transmitted a message in order to do a test. As far as preventing nuclear war, his ships block nuclear weapons. A joint project took place from November 11, 2011 to January, 2012. This project blocked the cabal faction's access to nuclear weapons. It ended in February 2012 when 99% of the weapons were blocked. The nukes were stopped in June of 2012, but there are still some chemical and biological weapons out there. This was a huge victory because any existing bombs available to start a war were unable to be detonated.

Ashtara is the twin soul of Ashtar. She is also known as Aphrodite, Venus and Isis. She brings the goddess energy back to our beautiful Earth which brings more receptivity and unconditional love.

In 1996, a strong invasion by the Dark Side happened. The Reptilians on Earth went below and tried to destroy the underground movement. So, the Resistance asked for help from Planet X. Planet X did help by sending reinforcements. Planet X, also known as Nibiru, orbits our sun beyond Pluto. It only passes by our neighborhood every 3,600 years. Their civilization had lived underground on Planet X. An uprising by Planet X was possible because they were less brainwashed, and they were in control until 1999. It took them only three weeks to free that planet. Seventy million of them came to Earth by way of teleportation and cleaned out the Reptilian bases on Earth. These bases had been in existence for over 500 million years.

In 1996, 1999, and 2003, all military bases on the Earth were cleared of the reptilians. Dulce, Area 51, all black projects, all advanced and exotic technologies including scalar weaponry, UFOs and clones related to the reptilians were also cleared out. I believe that there are other cabal groups that still use some of this weaponry, but they are watched very carefully.

From 1945 – 2010, The World Health Organization, which is owned and run by the Rothschilds made everyone on Earth get vaccinations which included microchips for mind control programming and shutting down our psychic abilities. As of June 2012, these microchips are no longer effective.

There is a lot of disinformation on the internet right now. Pay attention to fake websites, for example, not all chemtrails are real and most are being neutralized by the extraterrestrials to prevent further damage to our beautiful Mother Earth. Fluoridation is more serious because it can shut down the brain. The dark side was attempting to poison our air by various means in order to shut down our thought processes and our psychic abilities. This has, mostly, been neutralized.

I have been told that all positive Light groups on Earth are considered The White Knights. A very wise man I worked with in Sedona, Arizona, referred to them as the White Brotherhood. The name has nothing to do with race; the white designates the side of the Light. There are many positive surface groups operating on the Earth at this time. There is a positive military that has been formed that is different from the military we see every day. Some of the members of the military may belong to both groups, but do it privately so as not to cause a problem with their normal job in the Marines, Air Force, Coast Guard, or Army, for example. These positive military have formed in Russia, China, the United States, and other countries. They provide logistics and personnel as needed to defend the Light.

The Templars are another positive group on the Earth at this time. In the Thirteenth Century in Jerusalem, under the Solomon Temple, was found information depicting the life of the Prophet Jesus. The Catholic Church paid the Templars to keep quiet initially, and it was only later that they began the tortures, arrests and deaths of the Templars because they threatened the existing mind control programming that was being performed by the church. Remember, in the thirteenth century, the church was seen by everyone as the controller of the masses. When the time comes, all of these cabal leaders will be arrested, just as they did to the Templars. Also, keep in mind I am not talking about your local priests. I am referring to very secret and very high up. In fact, the new Pope is seen very differently. In my opinion, he is definitely from the Light, and is probably here to help us all through the ascension. No one has ever said that to me, but that is what I feel from my heart. He just seems lighter to me than those of the recent past. These thirteenth century people are the people who were known as the Illuminati.

The White Dragon Society consists of old ancient Chinese families that have expertise in banking and are in control of huge wealth. They are fighting to bring in a new financial system. According to my teachers, the cabal is not happy about this and want the Chinese back in the fold, but it is not to happen. They are fighting for a new financial system that will be fair, and world-wide.

The Brotherhood of the Star is an occult of very advanced beings, who bring higher ideals to us on Earth, and they project these ideals and impressions to those who are ready to hear them. Apparently, there are about 500 actual members.

The Order of the Star was formed in Atlantis. They are here to transform all darkness and to heal humanity. This order is made up of 144,000 beings. Some of us belong to the Order of the Star, although most of us have not been awakened to it yet. They are here to assist with first contact and to heal humanity. There will be a big need for healing within the masses after first contact. One of the reasons is that these beautiful beings, extraterrestrials, angels and ascended masters, will be teaching us the truth about our existence and it will be very shocking to most people. I have touched on a few of the things in this chapter, but it is only the tip of the iceberg. We will need to heal the anger that will undoubtedly crop up when we hear the truth about so many things. Any negative feelings that may develop about this will have to be cleared and transcended in order to continue toward the fifth dimension. And, they will be. That is what so many Light Workers have been trained to do. It is what I have been trained to do.

The Light Workers are the backbone of this movement. They meditate and invoke the Light. They are a transformational source for the planet, and there are millions of us. Chances are, you are too.

After first contact and meeting our extraterrestrial brothers and sisters face to face, and seeing the angels and ascended masters, people are going to need some time to grasp it all. In addition, when we learn our true history, there will be much to heal as a result. This is where the trained Light Workers will come in.

Part VIII

Life in The Fifth Dimension

Chapter 16

The Event and The Lifting of The Veil

I'm touched by the idea that when we do things that are useful and helpful-collecting these shards of spirituality-that we may be helping to bring about a healing.
—Leonard Nimoy

What is the event? The event is where we basically get out of the Matrix and escape this black hole that we were placed into so many thousands of years ago. When we refer to the veil, we are talking about making us into third dimensional beings where our memories were limited to just the life we were living in. Additionally, the layer around the surface of the Earth was used by the Archons to keep us in quarantine. Like I mentioned before, it is an actual structure in space-time where tiny black holes are created. It is an anomaly in the space-time continuum which can also affect the propulsion of spacecraft, making it very difficult for them to approach. That is one of the reasons so many UFO crashes have occurred here. I recall one time when I was on a week-long training with Dr. Greer's CSETI group in Joshua Tree, after our meditation, instead of making contact right away I could clearly see a mesh-like blanket covering the earth. I mentioned this to the group and Dr. Greer acknowledged that I was seeing that. It appeared to me like a chain-link fence that one would see around a prison. It is my understanding that this now is being cleared. That being said, however, our consciousness level on our planet does play a part in how fast everything will happen. I do believe that we must reach a critical mass of people vibrating on a higher level before everything will shift, just like the hundredth monkey theory suggests. Beyond this is the wonderful Love Energy that we have been blocked from for so many years. It is 15 to 20 miles on the other side of the veil.

Once the veil is removed, purity and harmony will be experienced by everyone, and we will anchor this purity and harmony on the Earth. The true state of liberty, being a natural state, will return to the Earth. We will be able to feel the tachyon energy from space that will enable us to be more balanced, and we'll be able to maintain our true reality of peace and happiness, ultimately creating paradise on Earth. At that time, billions of Reptilians and Archons and other members of the dark side who have committed such horrible crimes against planets and their life forms, will be sent to the Central Sun where they may be born again with a soul and a connection to God. These beings have lost their connection with God, The Source, and cannot be repaired. Remember, the Central Sun is where we all originate from when we became a spark of light and were given a soul. What it means for them to be sent there, but still be allowed to be born again with a soul, is that they will have to start all over again with life number one and relearn everything that they did not learn or did not utilize the first time. It is a trek many thousands of years back, but at least they are being allowed to do it. It is my understanding, also, that the remainder of the cabal that is still acting in that capacity on Earth will be given a choice to either turn to the light and take the consequences of their cabal behaviors or be taken with force to the Central Sun where they will not be allowed to start again. They will just cease to exist.

The Zeta Reticuli gray beings lost their contact with their emotions and were trying to come back from that. At the time of the Roswell crash in 1947, they were neutral, and then in 2001-2002, they all crossed over to the Light.

We are now to exit this portal, an energetic black hole around us after 25,000 years of being in a prison. It is that space-time anomaly. This exit will be the event horizon. It is an expanding dot of Light, and it is taking place right now. We are entering this brilliant Light. Those of us who are here have gone through the stages that we were trained for, but do not yet remember, and we are ready. The matrix is inside the quarantine, and is a computer program with artificial intelligence. There is a way to hack the matrix and crack the computer code. It has been explained to me that a flash of light is the mission, the ignition, the start. Apparently, we will know what to do when the time comes. It will take place when each of us, as shining lights, flash together and carry out our part of the plan.

The surface of our Earth is like being inside of a sandwich right now, and it is feeling pressure, intensity, and increased light, which is bringing up things in people that need to be released. This compression is made up of Light above the Earth, and Light from within and under the surface of the Earth. The positive pressure from the Light increases the intensity of what we all feel. Also, there is Light from the planet surface. The Agarthans, our inner Earth brothers and sisters, are providing pressure from below the Earth's surface. All of those things that are not of the Light need to be converted. When the pressure becomes so strong, the Event will take place. Things will go faster and faster up and until the breakthrough. This will be the time for the Event.

There will be a spiritual flash of Divine Energy from God, the Source, which is the Galactic Central Sun, through the solar system to Planet Earth. All galactic positive races of beings will receive a signal from the Galactic Central Sun, and then they will transmit to others. The Pleiadians, as part of their contribution to this event, will have all the conditions on the cabal, including intelligence., and they will tell the Resistance and surface operatives in all areas at that moment. Once the Resistance Movement receives that signal, it will be relayed to the underground to the operatives within the financial network, the political network, and all of the other networks controlled by the cabal. They will be given an offer to cooperate with the Galactic Federation of Light within a short period of time. They will not be given days to make that decision, but rather will have to make it within a few minutes. Those contacted will be given detailed instructions of what to do. They will be asked, "Do you wish to cooperate with the Plan?" There will be a global message broadcast through different media channels to announce the Event. The Dark Forces will be removed for crimes against humanity. Their actions must be balanced. This will all occur within fifteen minutes. Everyone will be surprised.

There will be an event flash from the Central Sun, which will be a communication and a wave of Energy. To quote from American Kabuki website, "The Event will be a special kind of light from the Sun that permeates the earth and humanity, it will calm humanity in the light of love energy—it's an energy not seen before on earth, the banking system will stop, accounts and currencies reset, and arrests will be made..." We will feel a strong energy first. Once the operation starts, there will be announcements within the media within a couple of hours. They will take over the satellite and television networks, and the messages will then be broadcast. The Light Forces will confuse any cabal still remaining. The higher-ups will be given evidence about the Event. The Event will be spread through blogs first and then through television. Those with a soul contract agreed to do this certain mission. The initial group alerted will be people in big important positions. Afterwards, anyone can get contacted. They will decide what we are to do according to our actions. We each have our own role to play in this event. We need to be effective. As always, the weakest part of the chain will determine the timing.

Let me talk about the new financial system now. It is hard to believe, but half of our jobs currently finance personal accounts of the cabal. The system is a computer program only, not a real system. The Windows Operating System has been used by the cabal to track money on the planet. Some of you may remember hearing about this, but in June, 2013, the Light Forces broke into the banking system and tested out a virus in the computer system. It crashed the entire system. So as not to panic everyone, the Forces of Light brought it back up on line quickly. Now aware that it works, they left the virus in their system, and when the time is right, they can bring down the system. Only a code is needed to activate this action. This is a back door to control all financial transactions. There are five steps to transfer to a new financial system. First, the virus will be activated. Second, the mainframes on computers at all banks will shut down. Third, for a period of time, no money will be accessible. Fourth, peoples' credit cards will not work, and the fifth thing is that all banks will close.

After the Event, people will be encouraged to get food and water as soon as possible. We will be encouraged to have enough on hand for approximately three days. It is important to have a little cash saved up at home because that is what you will need to buy anything. Also silver or gold coins will also work. In addition, a full tank of gas in all of your vehicles is a good idea because gas stations will not be open for a few days. It is being suggested to have enough fuel for one week. Some stores will remain closed and never open back up. I am not exactly sure why that is unless the store was a cabal endeavor. Apparently, we will keep our currency, but it will be re-evaluated. These are only precautionary measures to ensure that people have enough to eat and drink. It would now be a wonderful idea to come together with your communities, especially those who live on your block. We are entering an era of unconditional love and we can give each other support, if only moral support.

The financial system is going to be all about trust. Many people will panic because their money is not accessible. There will be a short period of confusion that will last a few days. There is nothing to worry about. No one will lose their bank accounts. That money will be preserved and returned to you after the reset. After the reset, paper money will again be useful, but eventually, people will lose trust in paper. When the new system comes online, the gold that the Nazi's stole from the Jewish people whom they abducted, and the Japanese gold will be given back to humanity. This gold was taken to deep underground caves for safe storage in February of 2012. The cabal, to cover this up, has been making gold plated tungsten bars to replace it in the Federal Reserve Bank. The cabal has no real gold now. After reset, we will finally have a gold backed system.

One of the things that the cabal was doing was taking the birth certificates of every person and trading them. They would gamble on the birth certificates they "owned" on such things as how successful the person with the birth certificate was going to be, or how many children they would have, and so on. We were just players in a huge game by the cabal. That was entertainment for them. That has now stopped. All business agreements that are legal will hold. Police forces around the world will be restructured. Everyone will be much more positive.

After the reset is complete, the banks will re-open. The outcomes are presented as part of the original NESARA document. NESARA stands for the National Economic Security and Reformation Act. Sometimes I have heard that the S stands for Stabilization. I really do not know which one it is, but that is probably pretty irrelevant in the whole scope of things. Actually, NESARA is an act that was passed by the American Congress. The global reset of currency is the beginning of NESARA, but even more wonderful is the global abundance program. NESARA should have been signed into law over eighteen years ago. It had been designed to be signed on September 11, 2001 at 10:00 am in the World Trade Center. We all remember what happened at 9:00 am and that truckloads of gold were stolen from the ruins of the World Trade Center. This gold was to be the first part of the gold-backed standard of our financial system. The truth about 9-11 will be difficult for people to accept, but the World Trade Center was brought down by the Cabal using explosives, not the nineteen alleged Arab hijackers.

NESARA mandates steps that will rid our government of the corrupt politicians who have really brought the legislative process in the United States to its knees. Also, on the way out will be the corrupt financiers who have stolen money from every taxpayer in this country. It is difficult to discuss NESARA right now because of our current paradigm-our way of thinking. Part of the new paradigm will be to release technologies that will give us free energy, clean up the water and air, and new vehicle technologies. It is a fact that many individuals who have tried to do this were murdered. For example, free energy could have been made available in the 1930s, but the huge multitrillion dollar oil industry would not allow it. Our military industrial complex has taken many technologies from the patent office that could have been a benefit to every person on Earth. Unknown to most people, the United States has a secret space fleet, and the United States has been flying to Mars since the 1970s. NASA was created for the public so they would not ask questions if something was observed that the cabal did not want them to see. My guess is that they probably launch from places outside of the United States or from some of our more private Air Force Bases, such as Vandenberg Air Force Base in California.

NESARA has been accepted by almost all of the governments around our planet. It is to bring peace to our planet and restore the rule of law in international affairs. Some of the provisions in the NESARA agreement are wonderful in my opinion. For one thing, the only tax will be a 14% tax on new items purchased. Humanitarianism will rule the planet. Everyone on the planet will benefit. New technology will be released, but the electricity grids will be kept going, at least for a while. Everyone will receive $100,000 from collateral accounts. All debts up to $100,000 will be forgiven. If one's debt is over that amount, it will be analyzed. Real outstanding debt will be taken from that amount or if it is not enough because your debt is way over that amount, you may be advised to file for bankruptcy. All countries debts will be forgiven. All mortgages will be cancelled out. Retirement accounts will be preserved. Social Security and retirement health care will be changed. Free health insurance will be provided for a new, advanced medical system. The average work week will be 3 – 4 hours a day, 5 days a week. All of humanity is to have prosperity.

Some additional provisions of NESARA are as follows. All of the world's currencies will still be alive and usable. There will be a re-evaluation after the Event occurs. There also will be transparency accounting with the banks that are allowed to reopen. All interest will stop. Fractional banking will stop. Much to everyone's happiness, I'm sure, is that the IRS will be dismantled immediately. All banks who have had strong ties to the cabal will be declared bankrupt. The Federal Reserve will be dismantled immediately. If anyone who finds out about the debt forgiveness aspect of NESARA ahead of time and then goes out and charges frivolous items on their credit cards thinking that they won't really have to pay for these items, will be in for a shock. That will not be acceptable and the person will have to pay those debts off. I believe the Pleiadians will be in charge of monitoring people and their use of credit cards and will make that decision. Food, shelter, and technology will be available for everyone. Gold will not be traded on the open market any longer. There will be no more stock market. All money in people's bank accounts will be frozen from reset until the new banking system comes online. If a person's funds were acquired legally, then they will be allowed to keep them. The cabal's money is considered illegal and it will be taken away.

When the money is released, the first money will be for humanitarian purposes. Task forces will be formed to handle this. The ground crew will be guided and watched over. The second phase of this is when our population will be reduced. No one will be killed. Instead people will either choose to leave or will be guided to leave. For example, many of us who are here are from different planets and we agreed to come here to assist in the Earth's ascension and humanity's ascension. After everything is done, they will be allowed to return to their home planets if they choose to. Also, there will be some people who are here that are not really ready for the fifth dimension. From what I understand from listening to Sheldon Nidle is that Heaven has declared that anyone alive on the planet at the time of ascension, will be allowed to ascend. However for some who have not worked through all of their karma and are really a long way from clearing themselves, may not be able to take the increased vibrational frequencies on their physical bodies and so will choose to go to another beautiful third dimensional planet to continue their spiritual growth until they are ready to ascend. There are no bad choices. Each of us will choose for ourselves when the time is appropriate.

Banks like Chase, which is a cabal-controlled bank, will go bankrupt. Production costs will decrease, so everything will settle into a system that makes more sense and is fair. All legal contracts will be respected. The police force will be restructured as protectors and not money collectors by giving tickets. Common Law will be respected, not distorted. Like I said before, most credit card debt will be cancelled. Speculation will not be tolerated. The Pleiadians will be tracking us. There will be new elections for Congress within four months of the reset. Monsanto, the corrupt part of Microsoft, will be made bankrupt immediately.

Most prisoners will be released and receive psychological counseling and training because they were forced to do things due to life conditions. Many will be released because they are innocent. The CIA drug trade will end, and drastic restructuring of the CIA will happen. When we are fully healed, we will stop eating meat. Remember we are all One, connected. I'm sure the animals will be overjoyed that we can appreciate them for who they are. When we get to first contact, I will share with you how some of the new technologies that we will be given by the extraterrestrials, will allow us to make food that looks and tastes like beef if that is what we want, and no animal will lose his life for it.

There will still be some bankruptcies, although I do not know what circumstances would cause it unless a person or company is in so much debt that it would be impossible to get themselves out of it. Companies will keep operating. Additionally, companies will buy back shares of stock and give investors their money back. Most of Congress will be threatened to resign or their position disbanded. Congress will close at the reset. New elections will be arranged within four months. Things will be handled more at the local level and less at the Federal government level.

The electrical grid will be intact, however, when the cabal goes down, we may be put into darkness until the new technologies come online or others go in and figure out how to fix the system.

All of us can help by being calm and explaining to our friends and neighbors what is happening. This will be the time to give out information and intelligence that has been gathered. During the first phase, just ensuring there is enough for everyone to eat and survive on will go a long way. During the second phase, once the vibration has increased, we will be able to travel to other planets if we desire to do so. The Lemurians are holding the vision of a paradise on Earth.

In terms of our educational system, they are based on a Jesuit program from the 17th century. The Renaissance wanted education for everyone, so the Illuminati updated the Jesuit program with mind control. I can see now, after being a teacher in the public-school system for forty years, how we were expected to teach our kids certain things and make them fall into line and believe certain things. Critical thinking was discouraged, and the "company line", so to speak, was the way to go. All spirituality was taken out of the public schools, and it was against the law to bring it up while you were teaching. The new educational system will be based on true spiritual ideals after the reset.

In terms of new technologies, many free energy technologies are available now but they are being suppressed by the cabal and will be made available to the masses once the cabal is gone. Factories will pop up as soon as possible after the cabal is no longer in control. These factories will produce energy machines that will create cheap energy for everyone. The production of the energy will be virtually free. We will have the ability to produce any physical object very cheaply. Energy for heating and propulsion will be very inexpensive. Our food production will require less effort on our part. Food will become less expensive when cheaper energy and fuel is available. When people are no longer worried about surviving, they will have more time to delve into their spiritual growth and creative potential. We will all realize what an abundant universe we all live in.

Our vehicles will also undergo changes. All engines will be changed to engines that produce free energy in existing cars first. Soon we will develop cars that levitate. Car computers will be upgraded to prevent crashes. Some of the higher end vehicles on sale now already have incorporated this technology in their cars. All transportation will become extremely safe and all pollution will be cleared from our environment. Chemical waste, air pollution, chemtrails, and water will all be purified and cleared. All ecosystems will be healed immediately. Nuclear power stations will be shut down and used for free energy generators on existing networks. All GMO (genetically engineered) foods will be reversed. Natural and original seeds will be introduced immediately to replace existing seeds, but it will take approximately one year to introduce. Rare Earth minerals will be readily available during this time. Old companies will be redirected to new industries. Inhumane treatment of animals will stop at the time of the Event. Time will change with the expansion of consciousness.

Chapter 17

Pre-First Contact

All journeys have secret destinations of which the traveler is unaware.
—Martin Buber[7]

First contact is about spaceships landing and making contact with us in masse. For me, personally, it will be an amazing culmination in my life. It will be an ending of one very special era and a reintroduction to another. I say reintroduction because I really feel as though I am a human from either the Vega star system who volunteered for all of the many incarnations on Earth or from the Pleiades star system. I have no evidence to speak of, that this is true, but it is just a deep feeling that I have. It is remarkable.

Remembering now the feeling I had while training with CSETI and having several spaceships land just beyond the crossing point of light and showing themselves enough that we could get a picture of one, was incredibly exciting and magnificent all at once.

SPACE SHIP LANDING

I can only imagine what a first contact landing will be like when it happens in our full visual spectrum.

Sheldon Nidle does an excellent job of explaining to us about the first contact through his webinars and DVDs. With Sheldon as my guide, I have taken copious notes which I will share with you now. Sheldon was taken on board spaceships as a child and worked with the Sirians who have trained him, and they are in constant contact with him. They do not channel their information to Sheldon. They are actually connected to him in some way. I will call it a live feed for lack of any other description at the moment.

When Sheldon talks about first contact, he likes to describe what kind of spacecraft will be landing. There are so many different types, and Sheldon feels that if we at least have a little knowledge about them the entire thing won't seem so strange.

There are several types of ships that he talks about, although he says there will be many other types as well. I got the impression though that these ships will be abundant. There is the Sirian Scout ship, which is the one Sheldon is really familiar with because he would spend a lot of time on those ships through the years. The Arcturian ship is next, the Orion triangle shaped ship, which is also a defense ship, and the Altarian Scout ship.

The Sirian ship creates a plasma beam as it is landing. The bottom of the ship is used for propulsion. The propulsion system creates a plasma beam upon which the ship rides. It also produces a plasma field which ties all elements into the ship into the same inertia-less field. This system has a field direction emitter, an energy rod, a field generator, a beam controller, and a beam generator. The ship rides above its propulsion wave and appears to surf the light wave. This effect produces a motion similar to that of a falling leaf. It has an inertia-less plasma field around it.

The size of the Sirian scout ships range from 100 to 300 feet in diameter. They have a capacity of carrying 5 to 15 crew members and passengers. Its traveling time is amazing. From the Earth to Sirius B, where the Sirians are from, takes 3 minutes. That is 2.5 minutes to set up navigation coordinates and 30 seconds for travel. Normally, these scout ships travel on interstellar motherships. The ships by design are round in shape. At the top of the ship is the flight control center and, if it is a larger scout ship, that is where the crew quarters will be located. In the center of the ship are the laboratories. Many of these ships are science ships. The bottom section of the ship is the passenger and storage section of the ship. At the very bottom of the ship is the propulsion system. It contains field emitters to strengthen the ship's propulsion field. They can be used as either deep diving submarines or spaceships.

The ship's plasma field is inertia-less which means that all objects within the ship's plasma field possess a unified movement. Consequently, all objects accelerate together. In other words, when the ship moves, any Being inside of it does not feel the ship is moving or is making a drastic turn. I can think back on how many times I have observed ships in the sky and then see them take off at "warp speed", and I wonder to myself how the occupants of the ship keep from smashing into the side of the ship. I was thinking in third dimensional physics terms then. The ship is riding on a wave of energy, like a ship on the sea. It has a bobbing leaf affect floating in the wind. These ships will appear to cloak and then re-appear a little lower each time when landing. They are making massive energy adjustments as they approach the Earth's surface. The ships during the first contact landing will not be making a normal landing for them. Usually ships come in as airplanes do. They fly forward and they land. During this event, however, they will be landing like a helicopter does, straight down and parallel to the ground. There is a wave of energy propagated on the Earth, and when the ship is landing, it magnifies this field as it is landing.

Most of the star fleets have some triangle ships. The Orion triangle ship operates differently than the Sirian ship. It has three major vector points on the bottom of the craft and as it is landing, it will be triangulating their vector points by bouncing the energy off each other in threes. There is also an energy point in the center of the bottom of the ship. This pod is a weapon. These types of ships are defense ships. This center pod can be used for propulsion or protection.

The Altarian scout ship is approximately 50 to 150 feet in diameter. It is shaped more like a saucer, but the top and bottom parts are shaped like a normal bell curve. The crew consists of galactic humans from the Altair system. Around the center of the ship are 48 to 72 semi-solid rings used as field censors to regulate the propulsion and navigation systems. Each flame shaped ring is about three feet tall. There are three different types of landing gear used by spaceships. This ship has four landing legs. Some ships have three. When the ship lands, it bounces like on shock absorbers. Once it hits the ground, it stays there, but the body of the ship bounces up and down until it settles. It uses very advanced metallurgy, which is what is found in space. Each strut is made out of a very special metal. The landing gear contour themselves to the Earth. Once the motor is turned off, the full weight goes to the ship, and the legs must hold it. When it lands, it bounces on the Earth's gravity. It is like bouncing a basketball. The crew inside will not feel the landing because the inertia-less field is turned on. When you look at the ship, it seems like there are no windows. That is because their metals have amorphous capabilities. They can change shapes. Their on-board computer is always looking through the gravity field. All the crew does, because the ship is interfaced with each of the crew, is tell the ship to create the windows, by a certain specification protocol, and the windows will appear. They can do that with anything. Everything about the ship is done through telepathy. In appearance, the ship is metallic, silvery, but seemingly no windows.

The mothership of the Arcturian ship is about 1,000 to 3000 feet in diameter. Their multi-purpose ship is approximately eighty to ninety feet in diameter. There are basically two sections of these ships-the bottom part and the top part, which is the crew section.

Many of these ships fly in a V-formation. By flying this way, it allows for maximum visibility. The ships bounce their energies off of one another. They can travel in a singular formation, where there is only one level of ships flying together, up to ten levels of ships flying together in a V. In 1952, there were several of these ships flying only about one-hundred feet away from the top of the Capitol in Washington, D. C. They appeared on radar, and the air force scrambled jets to chase them. This happened for several nights in a row.

So, when first contact does happen, those are the descriptions of many of the ships that will be involved. However, before this landing can happen, there is a pre-landing scenario that must have taken place first. Remembering in the last chapter, I spoke of NESARA. All of that is an important first step before the landing will be authorized. So, to re-cap of the pre-landing scenario, first the delivery of the prosperity funds to everyone must be complete. Next the United States government has to be replaced. This will be an interim government until later when elections will determine a new government. The IRS and the Federal Reserve Bank must have been abolished. The United States must have been returned to the American Constitution and to Common Law. The transitional American government will have been in power for at least nine months. The transitional government will announce the existence of the Galactic Federation of Light.

During those nine months that the transitional government is in office, many things must happen. We must end the wars in Middle East and Afghanistan, and anywhere else there is war. There needs to be a peace conference set up about the Middle East. This transitional government will replace the private Federal Reserve Bank with a Treasury Bank, called the Central Bank. The Internal Revenue Service, or IRS, will be abolished and there will be no more income tax. It will be eliminated because it is unconstitutional. It is essential for first landing that we have a more peaceful effect on the Earth. Once those wars end, the Galactic Federation will let our world leaders know that peace is at hand. Federal Reserve fiat notes will be replaced by the new precious metal-based currency. This transitional government will return the cabinet system to the constitutional requirements. For example, the United States Post Office will be de-privatized.

When all of these things have happened, which will have met the requirements for the Galactic Federation of Light to initiate first landing, we will experience one of the most wonderful things that any of us could have ever imagined.

Chapter 18

First Contact

A kind of light spread out from her. And everything changed color. And the world opened out. And a day was good to awaken to. And there were no limits to anything. And the people of the world were good and handsome. And I was not afraid anymore.
—John Steinbeck, East of Eden

The idea during this time is that we Earth humans will be prepared enough for this event that we will look forward to it in joy, without any fear. There is nothing to fear. First, the new governments around our planet will introduce its people to the Galactic Federation of Light. Then there will be global telecasts about first contact. The trained liaisons will begin their education projects. Then the mass landings will occur in the prescribed areas. Lastly, and after a time of education by our galactic mentors, Earth's society will move to inner Earth.

Before making the opening announcements, the Galactic Federation of Light will conduct psychological and logistical testing to prepare everyone for the broadcasts. These broadcasts are to be delivered by way of television, radio, or telepathic messages. In other words, if you are watching television or listening to the radio, there will be a world-wide interruption of programming to make the announcement. Suppose you are a farmer, for example, and you are out plowing your fields, there will be a very soft voice that appears in your head, calming you down and then delivering the announcements telepathically. Everyone will be listening to the announcements at the same time. During these announcements and subsequent announcements, the schedule of the landings will be announced worldwide. These broadcasts will not only introduce the Galactic Federation of Light, but will explain the reasons for coming in such massive numbers. I believe the answer to that is fairly simple. There are millions of people on Earth, and each one of us is going to have our own extraterrestrial mentor, so that means there has to be as many of them as there are of us. That is my guess, since I have not heard the announcement. Then, the Galactic Federation of Light will review the landing protocols. For example, it is probably not safe to go running up to the ships until the plasma fields have been cleared from them after the landing. I understand that will take about ten minutes to happen. After the landings, the Galactic Federation of Light will ask for our feedback for what we have just experienced. They will want to know how we are feeling and what we are hoping to get from this. What kind of world are we hoping to create? It is really important to be able to answer that kind of question in a well-thought out way. Saying something like, "Oh Gee, I want to ride in a spaceship", is probably not the answer they will be looking for.

Next, they will talk to us about the landing logistics. From the time the spaceships appear in the sky, actually land, and give their greeting announcements, will take approximately two hours. First, a fleet of scout ships will move to their assigned areas, and lock in their landing coordinates. These ships will be from the 50 different Star Nations of humans. They will look just like us, although they might be different colors. When God created all of us, He most likely wanted variety, so He created many different types of intelligent beings in the Universe. Humans actually come in many colors, such as orange, blue, two shades of green, yellow, pink, a purple color, red, and probably some I have not thought about. Personally, I think it is really cool that this is the case. Anyway, we are only familiar with white, black, brown and red humans. Remember, it does not matter because we are all One.

Once those scout ships are locked into their coordinates, at the appointed time, the other ships will uncloak themselves and be visible to us. They will link up with their heavenly companions. Remember, the angels and the ascended masters will be here. Just before the ships land, special calming energies will be sent around the globe over a thirty-minute period. All guns, missiles and other such weaponry around the Earth will be jammed from firing. All of the defense ships will go to their pre-landing positions and maintain the calmness and jamming of the weapons. All of them will await the first contact green light.

As the ships are landing, they will begin to rotate within their area like a corkscrew. They will do this for about 2 to 10 minutes. They are waiting for the final procedure to be given the go-ahead. Next the landing lights will all go on. There will be many different colors, pastels to dark colors appearing around them. According to Sheldon, it will be very different than we have ever experienced. Next, the landings will actually occur. All of the windows in these spaceships will now open and there will be ET beings behind them waving at us and greeting us in our own languages. The angels, ascended masters, and heavenly beings will be beside the ships as they land. The energy fields around the ships take about ten minutes to dissipate so we will not be allowed to approach the ships during this time. Heavenly trumpets will be heard around the Earth in the sky. It has been described to me as the ultimate heart energy. As we all stand there watching, the lights, the heavenly beings, the trumpets, and the calming colors will dissipate gradually. The Galactic Federation will broadcast to the crowd to stay away from the ships until it is safe. Then the Fleet Commander will deliver a message to us. Then all 50 different human star fleets will be delivered to us. The commander of each will meet with every major government on our planet. From that we will all move forward to become galactic beings.

Be a role model for your neighbors. Be a model of calmness and acceptance. Be a force of love centeredness in your community. Reassure your community of the Galactic Federation's mission to return humanity to full consciousness. It may not feel like it yet, but the time of the landings is close. These will be the most incredible series of moments for this planet. We are now moving toward our new world, one that we are creating together.

One of the very important things that will be happening is that we will be receiving Galactic Federation technology. Their prime purpose is to use their technology to aid in our getting over our fears and readying us to accept new perceptions needed for living in our new reality. Their message is to not be afraid of what will happen or what we will see. They want us all to be in Joy. They want to make us be able to maximize our talents, and know that we are limitless, we can do whatever we are capable of, and so just go for it!

Chapter 19

Our First Days

The evolution from human to divine consciousness involves healing duality and its legacy of karma and disease at the cellular and atomic levels.
—Sol Luckman[8]

Now that the landings have happened and we have been informed of what is happening to us, the really cool stuff begins. First devices will be installed in our homes and offices that use the Galactic Federation technology. Next, we will be introduced to magnetic lifter technology. Also, we will be taking a tour of the motherships. The new technologies and time tables will be explained to us. We will receive intensive education and training on our history, and on consciousness. I mentioned some of our real history a few chapters ago, but now we will be hearing it from the Galactic Federation. If I said something that turns out to be a little different from their version, then, of course, go with their version. My comments came from my lessons learned, and my knowledge is probably not complete yet. Their primary purpose is to use their technology to help us in getting over our fears and readying us to accept new perceptions needed for living in our new reality. It will make us be able to maximize our talents. For example, if your joy is to paint, you need certain items to do that. Maybe it is the canvas to paint on, the easel, the paints themselves, and the various brushes.

With this new technology, you ask for what you need and it is given to you. When you are finished, you simply give it back to the machine. The extraterrestrials want us to feel joy when we are using this new technology. They do not want us to have any fears. We are limitless.

This wonderful and amazing technology trains us to apply our telepathic abilities and learn to adjust to artificial intelligence devices. With an interface between artificial intelligence and our abilities it will be about how we think, and the mode of how we think. Artificial intelligence becomes a complete extension of who and what we are.

There are some pretty amazing technologies that we will be learning about and how to use. The first is processor technology. All of these technologies will interact with us and interface with us, so when we work with the machine, it will be like part of us. As an example, let's say you wanted to have a luau. You plan what food you want to have, what plates and utensils you want to use, the table arrangements, what drinks you want to have, what decorations you want to have, and even what clothes you want to wear. You don't need to write this down because telepathically, you are going to be interfacing these desires to the machine. I guess you push a button and just like magic, everything you asked for is there. At the end of the evening, when everyone is gone, you take all of the plates, left-over food, dirty dishes and utensils, and decorations, trash, everything, and you put it back into the machine, and poof, it is gone. Your area is not cluttered with stuff, and you can access it any time you want by just interacting with your machine. My comment is, "How cool is that!" This technology will seem like magic to us at first.

This general processor technology invites us into a world that is freed of agriculture and forest products. It also allows us to maintain these technologies in different sizes. In other words, the technology can resize itself. We will be interfacing with these technologies telepathically. All of these technologies are about Love and Divine Service.

Whatever we want, we can have. We will be creating a world where you are totally independent of the ecology of Earth. We will no longer be killing animals for food. Let us say that you still were craving a juicy steak. Tell your processor what you want and the processor will produce food that tastes, smells and looks just like it. When you put it in your mouth, you will not be able to tell the difference, and no animal will have died for you to have it. Another amazing thing is that the foods you now eat will be fully absorbed by your body. Everything. There will be no waste, so you will not have to go to the bathroom any more to relieve yourself. I like that idea all ready. Imagine what we will save on toilet paper alone.

The technology to restore the ecological balance to Mother Earth will show us how she is really a living, breathing entity. The technology also provides us with several transportation and communication devices that can make us more aware of what a reality is. We also will begin to see the connection of humanity, and we will feel the energy of the breathing of the Earth.

The next technology we will be introduced to is magnetic lifter technology. This is about using telepathy and receiving and giving instructions through the use of telepathy. What they plan on doing is to put us in a small ship and train us to lift and move the ship with our minds. That sounds like fun.

The tour of the motherships is designed to be a fun experience. They want us to have no fears. They will teach us about all of the technologies that they have on these ships, and everything else about the ships as well.

Next is our education training. Education is all interactive. You sit down in front of the machine, it could be a computer or anything else, and it has rods that come up and a hologram will appear right in front of you. Then it will move forward and envelope you and your mind so you experience whatever you are learning about, first hand. Let's say you wanted to know what it was like to be on Apollo 11 when it landed on the moon. All of a sudden you will be there. For lack of better words, I will say that through the use of something like virtual reality, we are pulled into that event. It becomes like we are really there in real time. We will know, see and hear what the astronauts are seeing and hearing, and what they are thinking. We can even interact with them if we wish. Reading a book would be the same. For example, when you are reading something, you will be brought right into the story as though you are really there. Sheldon Nidle said that when he was taken on board the Sirian ships as a child, they used to let him go into their massive libraries, to read and learn. He said when he came back to his third dimensional reality, he would sit down to read a book, and of course, it wouldn't do that. This used to upset him a little because he wanted it to act the same way.

We will receive a general education into who and what we are and where we are going.

When we go on trips to the various ships, the Galactic Federation has many goals for us in mind. One of the goals is to get us used to the technology and how galactic society operates. Another, very important one, is to introduce us to our inner Earth neighbors, the people of Agartha. To these wonderful beings, everything is second nature. Everyone on the ship is fully potentialized. Galactic humans love to interact with each other by way of discussions and the like. We are to see and learn how everyone interrelates. They will want us to interact with them. Everything is completely One. The Agarthans want to meet us and interact with us. They will take us down to inner Earth so that we can see how their societies work.

Other trips to the ships are to demonstrate how their science and personal philosophy affects their daily lives. Additionally, they will share with us how they carry out their various science and exploration missions. They are also going to explain a divine timetable to us for quickly bringing us back to being fully conscious beings. They will want to know how their philosophy affects you personally. They will want to know how we are feeling at the time and what we are thinking about all of it.

So, the timeline for all of this after the landings is as follows.

The First Week: We are to interact with first contact personnel and ascended masters.

The First Month: This will be the start of the technology transfers and the beginning of our education program.

The Second Month: Any questions that we have will be answered up to our soul levels. We will begin pollution cleansing and the renewal of Earth's ecosystems. We will also be taught to heal ourselves at an unbelievable level.

The Third Month: We will start full consciousness training and finish the reunion with inner Earth.

The Fourth Month: We will begin our evacuations to inner Earth and to the fleet. We are now ready for the final process, which will be our metamorphosis into fully conscious beings. I will go more into this process in the next chapter.

As part of our education, we will be introduced to the Galactic Federation of Light. A full history of the Galactic Federation and its predecessors will be presented to all the people of Earth. We will explore the spiritual and philosophical understanding of humanity and its place on the Earth. The general constitution of the Galactic Federation is to be distributed in most of the major languages of Mother Earth. All books are interactive. We read it and become it. The book suddenly comes alive.

In the immediate post landing world, the Galactic people will want to introduce themselves to us and get to know us better. They intend to introduce us to the many diverse star nations that make up the Galactic Federation of Light. Although there are many other humans that are represented, there are other sentient beings that are not human. Some may even appear scary to us. Part of that is because we have been so programmed to think that anything that looks "monster-like" is evil. The Galactic people want us to get over that. Remember even in our existence now, when we meet someone who may not come up to our image standards, we should be looking past the physical and into the person's heart. You are not looking to date everyone you meet, so meet others heart to heart.

They also intend to explain to us in detail how to earn formal membership into the Galactic Federation of Light. The question of how we are going to be returned to fully conscious beings is now at hand.

Chapter 20

The New Chakra System

Wisdom begins at the end.
—Daniel Webster

During this time, we must hold the energy and keep our vibrations up. The fifth dimension is all about cooperation, love, and unity. This next information was given to Sheldon Nidle by the Ascended Masters. Remember they have a direct line to him, not a channeling connection. I received this information by taking a webinar from Sheldon, and these are my notes of that webinar.

After having first contact with our beautiful extraterrestrial brothers and sisters, and learning some of the new technologies, the actual ascension process begins. The ascension process is now mainly affecting three areas of our physical bodies: The brain and head, the neck and upper heart chakra (thymus), and the upper torso.

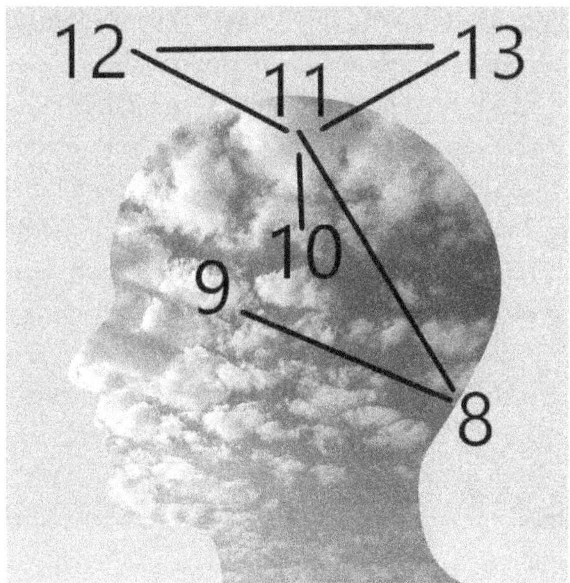

Our New Head Chakras

8 Well of Dreams Chakra
9 Pituitary Chakra
10 Pineal Chakra
11 Crown Chakra
12 Universal Female Chakra
13 Universal Male Chakra

Heaven is putting new chakras in our head. The whole thing is changing the nature of our brain. Our brain is mutating to accept a greater consciousness. Above is a drawing of our new head chakras: There are six chakras in the head including the crown chakra, which is still there. They are Chakra 8-the well of dreams; Chakra 9-pituitary chakra; Chakra 10- pineal chakra; Chakra 11-new crown chakra; Chakra 12-universal female chakra found above the head; and Chakra 13-universal male chakra found above the head.

The Universal Female Chakra controls the left side of the body and the Universal Male Chakra controls the right side of the body. These two chakras will merge together and our body will come into complete balance. The male and female will merge together and become equal.

As the energy enters the Crown Chakra, it moves down to the

Pineal and Pituitary Chakras. The Pineal controls the activity in the brain, and the Pituitary controls the hormones-the endocrine system.

The Well of Dreams located in the Occipital Lobe of our brain, merges all of the activities of the Occipital Lobe of the brain, such as reading, vision, and now we will become visionary. We begin to take the information from the physical and spiritual sides and mold it together. This information goes into the Well of Dreams, and then from there, goes to the Pituitary and Pineal centers. It is bringing spiritual, emotional, and the physical centers together. It is now more than just the logic of physicality. It is now the intuitive and spiritual logic as well.

Next we have the new Throat Chakra, which is chakra seven. Our throat is mutating to accept a greater consciousness. It communicates between the body and the brain. This area is all about balance. That is what the vertebrae in the neck are for. Also, speech and nourishment are handled by this chakra. This chakra is being nourished not only by food, but also by spiritual energy. We will be able to communicate not only physically, but now inter-dimensionally as well. It is moving up to an energy that works in both the physical realm and the spiritual realms.

Next our chakras are upgrading our upper torso area. The three chakras located there are the Thymus Chakra, which is Chakra six. The thymus is about being courageous in physicality. It has to do with our immune system. The Heart Chakra, which is Chakra five, says, "I am Love, I am of Heart, and I am of Life."

The Diaphragm Chakra, which is Chakra four, says things like, "I have tensions. I have things that I have gone through that cause stress at times." We will now be learning how to take any negative energies in our body and turn them into positive energies. All of those feelings of fear that we have had, not feeling like you belong, and so on, will now be changed to feelings of "I belong here, I am a sovereign being, any stress I take on I can handle it because I can convert it into love and light energies."

Our physical form is becoming less dense and it is changing itself by bringing in new energy centers in the body. So, we are rebalancing ourselves and changing our densities by upping our frequencies. All of our body systems are coming alive in a new sense.

Something else that is coming up for people now has been referred to as ascension symptoms. There are several of them. While some of these could be signs of other medical conditions, if you are concerned you should consult your health care provider. The first symptom is deep headaches that suddenly appear and then disappear. Additionally, pains in your sinuses can suddenly appear and last for a day or a few days. You might also display head cold symptoms that cause a stuffy nose, general aches and/or blurry vision. In terms of the sinuses, all of the stuff inside our nose-the mucous, dust particles, and so on, has to come down and clear out. All of this is happening because our new chakras must have room to move into our head. In other symptoms, you may have difficulties in swallowing and/or a deep soreness in your throat. You could have sudden chest pains, odd heart palpitations and/or a stabbing pain in the upper chest. If you are a person that worries about having a heart attack, having these symptoms may be a good reason to check with your doctor. You may also experience trouble breathing, rib pain that resembles a broken rib and/or a pain that seems to encompass one or both lungs.

Now we are being asked to integrate the new chakras into our chakra system. We are going from limited conscious beings to fully conscious beings. The new chakras are part of becoming a fully conscious being. It also means that our RNA and DNA have to change. The parasympathetic, sympathetic, and meridian systems are waking up in our bodies. Our eyes will get a lot bigger when we are fully conscious beings, which will allow us to bring in more of the light.

Chapter 21

Returning to Full Consciousness

We can never obtain peace in the outer world
until we make peace with ourselves.
—Dalai Lama

In order to go into these final stages of becoming fully conscious beings, we need to have had first contact, and learn about some of the new technologies. We also need to have our Chakra System upgraded so that it can handle the higher vibrations. Remember, also, that everyone is being given the opportunity while still in their physical body to ascend with our physical bodies intact. The people who are allowing themselves to become sick so that they will die and get rid of this physical body, will still be ascending to the fifth dimension. By dying and losing the body, one gets to ascend right into the Heavenly skies with a light body. If they want to reincarnate, they may. According to St. Germain, one of the reasons that people are choosing to leave the body now before ascension is that they feel it will just be a lot easier on them to do it that way. Most people, I believe, are choosing to ascend with their physical body intact. It will be an exceptional experience and people want to feel and experience it this way. Transforming with a physical body is the hardest way to go. We will be taking our carbon-based body and transforming it into a crystalline body of Light. The physical body needs to adapt to the increasing amount of Light coming into the Earth. We also need to be more Love and become the Love and know that we are from Source. It takes time because it is a harder process to go through. Others may actually choose to die and stop this life's contract, and reincarnate on another third dimensional planet and continue where they left off in this life. They will eventually ascend, but on a much slower time scale. It is all about personal choice.

Those of us who are choosing to ascend with the body are the strongest souls on Earth because the ascension and transformation of a physical body into a crystalline Light body is the toughest one ever. Remember this is a first in the Universe. The reason humanity is being allowed to ascend to the fifth dimension all at once as a group is because we were once fifth dimensional beings. We were stripped down to third dimensional, limited conscious beings by the Illuminati, and it was not our fault. We have been fighting to get back to higher consciousness for millennia. Because it is the time for Gaia's ascension, Heaven has interceded with the Galactic Federation of Light and the Ascended Masters to help and guide us through the process.

So, the next question is, "How are we going to transform these bodies all at once in a way that will not harm us?" The way is through the metamorphic Light Chambers. These chambers are wonderful, magical devices that will allow us to go from limited conscious beings to fully conscious beings. Each chamber is designed personally just for each one of us. The use of the chambers will occur once we have been taken to Inner Earth. Remembering the time-line, that would be approximately four months after the first landing.

Let me describe the Metamorphic Light Chamber to you. First, these are living machines that tie directly into your unique life energies. They are programmed with the latest information about you up until the moment you go into the chamber. These chambers are living artificial intelligence machines. Each of us has a mentor assigned to us. During a three-step process, you are returned to full consciousness. The machines are controlled by your angelic councils and guided by your galactic human mentor.

Each person will lie on a platform and slide into a chamber with their feet first. This metamorphosis chamber is in a room whose color changes according to the auric energy of the person in the room. The chamber has doors that flip open. When closed, it is seamless and without evidence of doors. These are not claustrophobic chambers, but they are actual live chambers that will be interacting with us. We will be like in a deep sleep. I have heard the analogy of the caterpillar turning into a butterfly used to describe this process.

Once you get into the chamber, you will be bathed in Light and Love energies and colors that will allow your body to accept these energies and change. So, here is the process. First you will be in a huge, big round room. When you look at the room you will see that there are your personal angels present. Your body angels will be there as will your personal guardian angels. There will be special Heavenly music playing. It will be very similar to the music that was played for you during the first contact landing. The energy is calming, and will allow us to sleep and get into our deep hibernation patterns that are required for our transformation. There will also be your guide, your mentor. Your mentor is a highly spiritual being. He is a physical angel. The machine is being controlled by Heaven and the mentor. Everything we do in the chamber is about transformation and preparing us for change and becoming fully conscious beings of Light.

Looking at the chamber a little more closely, it is an organic life form. It has the ability to interact with you at all times. There is technology put into it that allows us to change. When you lie down on the bed and the pillow, they adjust to your body, and it is almost like you are floating on air. As you hear the music, you are slowly rolled into the chamber.

Around the door opening in the chamber, there are two layers of lights that extend outwards. The lights represent 21 pastel colors that go around the door entrance 360^0. The frequency and order of the colors have been designed for you personally for your own transformation. These two lights facilitate reconnecting your RNA/DNA in your body, reconnecting the meridians, fields, and our regular nervous system. All of this will be reconnected so we are totally in contact with our body. This will allow us to go into our light body and go wherever we wish to go anytime we wish to do it.

These special devices are perfectly calibrated to your present energies and life patterns at the time you are entering the chamber. These chambers are built to exact specifications. They are to complete the remaining operations that are to return you to full consciousness. Like all of our devices, these chambers are living, organic beings of Light.

Metamorphosis Stage 1:

As you are lying there in the chamber, the colors will rotate while pulsing. There will be orange, pink, and blue colors. The first thing that happens in the chamber is that you will be connected to the "I AM Presence" which is your Divine Higher Self. This continual rotation of colors is affecting your RNA/DNA and our connections to the chords. Next, you will have your previous link between the gold cord, which is the crown chakra, and God, the Source re-established. During this stage, there is a general pink ambiance around the body. The Gold chord is at the crown and the silver chord is at the solar plexus. Our auric glow is starting to be more visible. Then, you will have the link between the silver chord and the solar plexus chakra upgraded. The next step is to transform all RNA/DNA into your former 12-strand prototype. You will become spiritual, emotional, and physical beings all at once. You will become a physical angel. It is starting a process where you will turn into a light body.

At the end of Stage 1, there will be two results. First, your physical body is now prepared for integration with the full array of your spiritual bodies. Our light bodies have 14 layers. Second, your remembrance process (ending our amnesia) has now begun. This is where you remember past lives, your Akashic records, who you really are and so on.

Metamorphosis Stage 2:

Here you connect to Heaven to integrate your spiritual bodies. You finish the full activation of the twelve-strand genetics and start your inner body glow. As you begin to come on to star tetrahedron energy, your body starts to glow. Your physical body's density will lower to allow all of your various bodies to merge. Then your soul's many present and past life memories will manifest.

In the metamorphosis chamber now, violet colors come in, and this is about remembrance. Then turquoise comes in, and this is about spirit. Greens come in because this is about Heaven connecting to the physical aspects. You are integrating the spiritual body itself.

Now there will be an outline of a whitish-yellow glow around your body. You are integrating yourself mentally, spiritually, physically, and emotionally. You are bringing together your fully conscious self.

Next in this stage, our aura needs to be cleaned. All of us have aspects in our aura that have to be cleansed. So now, we begin to cleanse our auric field. When the process starts, it starts to move all of these energies downward from your head to your toes until finally, your auric energy is clean. Cleaning the aura helps to stabilize and manifest the Light Body.

At the end of Stage 2, there will be two results: First, you are beginning to accept your fully developed light body. Second, you have begun to finish off your rejuvenating and to alter your size and personal appearance. You are becoming angelic. You are becoming a true angelic and physical being. You can become anywhere between nineteen and twenty-five years of age, wherever you felt the best about yourself, and you will have your maximum abilities, but as a young person. All of that programming from millennia of living on Earth as a limited conscious being that said, "As you age, your body will get old and will shrink. You will wrinkle due to the constant radiation from your polluted environment you are living in." All of that programming goes away. You now have the ability to change your appearance-how you look physically, your height, weight, skin color, color and style of hair, how your body looks, and whatever else you can think of. Additionally, you will be able to change your appearance any time you want. You will not age. You become a truly immortal Being of Light.

Metamorphosis Stage 3:

This is the final stage. Here you will connect to the Light Body. While still in the chamber, you will finish the integration of your physical, spiritual, and Light bodies. Now you will manifest your many physical and spiritual abilities such as telepathy, telekinesis, etc. You will also connect to your Heavenly lineage and your Heavenly councils. Finally, who you are in Heaven is a part of who you are now in your body.

Now having changed yourself back into a fully conscious being of Light, it is time for the Ascension itself.

Chapter 22

Ascension

Be the change that you wish to see in the world.
—Mahatma Gandhi

The ascension process is now mainly affecting three areas of our physical bodies. These are the brain and head, the neck and upper heart center (thymus) and we will have a very strong immune system, and the third is the upper torso.

In transforming the head chakras, we need to revisit the Metamorphic Light Chamber. A quick review of the process is as follows. Remember, these are living machines that tie directly into your unique life energies. During a three-step process you are returned to full consciousness. The machines are controlled by your angelic councils and guided by your Galactic human mentor. Each person will lie on a platform and slide into the chamber feet first. This metamorphic chamber is in a room whose color changes according to the auric energy of the person in the room. The chamber has doors that flip open. When these doors are closed, the chamber is seamless and without evidence of doors. All of this transformation in the chambers will happen in Inner Earth. All planets are hollow. Fifth dimensional beings live inside the planet, not on its surface.

The People of Inner Earth: After the fall of Lemuria on the surface of the Earth, the Agarthans escaped to the Inner Earth to get away from the Illuminati before they built a matrix on the planet. The Agarthans are working with the Ascended Masters and the Galactic Federation of Light to turn the surface realm back into a 5-D reality. As I mentioned before, the Agarthans are a remnant of ancient Lemuria. The Agarthans are cousins to Galactic Federation full conscious humans.

Inner Earth is a semi-tropical, beautiful place. There you will find things written in ancient Lemurian writing, and crystal cities. Remember you just morphed from having a carbon-based body that was limited consciousness to a crystalline body of full consciousness. The Inner Earth has large oceans in many parts of it. Also known as Agartha, it is an amazing place. In some areas they have remnants of ancient Lemuria that they have kept as reference, such as some of the old beautiful buildings from the ancient times. Notice this picture of Inner Earth:

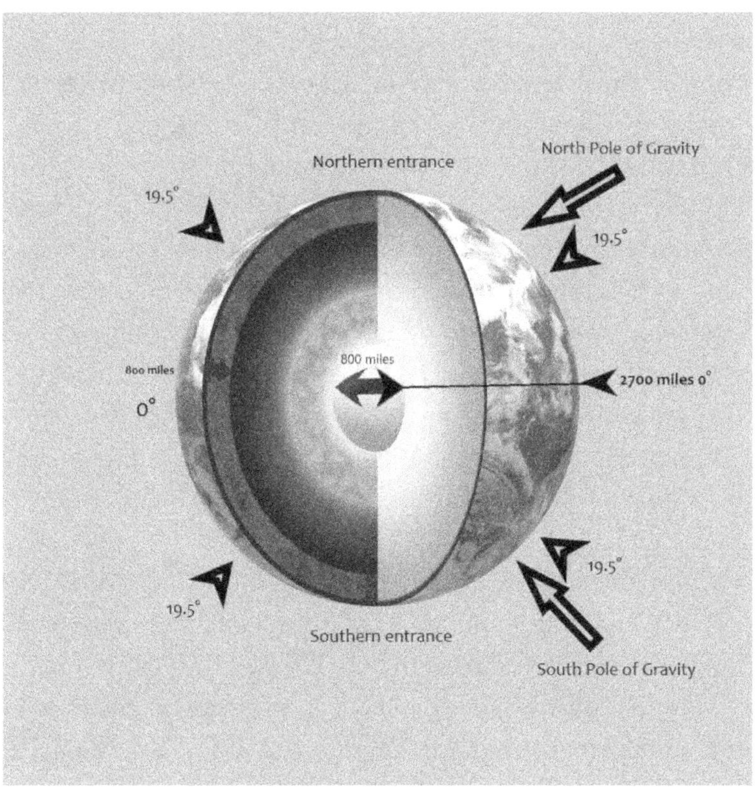

Drawing of the Inner Earth by Artist Haifa Dagachi

Next you will be introduced to Crystal City technology. First is the Replicator. Like the machine you were learning on during the first contact training, this will be similar. You will use this machine for food, clothing, furniture, and other necessities. As for meals and the mess afterward, no dishwashing is required. All items are returned to the machine. The Replicator turns the waste back into energy. It does not use resources such as wood, just energy which is infinite. The Replicator is an essential technology. It can convert zero-point energy and the zero-point field into matter. This matter will be an exact copy of the food or drink that you want.

The next essential technology you will learn to use is the communication device. It has three parts. The first is a multi-media communication device that uses holographic technology for 3-D conversations. For example, say you want to contact your brother who lives a couple of doors down from you but you do not feel like walking over there. If you use your communicator to call him up, and he answers the call, there will be a holographic 3-D image of him projected into your room. It will seem as though he is really there with you in your room. Actually, he will be in two places at once.

The next essential technology is the sonic shower which permits you to take a refreshing one-minute shower. You will be completely clean and sanitized. Additionally, there will be no need for toilets because the food you now consume is 100% digested and used in your body. There is no waste to get rid of as everything is utilized.

The last essential technology is the body adjusting bed which forms to your body and creates the illusion that you are floating on air. This will be similar to the effect of being on the bed and moving into the Metamorphic Light Chamber.

Now for the Ascension part. You are in a process that is nearing its most vital and critical phases. This is the actual movement to Inner Earth and your own Light Chamber. The final operations are being done under the auspices of your Galactic Federation mentor. These mentors are also to be in charge of your trainings. Ascension is a gift of Divine Grace from Heaven. It allows you to become useful Galactic citizens that work in the Divine Service to others. This process is the result of a joint effort between Heaven, Inner Earth, and the Galactic Federation of Light. You are on a Divine mission. You are a mighty warrior of the Light who is now about to manifest who you are. You are about to earn all those things that allow you to be at peace with all the world and you will now be able to dispense the dark. They are here from Heaven to bring the Light on this great world and to transform it once again into the great world of Light that it once was, and that it is meant to be again.

At the end of one of Sheldon Nidle's webinars where I got some of this information, several people asked Sheldon questions which I will share with you here. When Sheldon gives a response, he is in direct contact with the extraterrestrials and they will assist him with the answer if he needs it.

Questions #1: Is this the first time that mass ascension has happened?

Answer: Ascension has happened before many times on planets, but not mass ascension like we will have on Earth. The reason we will all ascend like that at the same time is because we were all once fifth dimensional beings on planet Earth and were stripped of that by the Illuminati without our knowledge. So, when Gaia ascends, so will we if we choose to.

Question #2: Is there any order who enters the Light Chamber first?

Answer: No. There will be massive change all at the same time. We need to all be ready to contribute to our new Galactic Society. On the Earth's surface, our planet will be changing to a 5D outer world, and that is why we will not be on the surface.

Question #3: Will there be people who will not ascend?

Answer: Ascension is for everyone. If you are still alive when all of this begins, then you will become a fully conscious being. The exception to that is if a person does not want to ascend to the fifth dimension now, then that person does not have to. It is whatever the person's life contract says.

Question #4: We are a water planet. Are there any other water planets in our solar system?

Answer: Yes, there will be four. Remember all of the planets in our solar system will be moving into the fifth dimension also. Venus will be turned back to the way it once was. Mars will become a water world once again. The asteroid belt which used to be a planet until it was broken up into pieces will return as it once was. It was a planet that was three times the size of Earth. She will be known as Pax, which means "Goddess of Peace."

Question #5: Do the Agarthans who already live in the Inner Earth miss seeing the stars, since it always looks like it is noontime 24-7?

Answer: Because of the central sun, it does always look like it is noon, although the sunlight is diffused somewhat. The Agarthans can fly in space any time they want to, so they do not miss the stars. When they go to the surface, they enjoy seeing the stars if they visit at night, but they can travel in space at the speed of mind, so there is no problem there.

Question #6: How will people be transported to Inner Earth?

Answer: Some will be teleported, and some will go by spaceships. Because they are fifth dimensional and above spacecraft, they are able to fly right through the Earth, just like going through walls.

Question #7: How long will it take us to become Galactic Humans once again when we enter the Metamorphosis Chamber?

Answer: It will take three days. There will be one day for each stage. When we exit the chambers, we will have earned our Wings of Light.

Question #8: What will happen to all of the animals?

Answer: All plants and animals will be teleported to a special place. They will change also and then be brought back. Then when you want to communicate with your cat or dog, he/she will be able to understand you and you they. Imagine the conversations we will have.

Part IX

Stargates, Portals, and Raising Mass Consciousness

Chapter 23

Stargates and Portals... What Are They?

Time is the most undefinable yet paradoxical of things: the past is gone, the future is not come, and the present becomes the past even while we attempt to define it, and like the flash of lightning, at once exists and expires.
—Charles Caleb Colton[9]

Wikipedia defines a stargate as an Einstein-Rosen bridge portal device within the universe which would allow practical, rapid travel between two distant places. Wordnik.com defines a stargate as a hypothetical device consisting of a traversable portal, such as a wormhole, that can transport a person to another place that is light years away, and it can be done instantaneously. So, the definition of a stargate has become pretty standard now. As I will present to you, however, the word, "hypothetical" really no longer fits because there are man-made stargates as well as natural stargates all over the place.

NASA, The National Aeronautics and Space Administration, has discovered that portals exist naturally around the Earth. They tell us that accessing them with a device of some sort may be much easier than was once thought. These portals, according to NASA, are formed with the mingling with the Earth's magnetosphere and the solar winds coming towards the Earth. These stargates open and close up to a dozen times each day.

So, a stargate is an interdimensional energy alignment between two points in interstellar space which allows high vibrational energies to pass through long distances of space and the space-time continuum. Since the vibration of the Earth is speeding up as it enters the photon belt, these alignments are even more crucial at this time. Stargates allow interstellar energies of higher vibration to permeate the etheric grids of the Earth with these in place therefore allowing the energies to integrate completely until the forming of the grid structures of the Earth. These sacred site entry vortices are opened once every three months on the equinoxes and the solstices. They also open at times of significance and astrological alignment in Earth's history.

There are different kinds of stargates. There are stargates out in the heavens and there are stargates on the Earth. Star-seeds, and I am using that term to indicate those of us born in the late 1940s and 1950s who became active and awake in the 1960s, as well as the Indigos, Crystal children, and any other group that came to the Earth to be ready for the Earth's transition to the fifth dimension as the Age of Aquarius gets under way, have awakened and are continuing to awaken in large numbers. There are still many who are choosing not to awaken, however. Earth is a planet of free will, so it is entirely up to the individual if he/she wishes to participate. So, when I say, 'Star-seeds', I am speaking about all of those groups. Each group has a different job to do but it is all to assist in the Earth's transition to the higher dimension and 1000 years of peace. As each of us awakens, we discover we have more and more abilities that are coming to us because of our awakening awareness. When humanity's consciousness is ready to receive the light through various stargates from a particular star, constellation, or other solar systems, we will receive it. There are starlight codes that are anchored into the physical realm through those awakened individuals and for whom that is part of their mission. If an awakened individual realizes that it is his/her mission during this time, it is likely that he/she will be living near the appropriate vortices, sacred sites, grid coordinates or dimensional doorways around the Earth so that they may anchor this energy. It is a beautiful job to have, although they all are, because by anchoring this energy around the Earth, this energy then radiates out for those of us who have awakened and are ready to open up to those higher frequency vibrations of love. This will awaken our consciousness more fully.

This type of stargate is a doorway that will open in our solar system, galaxy and into interdimensional space, that brings in a higher frequency to the Earth at specific times in order to assist transition of the planet. The doorway is held open to all individuals who are awake enough to receive the higher vibrational frequencies. This means that a shift in consciousness has occurred for all beings.

There was a stargate opening that occurred in August of 2013 in Castor and Pollux in the Gemini constellation. Castor and Pollux are twin stars whose stories come from Greek mythology. This stargate opening and anchoring that took place then, created a place of release from the Earth and the people also, which shifted the collective unconscious away from so much destruction, violence, and death. As more and more of these stargates open, we will begin to feel the shift in us and on our planet.

As the Earth moves through the photon belt, the energy dissipated will enter the humans on the planet and will begin to harmonize and balance everything. This will allow us to assist the Earth to shift with ease. This will help to release much of the doom and gloom scenarios that have been predicted. It is because of the shift in group consciousness which helps to release it. However, it does not mean that all of the negative effects will be dissipated. These shifts can only happen when they are in total and complete harmony and aligned with the greater ascension plan given to us by The Source, or God. We are asked only to realign things back to the original balance point. It does not matter if it is the Earth herself, a human, or an incident on the surface of the Earth. It is this balance point or the point of zero polarity that is sought. We are all messengers of the Light, creations from the Source, and we are all One!

We are raising the vibrational frequencies of physical Earth and anchoring them into the etheric Earth grid systems. In so doing, those of us who are sensitive to those incoming energies will raise our personal vibrations and begin to remember these higher frequencies within our own energy fields. Remembering this will allow the human energy field to reactivate. It will then move us along to the next level of consciousness and therefore, advancing us along our path of spiritual remembrance. By doing this, we will remember the light bodies which we have. This will also allow us to open and utilize new energies, the etheric structures of our physical bodies, which will bring us closer to the galactic bodies of light which is what we are trying to achieve. These alignments accelerate the Earth's healing process as well as our own. We connect on very high frequency levels to the perfection of the Earth and ourselves as one consciousness tied in infinite time and space for the Source of all of us.

Chapter 24

Stargates For Teleportation and Multi-Dimensional Travel

The bottom line is that time travel is allowed by the laws of physics.
—Brian Greene[10]

Stargates are now starting to energize more because we have shifted into higher frequencies of light and vibration. As we each begin to become lighter and begin to love ourselves more and more, and others unconditionally, and begin to feel our own peace within ourselves, these gateways will open for us and we will remember things we used to be able to do, such as teleportation, bilocation, even being invisible. Living in the realities of the third dimension created the dualities and the illusions which we have been living under and believing for so long. But, thankfully, not all of us are buying into that illusion any longer, which causes the matrix of light to get stronger and allows the stargates to open.

The major stargates on the Earth, which I will go into detail about in the next chapter, are transferring their codes to the places of the new fifth dimensional Earth, and there are stargates opening now at portals in the new Earth. As we move more and more into the new Earth, and the expansion of our hearts and the love that each of us are, we expand

and amplify those energies through us, and therefore the entire cosmos, which causes the stargates to open on the physical plane to assist us in being who we truly are once again.

In the last Golden Age, we were an advanced civilization. We were Galactic humans. We had the ability to teleport from place to place, travel through star systems, align star energies and the Sun with the Earth to keep balance, and we were Galactic citizens. We misused our special powers on Atlantis because the people in power began to use the technologies and knowledge we had for greed and the controlling of the masses. Very similar to what is happening today. We used our skills on Atlantis to the point where we manipulated so much of our technology that we destroyed the surface of the Earth, sunk Atlantis, and lost all of our galactic powers. Now, as we awaken to the power of love, we realize the doorway for us is our heart and the wisdom to handle such abilities once again through the Source, or God. We had reached a point on the third dimensional Earth that we had the technologies to blow ourselves to bits, but we did not have the spirituality to stop it. We are in a battle now against the dark cabal, the dark side as I refer to them, but people are awakening more and faster than ever before to the realities of our situation, and are standing up and saying, "No more!"

As we shift in consciousness more and more, we will find that with practice we can bilocate, teleport, and become invisible with divine will. I can speak personally about bilocation and invisibility. When I am calm and my mind is clear and I put myself into a meditative type state, I have been successful in both remote viewing and bilocating. I have a story about invisibility. In 2009, I was participating in a week long CSETI training in Rio Rico, Arizona. We had just finished the inside training for the day and I was waiting in line at a table that had a book for sale that I wanted. When I got to the front of the line, I told the woman there that I wanted to buy two books, one for my friend at home. She was looking right at me, so I kept talking. I had my money in my hand and was trying to give it to her when the person behind me moved up to the table and started asking to buy the book. The woman at the table reacted immediately to her and took her money. I stood there dumbfounded wondering if I had done something inappropriate to cause this woman not to notice me at all. I was a little hurt and as I walked away an acquaintance of mine saw my reaction and came up to me. I asked her if she had observed that interaction, and she said that she had. She said, "Don't worry about it. She did not even see you. Your vibration is very high today and she is not vibrating on your level, and she really does not see you." I was amazed by that but started thinking about my day up to that point, and realized that my vibration was much higher than normal for me. It probably was because of our group activities and training for the day and I had been really into it. I had been in an altered state of consciousness for most of the day.

As we resonate more and more in the world, but not of the world, we will naturally become invisible. It is due to our vibration being much higher because of us unifying our lives, emotions, and thoughts. Therefore, we do not get involved in the wars and other games being played out in the third dimension. There is no judgment towards these lower vibrational, fear-based worlds because we are no longer vibrating there. It is as though we simply cease to exist in them, and so we become invisible to the lower frequencies and vibrations. Once our light frequencies and vibrations are higher, then invisibility, teleportation, and bilocation will happen naturally. The Earth stargates are opening but only to those who have love in their hearts and are not working from agendas or power trips. There are stargates that those who are fighting for power are trying to gain control of around the Earth, such as the one in Iraq, for example. They are still fighting over them, without realizing that hatred and fear in one's heart makes it impossible to access them.

Chapter 25

Natural and Man-Made Stargates Around the Earth

It is difficult to live in the present, ridiculous to live in the future, and impossible to live in the past. Nothing is as far away as one minute ago!
—Jim Bishop[11]

Simply put, a stargate is a shortcut. They exist all around the Earth, but we have lost the instructions on how to use most of them. Many ancient Earth civilizations speak of portals and traveling to other worlds and connecting with those civilizations. NASA has said that portals do seem to be hidden within the Earth's magnetic field. I want to mention several ancient stargates that still exist today, and phenomena that seem to open up holes in the time-space continuum that things can be caught up in and transported to other dimensions. I would call these phenomena, portals, because they do seem to propel people, ships, and aircraft to other dimensions. These seem like natural phenomena, unlike the man-made stargates that exist, but they seem to cause anyone caught up in them to travel to other dimensions.

The first is the mysterious disappearance of many boats and aircraft while navigating across Lake Michigan in the United States. There are seemingly two separate phenomena occurring here, but I believe they are connected and working together. Whatever causes this phenomenon though is indeed strange and interesting.

In 2007, archeologists looking for ship wrecks in Lake Michigan while scanning the bottom of the lake, discovered a huge boulder with a prehistoric carving of a mastodon. Even more interesting was a series of stones arranged in a Stonehenge-like manner. The petroglyph found on this rock is thought to be at least 10,000 years old. This would match the time line with the post ice age presence of both humans and mastodons in the northern Midwest. Stone circles and other petroglyph sites are located in the area. These particular series of stones are arranged in a circle 40 feet below the surface of Lake Michigan. These were placed there before water from Lake Michigan covered the region. This has been referred to as America's Stonehenge. According to researchers, the stones located at the bottom of Lake Michigan all measure the same distance across, something that we would not find if we were looking at a natural formation. This rock formation looks like other structures found in England and France. Also, it resembles those at Nabta Playa, so it is unlikely that it is a natural formation. Nabta Playa was once a large dry lake-like basin in the Nubian Desert, which is located about 500 miles south of Cairo, Egypt. There are a great many archeological sites there. An advanced urban community was there about 11,000 years ago. This civilization left behind a huge assembly of stones, which scientists have studied and said this is the oldest known astronomical alignments of megaliths in the world. Playas are dry lakes.

Ancient stone circles, such as Stonehenge, have been thought to have been used for time travel in the past. Did civilizations in the past use large crystals in the center of these circles to create electromagnetic energy that opened up holes in the time-space continuum? It has been written in the stories about Atlantis that they used huge crystals for electricity and for creating portals for time travel. What about the stone circle found in Lake Michigan in the Michigan Triangle? It has been suggested that there are buried crystals found in these locations that still emit power creating electricity and electromagnetic fields.

There have been many documented reports of ships, boats and airplanes disappearing over the Michigan triangle never to be seen again. Sometimes, though, people experience a strange phenomenon that causes them to seem to be caught up in some kind of vortex and a loss of several hours of time, but they do return. One such story is that of Kathy Doore.

Kathy Doore set out in her yacht one evening with her crew. It was a clear warm night with winds of 7 – 10 knots and flat seas. After a few minutes when they were well under way, they encountered a very strange fog. It seemed to come on suddenly and out of nowhere. This fog engulfed the boat. It became very cold. The visibility dropped to zero. They became disoriented. Kathy leaned over the rail and noticed that the surface of the lake was calm with little movement. She reported next, when she stood back up, she became extremely cold. In fact, she said, she was freezing. She turned her attention back to the helm to ask her crewmates if they were cold and they were no longer standing next to her. She was suddenly alone at the helm. She located them standing on the aft deck, where it was several degrees warmer. They were also perplexed about their situation and she then realized that no one was steering the boat. The captain swore that he had not been steering the boat for the last ten minutes, and yet, just one minute before, she was certain he was standing right next to her at the helm. Surrounded by dense fog, the boat began to slowly and deliberately turn on her axis completing three perfect 360^0 turns, without ever crossing the wind. Then just as suddenly as it had appeared, the fog disappeared. As the weeks passed, she realized that they had lost two hours of time during that incident.

In the past, many planes have disappeared while flying over Lake Michigan. Other ships have disappeared never to be heard from again. This strange fog seems to come on quickly and then leave as quickly as it came. In 1950, Northwest Airlines flight 2501 disappeared over Lake Michigan. No wreckage was ever found. Did a hole open up in the time-space continuum and send the plane into another dimension from which it could not return? No one knows.

There is a phenomenon known as electronic fog which seems to partly be created by the ley lines of the earth that are connected by ancient ceremonial sites. Electronic fog is a grayish cloud of electromagnetic fields that get formed above water, such as lakes or oceans. It seems to appear out of nowhere and completely engulfs a ship or an aircraft. The fog then keeps moving along with the ship or plane. It is as though this fog is attached to them. This fog has been reported over areas where submerged ancient ceremonial sites are found, such as in Lake Michigan. There is a triangle shape in Lake Michigan where this phenomenon has occurred. Drawing imaginary lines to create the triangle, it starts at Manitowoc, Wisconsin and crosses the top of Lake Michigan to Ludington, Michigan, then runs down to Benton Harbor, Michigan, and back up to Manitowoc, Wisconsin.

The Lake Michigan triangle accounts for a number of mysterious events, beginning in 1891. Strange things could have happened before but simply were not written down. In 1891, a schooner named the Thomas Hume started out over Lake Michigan to get lumber. The Hume disappeared, along with its crew of seven sailors. There was never even a trace of the boat that was ever found. What caused this disappearance?

Another strange case occurred in 1937 when Captain George R. Donner disappeared from his cabin after guiding his ship through icy waters. The captain had gone to his cabin to rest, and three hours later one of his crew went to his cabin to let him know that they were nearing their port. His cabin door was locked from the inside and when the crew member got no response from the captain, he broke into the room only to find it empty. A search ensued, but no clues were ever found and Captain Donner's disappearance remains an unsolved mystery.

One of the most mysterious events that took place over Lake Michigan occurred in 1950 when Northwest Flight 2501, carrying 58 passengers, crashed into Lake Michigan. The plane was never found. In 1950, this was the deadliest commercial airline accident in American history. The pilot had just before asked the control tower to descend to 2,500 feet because of a severe electrical storm which was hitting the lake with very high velocity winds. The plane suddenly disappeared from radar. The plane wreckage has never been found to this day, and the cause of the crash officially remains unknown. About two hours after this last communication between the pilot and the tower, two police officers reported seeing a strange red light hovering over Lake Michigan. This red light disappeared after about ten minutes. This led some to believe that an unidentified flying object had caused the crash. It has been argued that these vortices over these ancient stone circles are actually stargates that Star Visitors enter and leave the Earth from. This phenomenon has been reported over the Bermuda Triangle as well. There had been several sightings of spacecraft over Lake Michigan during that time, and still are today, actually. We will probably never know what happened to that flight.

The question arises as to whether these are two separate phenomena, each activated on its own, or do these two phenomena, the stone circle and the ley lines work together to create a hole in the time-space continuum where ships and planes slip into? Are there huge crystals buried under the lake in the middle of the stone circle that were used in ancient times to time travel by manipulating the electromagnetic fields? Until divers explore there and look for those specific possibilities, it is only conjecture. Or could these be stargates created by extraterrestrial civilizations to travel back and forth to the Earth?

We all know the stories of the famous Bermuda Triangle. This triangle covers the Straits of Florida, The Bahamas, and the entire Caribbean island area, and the Atlantic Ocean east to the Azores. Christopher Columbus, during his voyage, wrote in his log about bizarre compass bearings in the area. This region actually got its name when a writer, Vincent Gaddis used the term Bermuda Triangle in a cover story for Argosy Magazine about the disappearance of Flight 19. Flight 19 was the designation of a group of five aircraft, Grumman Avenger torpedo bombers, that were in an overwater navigation training flight from the Naval Air Station in Fort Lauderdale, Florida. It disappeared on December 5, 1945 over the Bermuda Triangle. All contact was lost from this group of aircraft. The flight's leader was Lieutenant Charles Taylor who was an experienced pilot and a veteran of several combat missions in World War II. Shortly after the patrol turned north for the second leg of its journey, the Lieutenant became convinced that his Avenger's compass was malfunctioning. He believed his planes were flying in the wrong direction. Then a strange weather front blew in and with it, rain, erratic winds and a very heavy cloud cover. Flight 19 became hopelessly disoriented. Eventually all contact was lost with the flight. A pair of PBM Mariner flying boats took off from an air station north of Fort Lauderdale, and just 20 minutes later, one of them suddenly vanished off the radar. The remains of the Mariner and its 13 crew members were never recovered. Flight 19's disappearance was accompanied by many strange occurrences and many unanswered questions. None of the pilots of flight 19 used the rescue radio frequency or their aircrafts' ZBX receivers, which could have helped them go toward Navy Radio towers on land. The pilots had been told to switch the devices on, but they either did not hear the message or they chose not to acknowledge it. Many people believe that the wreckage of Flight 19 and its doomed rescue plane may still be out there somewhere in the Bermuda Triangle. No trace of them has ever been found.

Albert Einstein hypothesized that a curvature of space would cause light to bend through it. Some theorists believe that "time" as a force of nature, can also get bent or twisted out of shape based on one's location. The Bermuda Triangle is one location on the Earth where the fabric of time seems to be very thin. Travelers can easily slip through it and come out on the other side of a completely different time.

It is also believed that the lost city of Atlantis lies beneath the ocean in the Bermuda Triangle. Edgar Cayce, the famous American psychic referred to as the sleeping prophet, claimed to be able to channel answers to questions pertaining to Atlantis and had even documented many of his 'readings' between 1924 and 1944 regarding the lost city of Atlantis. He claimed that the Bahama Banks were the last part of Atlantis to sink into the ocean. He also mentioned Bimini, the island. He said there was a series of energy crystals lying in that region that were once used to power the city. These electromagnetic forces would be able to cause interference with ships and airplanes electronic systems, which would cause them to disappear. Cayce did not hypothesize why these forces would make something disappear.

Then in 1968, a scuba diver named J. Manson Valentine, discovered a series of laid stones at the bottom of the ocean that seemed to form a road, therefore proving the existence of Atlantis. Could this be the

Bimini Road off the island of Bimini in the Bahamas? All of this just adds to the high strangeness associated with these triangle areas.

Whatever is causing these disappearances in these areas of water that have some sort of ancient structure under water, remains a mystery, but I do believe that something in these areas causes openings in the time-space continuum to open from time to time, and these ships and planes pass through them. NASA has said that there are natural stargates found around the Earth that do open and close at will, and they seem to be hidden within the Earth's magnetic field.

Portals and stargates are a means for people to instantly travel to and from vast distances connecting to the Earth where the portal or stargate is located. Stargates are man-made and portals occur naturally.

The stargate known as "The Puerta de Hayu Marca", or in English, "The Gate of the Gods," is located near Lake Titicaca in Peru. It is made up of a block of stone that is twenty-two feet by twenty-two feet. It has an inset door that is seven feet high and it is carved into the rock. The ancient Incas believed that the largest doorway was used by the gods to travel between planets, and the smaller doorway was reserved for mortals. To the people at this time, any being traveling through time in these stargates, would seem like gods. The technologies that these extraterrestrials possessed would have seemed like magic to the local people and therefore, they would think that the visitors were gods.

This mysterious structure is about twenty-two miles from the city of Puno, and is in an area which the local Indians believe is the City of the Gods. No actual city has ever been found, however, but the area is known as a spirit or stone forest. It is made up of strange rock formations that look like buildings, people and other artificial structures. The door of this stargate was carved out of a natural rock face and measures exactly twenty-three feet in height and width. It has a smaller alcove in the center of the base which measures just under six feet high.

In 1996, Jose Luis Delgado Mamani happened across this structure while hiking through the surrounding foothills. He was trying to familiarize himself with the area because he worked as a guide for tourists who liked the mountains. In talking to the native Indians of that region they spoke of a gateway to the land of the gods. The legend says that in times long ago, great heroes had joined their gods by passing through the gate. They were to receive an amazing new life of immortality. On a rare occasion, those same men returned for a short period of time with their gods to "inspect all the lands in the kingdom', by passing through the gate.

Another legend comes from the time of the Spanish Conquistadors and their arrival in Peru. They looted all the gold and precious stones from the Incan tribes. An Incan Priest, who was from the Temple of the Seven Rays, Amaru Meru, fled from his temple with a sacred golden disk. This disk was known as the key of the gods of the seven rays and was hidden in the mountains of Hayu Marca. This Incan priest eventually found the doorway which was being watched by shaman priests. He showed them the key of the gods, and a ritual was done. At the end of this magical ritual initiated by this golden disk, the portal was opened. Apparently blue light emanated from a tunnel inside. The priest, Amaru Meru, handed the golden disk to the shaman and then passed through the portal never to be seen again. When archeologists have studied the gateway, they have observed a small hand sized circular depression on the right-hand side of the small doorway. They have assumed that this is the place where a small disk could be placed and held by the rock. There have been people who claim to have experienced strange sensations when they are standing near the stargate such as anomalous noises, which included music and whispers, and also hallucinations of stars and columns of fire. Also, there have been stories that a certain energy can be felt echoing through the rock when it is touched.

People have noticed that the stargate at Lake Titicaca resembles the Gate of the Sun at Tiahuanaco in Bolivia, the second actual stargate found on the Earth that I will tell you about. It is located at 12,549.2 feet above sea level. It is near the town of La Paz, Bolivia. It is also apparently aligned by five other archaeological sites which together form an imaginary cross with straight lines crossing each other exactly at the spot where the plateau and Lake Titicaca are found. This was once the capital of a great empire stretching from Bolivia all the way into Peru and Chile. This city is full of ancient folklore, with the original inhabitants believing that the Sun god, Viracocha, had chosen this location to create the human race. Apparently, he used this stargate to travel from one dimension or planet to the other. This stargate was rediscovered in the 1800s. The gate itself is an arch made from a single massive block of stone. It is about 9.8 feet tall and 13 feet wide. It is estimated to weigh ten tons. Etched into its surface were various images of winged figures with curled tails and wearing what appear to be helmets, like a space suit might have. There was also a carving of the sun god himself, complete with rays of light coming from behind him as he very obviously displays two wooden staffs. Local stories say that this gate was used to travel from one dimension to another. The stargate is said to have been built by the ancient Tiwanaku culture of Boliva.

When the gate was rediscovered by European explorers in the mid -1800s, the gate was lying on its side and had a large crack running through it. It was damaged in some catastrophe. It is not known how this happened. It does seem to follow the legend, however, that it was destroyed and made inoperable in some event. The true purpose of the damage is unknown. Currently it stands in the place where it was found, although local people believe that it is not the original site. It is unclear where that site is located.

There are mysterious inscriptions found on the stargate and they are thought to be of astronomical and astrological significance which might have served the purpose of a calendar.

The third stargate to mention was found on the Earth and is located in Sri Lanka. This stargate is burrowed within the remote rocky outback and caves of Ranmasu Uyana. Also referred to as 'Gold Fish Park,' it is between the Thissa Wewa reservoir and the Isurumuniya Rock Temple. Many strange symbols carved into the stone were found there. This stone grid, is about six feet in diameter. Interestingly, there were four stone seats located directly in front of it. It has been hypothesized that the symbols stand for some kind of code key to open the stargate between worlds. Additionally, it is thought that it could also be an ancient star map, which is called the Sakwala Chakraya, which translates roughly into, "The rotating circle of the Universe," and is referred to more commonly as "The Stargate of Sri Lanka." Very little is known about this stargate or who created it at this particular site or even how old it is. The mystery surrounding this stargate remains just that, a mystery.

It is alleged that there is an ancient stargate that is lost and hidden at the Eurphrates River as well. Elizabeth Vegh, a stargate researcher, has written several books on ancient stargates, and she states that this stargate is buried under the ruins and remains of the Mesopotamian city of Eridu. So far, it has remained lost to us. It has been said that this stargate is connected to Sumerian gods and kings, which Vegh believes regularly used such stargates to travel around the universe. This idea of Sumerian stargates is supported by odd discoveries of scenes of Sumerian gods or kings using such devices. One such depiction shows a seal with a god appearing on a stairway surrounded by what seems to be columns of water. Another shows the god Ninurta standing at a stargate ready to push a button. He is shown wearing what seems to be a modern wristwatch. Ancient Mesopotamia, where the Sumerians lived, is often said to have had some of the most ancient of stargates. It is alleged that these gates were used by beings from another world to travel between Earth and a planet called Nibiru which is said to orbit our sun once every 3,600 years.

This leads me to the fifth stargate on Earth that I would like to mention. The stargates of ancient Egypt. Probably the most well-known of these stargates is the one referred to as Abu Ghurab. It can be found at the Abu Sir Pyramids. It happens to be approximately a twenty-minute drive from the Great Pyramid at Giza, Egypt. Most often, it is called "The Crow's Nest." This stargate is thought to have been built by the fifth Dynasty pharaoh Niussere approximately 2400 BC as a temple to worship the god, Ra. Unfortunately, this site has fallen into disarray over the centuries and now it is almost all rubble. It is believed that it once was around fifteen feet high, and most likely, copied the sun temple at Heliopolis, or On.

One amazing feature of this highly sacred site is a mammoth platform made from alabaster. This platform is formed in the shape of the Khemetian symbol Hotep, which translates to peace. Because the exact purpose of this platform has been lost in history, some theories prevail. One such theory was by Abd'El Hakim Awyan, a researcher of ancient Egypt. He asserts that this platform was used to harness and channel certain vibrations and Earth energies. These were used to emit a kind of harmonic resonance for the purpose of creating an amplified sense of enlightenment and awareness of the universe. This then allowed an individual to attune himself to the universe and to communicate directly with sacred spirits of the universe known as Neters. It has been told that Neters were beings that occasionally would visit the Earth through this Abu Ghurab stargate. At least for now, the true story of this stargate is unknown.

In the 1990s, the movie, "Stargate," was released to the movie theaters. It takes place in modern day Egypt, and a professor, Daniel Jackson, teams up with a retired Army Colonel, Jack O'Neil, to figure out the last symbol to a stargate that was discovered in Egypt which would open the stargate. The thing that really bothered me about this is that anytime we find something in our ancient history that could lead to technology that would free the Earth's people from relying on oil and electricity, the military always takes over and classifies everything so it is very difficult to get the information to the general public. I will make reference to this further when I discuss the next stargate. In the movie, Daniel does figure this symbol out and they pass through the stargate and come out on an earth like planet located on the other side of the known galaxy. This planet is ruled by a despot, Ra, who holds the key to allow the Earth travelers a safe return back to Earth. In order to get back to Earth, they must convince the planet's inhabitants, who speak an ancient Sumerian language, that Ra is a fake, and must be overthrown. I believe this movie is based on a real stargate that is located in modern day Iraq and is still functioning today.

Since I just referred to this working stargate, that will be the next stargate I will mention. There is an ancient Sumerian stargate that can be found in a huge ziggurat near Nasiriyah, which is a city about 60 miles south east of Baghdad. A ziggurat is a tower with steps and is rectangular in shape. It is in the form of a terraced compound. They were first recognized in the late third millennium BC. Some say they inspired the biblical story of the Tower of Babel. That story can be found in the Bible, Genesis 11:1-9. This stargate was discovered in the 1920s. When word got out that the stargate was there, and that it actually worked, there were many governments that jumped at the chance to find it and use it for their own purposes.

The Sumerians lived in ancient Mesopotamia which partly covers part of modern-day Iraq. The Sumerians were one of the first civilizations on Earth at around 3000 BC. For a period of time they worshipped The Annunaki who were their gods. In reality, the Annunaki were Star Visitors who came to Earth through the stargate, causing the Sumerians to see them as gods because of the technology. The Annunaki gave the Sumerians technology, and it is this technology that advanced their society so quickly at that time.

After its discovery in the 1920s, the Nazi's utilized heavy resources studying it during World War II. It has been alleged that the Anglo-Iraqi War of 1941 was started in order to gain control of the stargate and to exploit its use. Apparently, Saddam Hussein moved the stargate to a cave system underneath his palace in Baghdad and had learned how to harness its power. The United States got wind of the fact that Saddam Hussein had control of this stargate and started the war to gain control of it. Instead of weapons of mass destruction that had been alleged about Iraq in 2003, the real reason for the Iraq War at that time was for the U.S. military to take possession of the stargate for its own purposes. When Baghdad fell to the American forces, it happened to fall right in the middle of a highly guarded and fortified Green Zone. I would bet this is no coincidence. There have been a few whistleblowers who have come out to confirm that the United States wanted access to this technology. Dan Burisch is one who claims to have been part of a covert team that went into Iraq on a mission to find the stargate.

There are many projects that are deep black and are not controlled by our elected government. They have many projects that are above top secret and no one in our government is in control of them. Even the President of the United States is not in the loop. President Dwight Eisenhower in his farewell speech to the nation warned us about the Military Industrial Complex. Dr. Michael Salla, exopolitics, said, "Essentially more and more people are coming forward saying that they have been involved in these classified programs where these technologies are used quite regularly and that they can be found all over the planet. Iraq is just one place they are found. They [the stargates] are also located in Iran and Syria." It is why there is a big push for the United States to go into Iran and to intervene in the Syrian civil war. This is all very significant in what pushes international conflict. It does cause one to wonder why the big governments of the world are fighting in these countries. Having control of a stargate would be an important thing to have for a lot of reasons, good and bad.

Even though it is impossible for us to know for sure if these ancient stargates really worked and who built them, the stories handed down from generation to generation over the vast number of years make it all very believable. The most common of these stories handed down, are that "gods" that the ancients spoke of, were actually extraterrestrials who used their technology to create these stargates and travel through them. Another theory about them is that many of these stargate sites seem to lie on the places where ley lines come together and natural arteries of energy crisscross the Earth, and that they were somehow able to harness this energy to create some kind of wormhole or dimensional doorway. There is even another theory that some of these sites may have contained a small black hole or some other kind of vortex that would allow someone to travel through space and time. In my space travels when I was being taken on board spacecraft, the Star Visitors were taking me on a visit to their home planet. I asked them how long it would take to get there and they said that it would take 3 minutes to punch in the coordinates and then about 2 minutes to get there. He said they travel at the speed of thought.

The last stargate I will mention is located in the mountains of southeastern Arizona. Rob and Chuck Quinn, treasure hunters, in 1956, came into this area searching for gold and lost Spanish treasures. What they discovered, however, went beyond most people's imagination at the time. These two men in the past had experienced high strangeness in the area in the form of mysterious floating lights at night. This time they reported that they stumbled across an eerie stone archway just standing in the middle of nowhere. It measured seven feet high and five feet wide, and had columns of andesite which were fifteen inches in diameter. Andesite is a rock with a composition between that of rhyolite and basalt. Andesite lava has medium viscosity and forms thick lava flows and domes. Andesite is the volcanic equivalent of diorite. While it received its name from the Andes Mountains in South America, it is found naturally in Arizona. The archway they were looking at was just standing there among scattered and broken geodes which were glittering in the sunlight. Even though they were curious about what they were seeing, they decided to make a note as to its location and move along to hunt for treasure.

When Rob and Chuck later mentioned the archway to other people, a local Native American guide, named John, knew what it was they had found. John had heard many stories about this strange archway. He told them that on some occasions people who had ventured through the archway had disappeared completely, and when rocks were thrown through it, more often than not, they would not emerge on the other side, suggesting that there was some kind of portal hidden in the archway. John also had heard stories of the archway glowing, like shimmering, and he said he also had his own strange experience there. He told them that one time he had been trekking in that area and had observed a strange phenomenon. Although the day had been very dark and cloudy, the sky through the stone archway had appeared clear and blue, something which he could not explain.

The Quinn brothers decided to go back to the puzzling and somewhat eerie site, and when they did, they expressed that things only got stranger for them. They experimented with the archway by throwing rocks through it. At one point they even shoved their arms in, but nothing strange at all occurred. Now their skepticism was growing. But, on the following day, as they hunted around the site for treasures, Roy and another team member witnessed the portal shimmering for several minutes like a heat mirage would. Not long after this, they could feel pressure building up in their ears. They reported that this pressure lasted for several minutes before leaving. They were not able to repeat the effect. However, a group of treasure hunters passing by said that the stone archway indeed had some kind of unexplained force. They reported that they had been camping there when stones rained down on them from nowhere, and that the stones were warm to the touch. They then said that after that, nothing else happened to them during their trek.

Roy and Chuck did not forget the strange stone doorway, and in 1973, Chuck went out to the site once again. While hiking up the canyon, he stopped to rest. He noticed that there was another canyon that had not been there before. Believing that this was very strange, he climbed back down and entered the canyon from a different direction. He then realized that it was in fact the same canyon he had been in before except that he had somehow been transported 250 yards down the canyon he had hiked along, and to another slope that was facing south rather than west. This was a very shocking experience for him, and he was now convinced that he had traveled through some sort of portal and was teleported from one place to another. I wonder if the gateway arch is still there in that canyon and how many other stories people have told about this strange and mysterious gateway. Maybe I should add this to my future journeys to see for myself.

Chapter 26

My Stargate Assignment in the Valley of Fire, Nevada

Time is precious – spend it wisely!
—Anonymous

In 2014, I was working with my friend and colleague, Jeanne Love. Jeanne is a very gifted psychic medium, clairvoyant, earth healer, and someone who does healing on those who have crossed over suddenly, especially if it was an accident. Jeanne is known for having been contacted by The Space Shuttle Challenger crew after the Challenger blew up a minute or so into the launch sequence killing all seven astronauts on board. That is another story. Jeanne was given the assignment to take her team, there were six of us at the time, into the Valley of the Fire, Nevada, and psychically tear down the existing stargate tracts that were located there so that they could be replaced by gates that were vibrating at a much higher level so that the "dark side" could not use them. Through their carelessness over the years experimenting with time travel and not really knowing what they were doing, they poked huge holes into the channel tube where people would be while traveling through from one place to another. It was described to me like the water slides at a water park. Imagine if halfway down a steep water slide, a hole had been punched into the side of it. Then when a person gets in the tube at the top and starts sliding down, he would pop out of the slide in that hole and fall many feet to the ground, either injuring himself badly or killing himself. That is just what had become of these particular stargates. A traveling person would hit one of these tears or holes in the stargate itself and would fly out and be lost in space or be shot into another dimension, never to return from where he came.

In chapter three I mentioned that the two NSA agents who showed up at my presentation at the hypnotherapy convention told my friend, Diana, that I had something very important; some information that had been given to me, and it was tucked away in some part of my memory and I would not know what it was until it was time to use it. I had wracked my brain to try and figure out what it could possibly be, and I ended up assuming it had to do with the doctoral dissertation topic on DNA that I had wanted to do, and then changed my mind after being harassed and followed. It was not. They had been watching me and even tried to get it from me using remote psychic attacks, but my connection to angels and the Light protected me. What it had to do with was these stargate tracks that our team was going to go to and disrupt. Each of the six of us had a portion of a blueprint for those stargates that had been downloaded to us, probably from the Galactic Federation of Light years before. I am not even sure. Even though we were successful, I have been holding this event close to me and not sharing it much because the "dark side" did get involved and caused us disruption. I deliberately did not take notes or write anything in my journal in order to protect the integrity of what we were doing. I will give you a general overview of what we did, but I am choosing to keep some of the details to myself in order to protect what we did. It has been five years since we completed our three-day task and I am sure that subsequent teams have come in and completed their tasks after us. The goal was to ultimately rebuild the stargate there at a much higher vibration so that the dark side could not access it. As you can well imagine, this did not make them happy.

Jeanne's daughter had been given the entire blueprint and only became aware of it when she was lying on her death bed. She knew that she needed to get it down on paper before she passed so that we would be able to do what we were supposed to do. The blueprint was in the form of a hand and each finger represented the message and the part of the gate that each of us was supposed to do. There will be a picture of this hand at the end of this book in the epilogue.

Jeanne, Roy, and I, the three of us who were available to do this, went to Las Vegas and stayed in old Las Vegas instead of downtown where all the glitz and glamor was. We were not there for that purpose and we wanted to stay focused on our task. We went very near Thanksgiving but I do not recall the exact dates right now. The dates are not really important anyway. We left in the morning and had a pretty uneventful drive until we started reaching the Nevada/California border. We all started picking up some negative energy, but Jeanne, being our leader, was really being bombarded with it. The dark side knew we were coming and were not happy about it. Jeanne is powerful in the Light and she shows no fear! They were attempting to disrupt Jeanne psychically but she was ready and psychically deflected and countered. We had strange things happen with the car as well. We would be driving down a road where we knew we were supposed to be and before we knew it, we would be completely somewhere else, not realizing how we got there.

We checked into our hotel without incident. It was a big hotel which had its hay-day in the 1950s and 1960s. The rooms were wonderfully large and were set up like cabins. Jeanne and I had a two-bedroom room and Roy stayed by himself. Very inexpensive because it was off the beaten path. We got something to eat and settled in for the night so that we would be alert and ready in the morning for our first day out in the field. We each had a particular part of the stargate to tend to according to the blueprint, but we were each back-up for the other.

Dawn seemed to come quickly. We showered, went to get something to eat and set out to the first spot where we needed to work. See pictures. The first stop was mine, up in the mountains. It took us about an hour to get there. As you look at the hand blueprint, my fingers were the middle finger and the index finger next to the thumb. Those were the blueprints for this stargate. When we got there, I remembered that I had brought those balls with me that Bob, the hobo, had given me when I was six years old. He told me at the time that I would know what to do with them when it was time for me to use them. I suddenly remembered that I had them in my pocket and I pulled them out without giving it much thought. I was acting unconsciously, actually, not really knowing what I was doing. I could feel these balls vibrating in my hands, something that had never happened before since I had them. I began to realize that they were reacting to the stargate's energy. We all just stood there staring at the stargate opening and we began to see what looked like a heat mirage, like you might see in the desert when the ground gets so hot, wave like energy is produced. The interesting thing is that it was not hot, but very cold. It was about three weeks until official winter, so there would not have been a heat mirage there at that time. We knew that it was coming from the stargate.

Without thinking about what I was doing, I held one of the balls at arms-length facing the notch in the mountain where I knew the stargate opening to be. As I stared at the ball I was holding it in front of the stargate, and it began to spin rapidly. It looked like the animation one would see in a physics class of a proton, neutron, and electron spinning around an atom. As it was spinning, it was directly affecting the stargate opening because that area began to sparkle and react to the ball in my hand. The ball kept spinning faster and faster for about a minute, and then all of a sudden, the energy in the stargate opening shot out like a small explosion, creating sparkling energy all around it. Then it was quiet. The ball in my hand stopped spinning and became quiet. Before it had been hot in my hand, but now it was cooling quickly. We knew that whatever I was here to do, had been done. We walked back to our car from where we had gone, I placed the balls back into my pocket, and the three of us just stood there outside of our vehicle, staring at the stargate opening, which now looked like just sky and the notch in the mountain. We decided to drive up higher to be closer to it and we turned off on a little road that took us into the area a little way and we stopped. I had brought a rose quartz crystal with me that I had kept for the longest time, not really knowing why. I had decided to bring it with me and leave it near the stargate. I found a tree that was calling to me and I buried it at the base of the tree. The interesting thing about this tree is that it was dead. But one could see and feel how grand it had been once and could still feel its energy. I was drawn to it. Perhaps the dead tree was a symbol for the now "dead" stargate. We all knew that the next crew would be coming in about three months from then to begin building back the stargate at a much higher dimension so that the dark side would not have access to it.

All in all, we had been involved with this gate for about four hours. Instead of going to the second gate, we decided to explore around the area to see what was there. It took us about an hour to get back into the Las Vegas area, and we decided to drive towards Henderson, a town that runs right into Las Vegas, like a suburb of Las Vegas. While driving down the main road, we came upon a road that looked like it went into an area with a water tower, some gravel and other things. We decided to check it out so we drove down the road. As we approached the site, we felt very negative energy coming from there. I am getting goosebumps right now as I am writing this because I am remembering that feeling. Something was going on in the mountain that was there and we came upon a sign that told us it was military and that we were trespassing. None of us had any idea that the military was so close to us. As we turned around to go back to the main road, we made several observations about the place. We knew we were being watched and that gave us the creeps. We figured that they were not happy with what had occurred at the stargate that morning so we began to feel a little uneasy.

As we were driving back to town, we came upon another road that looked like it went to a few buildings and then just open land. We decided to drive down it, and when we got as far as the road would take us, we got out of the car and walked around looking for anything that seemed out of place. We took some pictures and watched. About that time, a vehicle with one driver came into our area and parked about fifty yards from us, kept his engine running and just watched us. There was really no reason for him to be there because there was nothing there to see on the surface anyway. We stared back, made eye contact so that he would know that we saw him, and then we went about our business. He just sat there and watched us for about fifteen minutes, then turned around and left. The energy in the area was uncomfortable, but we stayed a little while longer looking at a few rock formations and anything else that might tell us something. About ten minutes later, another vehicle drove up and stopped about where the other one had stopped. The man watched us for a minute and then got out of the vehicle and came over to us. He tried to act like just a person viewing the area, but he didn't do a good job. He asked us what we were doing out there and one of us said, "Why? Is this area off limits or something? We didn't see any signs." He said, "No, this area isn't restricted but it is just not a place people stop at very much." We said, "Oh! We were just leaving anyway." At that point we walked to our car, got into it, locked the doors and just sat there for a minute talking about what we thought was going on. The man just sat in his vehicle until we pulled out and began down the road. The man left too, but did not follow us. We decided to maybe check this area out again when it was not so busy. We were tired and went back to our hotel where we debriefed on today's events and then looked at a map to see where we would go tomorrow to the second stargate. The second stargate was Roy's stargate. It and the third stargate were located in the Valley of Fire. We ate dinner and then went to sleep for the night. We were exhausted both physically and mentally. We also knew we could be in danger if we were not careful.

After breakfast the next morning, we started out to the Valley of Fire National Park. I had never been there before that I knew of, although as we worked our way through it, I began to realize that this was the area I was taken on many occasions by my core group of Star Visitors when I was learning navigation, flight, surveillance and things like that. We stopped at the entrance to pay our fee to drive into the park and the many miles that it covered. The state park itself is a public recreation area and also a nature preserve. It is a very large area making up about 46,000 acres. The Valley of Fire gets its name from the red sandstone formations made up of Aztec Sandstone. The sandstone was formed about 150 million years ago by the shifting sand dunes.

The Moapa River Indian Reservation near Moapa, Nevada. It is the land of the Moapa Band of Southern Paiute Indians. The Indian reservation is made up of 71,954 acres. As of the 2010 census, there was a population of 238. This is important information because these Native Americans love the land and treat it accordingly. The reservation is crossed by the I-15 Highway, northeast to southwest. It is next to the Valley of Fire State Park in the southeast. The local road leading to the west park entrance belongs to the reservation.

What is important to note is that on this reservation, there is a 250 MW solar power generation facility called the Moapa Southern Paiute Solar Project. This project generates enough energy to send power to 111,000 homes. It displaces around 341,000 metric tons of carbon dioxide yearly. Another solar farm is being constructed on the reservation called the Eagle Shadow Mountain Solar Farm. It is a planned 300 MW solar project.

This entire area of the Indian reservation and the state park is on a flight path for unusual things coming out of Area 51, which is very close as the crow flies. It stands to reason that Star Visitors would be very comfortable working out of this whole area. We had ships observing us while we were working. I took a couple of pictures at the stargate locations asking any spacecraft to show themselves to us, which they did. We could not see them with the naked eye, but I "knew" where they were so I made sure that location was in the photograph. They appeared in my photographs. I can only speak for myself on these issues with the Star Visitors because they have been with me through everything that I have done relating to the topic. They were instrumental in the downloading of the stargate blueprints to me probably when I was a child going onboard their spacecraft every summer. Bob, the "hobo" has been with me in one form or another ever since. I will tell more about that in an upcoming chapter.

From 300 BC to 1150 AD, the Fremont people, who were basket-makers, and the later Anasazi farmers lived in the Moapa Valley. Their lifestyles probably involved hunting, religious ceremonies, gathering food, but with the lack of water, they probably did not stay long at one place. However, they left behind wonderful petroglyphs throughout the Valley of Fire!

Chapter 27

Wormholes, Stargates, Time Travel and Black Projects

War itself is, of course, a form of madness. It's hardly a civilized pursuit. It's amazing how we spend so much time inventing devices to kill each other and so little time working on how to achieve peace.
—Walter Cronkite

An interesting thing happens when one starts to look into black projects. What you thought you were looking for turned out to be something else entirely or it leads you to an alleged dead end. Dr. Dan Burisch, a microbiologist, is known for working in S-4 with an extraterrestrial they called J-Rod. Recruited into MJ—12 (Majestic) he was allowed access to many black projects. Dr. Burish confirmed that these five projects are real. They are Project Sigma, which establishes communications and also satellite surveillance; Project Galileo, a propulsion system; Project Sidekick, which is manipulating glass to regulate light rays on the gravity wave to act as a particle beam weapon to focus on a target; Project Aquarius, which is extraterrestrial biology; and Project Looking Glass, the physics of looking back in time. While all of these are worth looking into, it is Project Looking Glass that is worth mentioning here.

According to what is out there regarding classified technologies in black projects, it has been said that those programs are over a thousand years ahead of the public sector technologies. It is also allegedly speeding away from the public technology at a rate of 1,000 years per calendar year. I do not know who said that or when it was said, but I find it interesting enough to include it here, and frankly, I think it is totally possible. We, the people have been kept out of the loop completely. What is Looking Glass Technology? According to the literature that is out regarding this technology, it is basically a device using wormhole technology to see into the future or the past. It has also been connected to stargate technology which has allowed people to be shot into the future, apparently at first, with a very poor success rate, leaving the test subjects to die a painful death or to be lost somewhere out there, never to return.

Project Looking Glass ultimately allowed people to peer into their past events or their future. I have heard that the dark cabal, the 1% of the wealthiest people in the world who are currently in charge, were given regular access to this technology at first to look at their futures and then make changes in the now time to make things better for themselves in the future. This technology, however, could not focus on a detailed series of events in the future. Later, the access to this technology, was pulled back from the dark elite, but one wonders what decisions were made by these people that would allegedly make their lives better, but possibly worse for us? Apparently, Project Looking Glass came from an intelligence gathering technology that had been around and in use since the 1950s. It also seems like some of the Star Visitor technologies are making the technology even better. The aim of this program is to look into the future and see what scenarios are the most likely, given today's circumstances. Then the information would be transmitted back to our leaders so that they could avoid those future events by changing how we are doing things now.

I am attempting to explain how physics allows us to predict the possibilities of time travel. I have been told by people who have been close to some of these projects and are now retired, that time travel is not only possible, but our black projects have produced time machines and use them regularly. I am using the terms time machine and stargates interchangeably because they both, in essence, do the same thing, but with some subtle differences.

Why is this important for me to talk about here? In my many travels onboard Star Visitor craft over the years, and especially when I was a little girl on my grand-parents farm in Antelope, California, I could see how quickly we were traveling from one place to the next. I only had a 1940s automobile to compare the speed to, and I knew in relation to the spacecraft, the car was extremely slow. I mentioned before that I asked a Star Visitor how long it would take us to get to his home planet because that is where he was taking me, and he said three minutes to punch in the coordinates and two minutes to get there. They travel at the speed of thought. I'm guessing that the technology acquired in black projects is still not sophisticated by any means, but functioning nonetheless. Although, I could really be mistaken about that. I also want to share with you how two programs, Project Rainbow, better known as the Philadelphia Experiment, and the Montauk Project touched my life in some strange ways.

A wormhole is a tunnel of sorts that would connect two points in space-time together by a shortened route. I used to demonstrate simply to my physical science students the idea of a wormhole. I held an apple to show them this concept. I marked an X on one side of it and another X on the side just opposite of it. Then I asked the question, what would be the shortest way to connect these two Xs by travel? This demonstration usually happened before I introduced the concept of a wormhole. I would get answers such as going north over the stem would be the shortest route or going around the middle of the apple would be best. After we talked about this for a couple of minutes, I said, "*Okay! I am a little worm sitting on this X right here, and I need to get to the other X as quickly as possible. What if I chewed my way through the apple at this point? How long would it take to get to the other side now?*" The shortest distance between two points is a straight line. This, obviously, is a kindergarten view of a wormhole, but it allows one to visualize the concept more easily. Where a wormhole may differ from a stargate, is that a wormhole may actually allow for us to travel in time, but instead of connecting different places in space, like two planets, for example, it may connect different regions in time.

Wormholes were actually studied by Albert Einstein and his student, Nathan Rosen in 1935. What they predicted with their model was that the singularity, or the infinite density one would find in a black hole, for example, is connected to another singularity, which would result in a theoretical object referred to as a white hole. The black hole would draw matter into it, while a white hole would spit things out. If you look at the math, a white hole would be a time-reversed black hole. However, no one has ever seen a white hole, so there is a probability that they do not even exist. However, they are allowed by the equations found in general relativity. Because of that, scientists have not yet ruled them out as a factor. Therefore, a spacecraft or an individual entering a black hole could travel through the wormhole and come out of the white hole on the other side and in another region of space.

Einstein showed, at that time, what he presumed were two flaws with that theory. He opined that a wormhole is so unstable that it would collapse instantaneously in on anything entering it. The other flaw he presumed was that anything entering a black hole would be ripped apart by the super gravitational force inside the black hole and would never make it out on the other side. These two ideas are still presented in our third-dimensional physics classes today.

However, if one could get a wormhole to be big enough and stable enough to pass through, then a simple time machine like the one proposed by Kip Thorne at Cal Tech would look like this. "Make one end of your wormhole on planet Earth, and the other end of the wormhole is located inside a spaceship, which is currently stationary on the Earth. The end of the wormhole inside the spaceship will move when the spaceship moves. He postulated that one could travel through the wormhole either way, or even talk through it, and this travel and communication would happen instantly." Since Kip Thorne's wormhole model, there have been many wormhole-based time travel scenarios created by physicists. Some of these scientists have even proven that if a wormhole exists, it must allow for time travel in space.

String theory is what seems to tie Project Looking Glass and time travel together. According to Wikipedia, in physics, "String theory is a theoretical framework in which the point-like particles of particle physics are replaced by one-dimensional objects called strings. It describes how these strings propagate through space and interact with each other. Thus, string theory is a theory of quantum gravity." In an article by Andrew Zimmerman Jones and Daniel Robbins, called, "*Crossing Cosmic Strings to Allow Time Travel*", cosmic strings are actually theoretical objects that come before string theory. However, recently it has been thought that cosmic strings may really be complicated strings which were left over from the big bang. This has created the idea that they can be used to create a time machine.

It doesn't really matter where they come from, however, if cosmic strings are real, they should have a huge amount of gravitational pull. Because of this, they can also create what is known as frame dragging. Frame dragging happens when an object drags space and time along with it. This is in addition to the normal bending of space-time because of gravity and the movement of very dense objects such as neutron stars. As an analogy, think about an electric mixer and baking a cake. Assume that the cake batter is vanilla, and you decide to put some chocolate into the batter. Notice how it makes the surrounding cake batter swirl.

Let's say you are in your spaceship and you want to fly out to a large object in space, such as an asteroid. It is tough to visualize this because this path is in four dimensions. You can set a course to fly around this asteroid and arrive back at a point in time before you got to the asteroid. In other words, one can travel into the past along a closed timeline curve.

In 1985, Richard Gott and William Hiscock solved Einstein's field equations for cosmic strings. In 1991, they began to realize that two cosmic strings could allow for time travel. Here is how they explain this idea. "Two cosmic strings cross each other's path in a particular way. They move at very high speeds. A spacecraft, for example, that was traveling along the curves could take a very precise path and arrive back at its starting position, in both space and time, which would allow for travel in time." Several of these possibilities were worked out by Curt Cutler, a physicist who works at the Laser Interferometer Gravitational

Wave Observatory. This facility is used to detect cosmic gravitational waves and their measurements for scientific research.

Kip Thorne, a theoretical physicist at Cal Tech, had built a time machine in the early 1990s and he had been published in a major journal. Gott's time machine was actually the second one. What they found was that like other time machines, the spaceship could not travel further back than when the cosmic strings originally were put in a position to allow for time travel. Basically, time travel is limited to when the cosmic string time machine was activated.

Can string theory explain quantum entanglement? Well, what is quantum entanglement? This is a physical phenomenon that happens when groups of particles are produced and interact or share space in proximity to each other in such a way that the quantum state of these particles cannot be described independently. In other words, even though they may be separated by great distances, they no longer react independently without something happening to the other ones. String theory suggests that matter can be broken into tiny loops of strings that vibrate. The strings vibrate and move at different frequencies. This gives particles properties such as mass and charge.

We know from our own history that time travel experiments have been done since at least 1943. We can look at Project Rainbow, more commonly known as the Philadelphia Experiment, to see this. While this experiment was never meant to create a hole in the time-space continuum because the Navy was trying to make the USS Eldridge invisible to radar, it happened, nonetheless. Unfortunately, the results of the experiment went farther than any of them could imagine. They did not really know what they were doing and how dangerous it could become. The reports tell of men being frozen in time for months, also men traveling through time, and probably the most horrible, men being stuck in the bulkheads or the floor of the ship. They became a part of the structure of the ship itself. Most were still alive, but nothing could be done for them because they were melted into the ship itself.

Nikola Tesla, in the 1930s, got involved in the experimentation of movement through time and space. This project was moved to Princeton's Institute of Advanced Studies in 1939. They had learned how to make small objects invisible. Tesla and Einstein came to the same conclusion, that this technology would not be used for the benefit of humans. This notion became reality when the government wanted to use this technology during war. It still amazes me how greed and power take over these programs. From the technologies given to us by the Star Visitors and those we created, the first thought is to use it against each other instead of using them to benefit mankind.

The original testing for this experiment used test animals on the USS Eldridge. The animals had been placed in metal cages, and when the ship rematerialized after having been made to disappear, some of the animals were missing, some of them had radiation poisoning, and some had burn marks. It was never the intent of the Navy to use human test subjects. However, that all changed when on August 12, 1943, the USS Eldridge was tested in the Philadelphia experiment with a complete crew on board.

Even though the government has tried to cover up the entire incident by saying that this was really an attempt at making a ship invisible to magnetic mines, people have not bought it. Using a process known as degaussing, where the magnetic field of a ship is neutralized by encircling it with a conductor carrying electric currents, the ship was completely gone from the harbor for about four hours.

When the ship did reappear in the harbor, it was surrounded with a green colored haze. Some sailors were running around on fire, some were going crazy, some were vomiting, some had heart attacks, some died, and others were embedded in the structure of the ship. Others just disappeared and were never seen again. There is a story of two brothers who jumped ship when everything started happening. They jumped overboard, but instead of hitting the water, they were thrown forward in time 40 years to the year 1983. They had remembered who the person in charge of the experiment was and set out to find him. His brother, I believe, was sent back in time to the ship by accident. The other brother found the room where the time machine was located that could take him back to the USS Eldridge. He had to go back to turn off the equipment on the USS Eldridge. In the meantime, he had met a girl in the year 1983. Before he was sent back, the scientists promised to never experiment with this again, but we know now, that wasn't true because these men had connected to the year 1983 and the Montauk Project. The brother successfully went back in time to 1943 and was also successful in turning off the equipment, which closed up the hole in the time-space continuum. Just before the equipment was completely off, he jumped back into the time tunnel before it closed completely, and made it back to the year 1983.

The Montauk Project was really a continuation of this old experiment. Many of the surviving sailors from the USS Eldridge ended up in Montauk, New York in a time loop to 1983. A few of them came forward with their stories. It was also rumored that the people controlling the Montauk experiment were also going regularly to Mars. That story is still out there, and it would not surprise me if it were true. NASA has had a secret space program for years. Most people would agree with that. I have been told by Star Visitors that we have a colony on Mars of 100,000 individuals or more. Not all from Planet Earth. I'm guessing they live underground mostly because of the radiation probabilities. It would explain why our Mars rovers do not send back pictures that show life. Or maybe they do and we just are not privy to them. That is probably more likely. I got involved with the Montauk Project in a strange way. I believe, somehow, I was involved with it but don't understand why I would have been, but some very strange things started happening to me in the late 1980s and early 1990s. At that time, I had received my hypnotherapy doctorate and had opened a part-time hypnotherapy practice and was specializing in working with people who had extraterrestrial encounters and wanted to know more about what had occurred during these encounters. It was also the time that I was part of the Teacher-in-Space program and was working for the Challenger Center for Space Science Education, and in NASA education doing teacher workshops on space at the Jet Propulsion Laboratory in Pasadena, California. Additionally, my first re-encounter with the Star Visitors had happened in 1984 when I was on Bora Bora in the Tahitian islands.

From what I remember reading about this project, very psychic individuals trained in remote viewing who could hold coordinates in their minds for a period of time, were used in this program. I am going from memory now because I stopped writing down the things that were happening around this program because it felt very dark to me. I had read about Alister Crowley and his involvement with strange phenomenon, and an alleged connection to this project. As I recall, there was just a high degree of strangeness around the whole thing.

The way it would work is that one of these very psychic, trained individuals, mostly men I had thought, but I don't think that is necessarily true, would sit in this chair that kind of looked like a dentist's chair, but more comfortable. The person in the chair would be given certain coordinates that would open a hole in the time-space continuum and they would visualize those coordinates and hold them. If they were successful, a portal would open and a person could travel to where those coordinates were. I believe the person in the chair was given some kind of drug intravenously which would help him hold open the portal so that the people going through could come back. It is my understanding that many times, the person in the chair could not maintain, and the portal would close leaving people lost out in space somewhere. Once the portal closed, the person usually could not open it again at the same location. Additionally, they were experimenting with teleportation, which we have since mastered.

I remember reading the first book written by Preston Nichols and Peter Moon and was fascinated with it, but felt very dark about it. At the time I was seeing a hypnotherapy client who claimed to have been part of the Philadelphia Experiment. I am not mentioning his name because I do not have his permission and it was years ago. With all of the things I was involved with at the time, Teacher-in-Space, Challenger Center, NASA consultant, hypnotherapist, specializing in working with people who were encountering extraterrestrials, and now the dreams, added to the high degree of strangeness that was happening in my life at that time. I had been having strange dreams at night, that had been occurring for a while. The dreams actually began before I really knew anything about the Montauk Project, and in this recurring dream, I was in that chair and I was being told to open up the portal. I felt like I was doing it in the dream, because the next day so many memories would indicate that. I had mentioned these recurring dreams to my hypnotherapy client seeing what he could make of it. He told me I should read the Montauk book because it sounded like I had been there. So, I bought the book and read it.

About a month later, I got a strange phone call from my client telling me a Peter Moon was going to be calling me. I said, "Peter Moon? I don't know Peter Moon so why would he want to talk to me?" As you probably recall, Peter Moon was the co-author of the Montauk book. I asked my client where he got that information and he said that a friend of his from New York asked him if he knew Judy Cameron, and he said that he did. Again, I asked how he got my name, and my client said that he did not know. I thought that was all very strange, of course. I continued to have those unusual dreams about once a week, but nothing else was happening around that so I let it sink to the background of my life because I was very busy teaching and doing other things.

Approximately three months passed and I did not give that much thought, and one day, after teaching all day, I left earlier than usual from school. Normally I was there until around 5 pm in order to make sure whatever I needed for the next day's lesson was ready to go for the next day, but I was caught up, so I left school around 4 pm and was home by 4:30. I was just settling in after being on my feet all day and my phone rang. I was sitting in my leather reclining chair and had just put my feet up, and I was not really happy about having to get up to answer the phone. Remember, we did not have cell phones in the 1980s. So, I growled to myself, but got up and answered the phone. The man on the other end said, "Is this Judy Cameron?" and I said something like, "Who is asking?" The voice said, "This is Peter Moon!" It caught me by surprise. Even though my client had told me that Peter Moon was going to call me, I had actually put it out of my mind. I responded, "Peter Moon?" How did you get my name and phone number, and why are you calling me?" For those of you who are old enough to remember, in the 1980s, we could have unlisted phone numbers, and mine was unlisted. He said something like he had heard about me and the work with extraterrestrial contact I was doing and how I was interested in knowing more about black projects. I had not yet had my encounter with the men from NSA when I was speaking in 1994 at the hypnotherapy convention because it had not happened yet. All of this was rapidly going through my mind as I stood there waiting for a response. Peter said, "I am going to be in Los Angeles in a week and I would love to meet you and talk to you. Would you be willing to meet me?" I was a little apprehensive, but because of my constant search for adventure and the search for the truth, I said that I would. He said he would call me with the details a few days before.

Peter did phone me a couple of days before his arrival to say that he was coming. He said that when he got to his hotel, he would call me with the address. He called me two days later and gave me the address to the hotel. Keep in mind also, we did not have GPS in the 1980s either. Also, there were no personal computers. So, I had to get out my Thomas Guide to find the address. I expected that he would be staying at one of the big hotels in a good area of the city, but I was wrong. The area of Los Angeles that he was in was not one that I would normally venture into by myself, and especially at night, but it wasn't the worse section of town either. It was kind of in the lower middle, as I recall. One of the things that I have been able to rely on all of my life is that I am truly protected by the Light. I have guardian angels who are probably assigned to me because I would do dangerous things such as this. When I use the term, *dangerous* here, it was in the sense that I was going into an area of LA that I had never been, at night, and meeting a man whom I had never met and who was involved with a very dark program, the Montauk Project. Plus, I did not know Peter at that time, although I am very psychic, and I did not get any negative vibrations from Peter when I was talking to him on the phone. So, I was not fearful at all. Maybe a little apprehensive and on guard, which is certainly a good way to be so that you can be ready to protect yourself if needed.

Before I left home, I gave a copy of the map to my husband, Richard, and told him where I would be, and that if I was not home by two am, to call the police. I then left on my 45-minute journey into LA. I also put my angels on notice to stand by in case I got into trouble. I was not anticipating anything going awry, but it never hurts to be prepared.

It took me a little longer to get to my destination than I had anticipated, so I was about a half an hour late. I arrived at 6:00 pm. I parked on the street and went inside to the office where I told the man behind the desk who I was meeting. Peter had already given him my name, so this man was expecting me. He gave me Peter's room number and told me to move my car off of the street and into their parking lot, which was more protected. I thanked him and moved my vehicle. Peter's room was upstairs and I knocked on his door when I got up there.

When Peter opened the door, I relaxed because he was sending out positive vibes. We greeted each other and I sat down and we started talking. I spoke first. "How did you get my name and phone number, Peter?" I queried. "My phone number is unlisted," I continued. Peter responded, "A friend of mine who is involved with this project gave me your name and phone number and told me that I should call you because you were having strange dreams or something like that!" "Really?" I reacted. "How did your friend come by my information?' I knew that I had not shared anything about my dreams of Montauk except with my hypnotherapy client who was involved with Project Rainbow. Then it occurred to me that my client was also friends with this same person, and my client must have shared with him about my dreams. It makes sense that could happen because the two experiments are tied together. So, looking back, that is how my client knew that Peter Moon was going to call me.

Our conversation continued with Peter asking, "I understand you are having dreams that you think may be connected to Montauk. Would you tell me about them please?" I responded by saying, "Only if you keep what I am telling you with you only unless you ask me first and I trust who you want to share it with." He agreed. I told him I had read his first book and that some of the things in it matched some elements in my dreams. I said, "In my dreams, I have been in that chair and I was given some coordinates and told that I was to let my mind go there and open up the coordinates I had found." I continued, "It all seemed so real and like I was really doing it." I sat there perplexed for a moment before I went on. "I just hope and pray that I did not hurt anyone in the process." Peter seemed to have been attentively listening to me as I told my story. He then said, "to my knowledge, only male servicemen who were very psychic and trained in remote viewing, were used as subjects." I responded with, "Wow! My dreams certainly feel real." He then asked me if I knew how to bilocate and/or remote view. I said, "Interesting that you should ask that question. I have been trained in remote viewing and I have been reading on bilocation and have been practicing that on my own. I have been successful a couple of times bilocating to my mom's home in Sacramento. It is easy to practice with her because I can call her up the next day and confirm what I saw in her room when I was there." Peter thought for a moment and then commented. "It is entirely possible that you are bilocating into that room at Montauk, where you would be seeing everything, and you might be assuming that it is you who is doing the work." I must have had a worried look on my face because Peter said, "Are you concerned about that?" I told him that I was because I thought it would be entirely possible that the people running the program could detect me if I was there in some form. Peter explained, "They probably do know that you have shown up a few times, but they will most likely leave you alone so long as you don't do anything with the information." I told him that my interest in it was along the lines of knowing the truth, about how to do it, but that it was a little too dark for me to want to be too close to it. I explained that the work I do with the extraterrestrials is of the Light, so I do not want to mess that up in any way. Then I went on to say, "However, I am really curious about a lot of things. I just don't want to end up dead or in another part of the galaxy because I experimented with things I knew nothing about."

As I looked at my watch, I realized we had been talking for over two hours. It felt like I had just arrived there, but it was now 8:00 pm. He asked me if I would be willing to try a little experiment. He wanted to know if we put our energies together if we could move objects. Even though I knew there was some risk to that, I said yes because I am always curious and therefore prone to experimentation, so long as I feel it is safe. In this instance, I could see nothing to really worry about. We agreed that we would get into a meditative state for about twenty minutes, and then we would focus our energy on a vase that was on the table to see if we could get any movement out of it. We got into a meditative state and stayed that way for about twenty minutes until we both were in an altered state of consciousness. We then both directed our energy toward this vase. After about five minutes, I started to feel really strange. As I looked at the vase, there were wavy lines appearing around it. Something told me to break away from it like now, which I did. When I broke my focus and came out of my meditative state, it caused Peter to do that too. I said, "Oh, my God! What just happened?" Peter commented, "Our combined energies were affecting that vase." I agreed, but said, "Yes, but how were we affecting it? If we had continued, could we have opened up a portal of some sort?" I asked him what he had experienced. He said the same as me. Neither one of us could really answer that question adequately because we had nothing to base our experience on. For me, the fact that I saw wavy lines around the vase tells me that we could have done something that we could not come back from. I decided that it was enough for me to have experienced something like that, but never again. There were too many factors that we had no control over, nor did we understand them. I said, "Well that was interesting and exciting, but also very scary. I do not want to do that again." "You are probably right," he said. "It was a bad idea!"

By then it was 10:00 pm and I was ready to go home. I had an hour commute to get back to Fullerton, and I had to teach the next day. So, I thanked him and bid him farewell. He came out to LA two more times and I met with him and we talked about what was going on, but that was as far as it went. It was during this time also that I had started my training with Steven Greer, MD for CSETI, and my friend, Diana, and I were doing our trips around the southwest experiencing unusual things and learning a great deal. Because of that, I decided that I should not meet with Peter again. Peter is a good guy, and has a lot of knowledge about a very dark program. I am happy that I met him.

Before leaving this completely, I wish to comment about the question some people are asking, "If time travel is possible, why are we not seeing people from our future?" When I lived in my Fullerton home, time travelers used to pop in and out all the time. There was a portal in my house that had been opened when my father passed away there. I chose not to close it, but to only make it available to beings of the Light. I had two very large guardian angels and star visitors guarding the entrance. I only closed it two years ago when I lost my home and had to move.

One of the more interesting events occurred when Richard and I were in the living room watching television one night. The entry hall from the front door opened out to the living room, so that area was like being in one large room. All of a sudden, a young man about twenty years old, suddenly popped into the entry hall from the ceiling. He landed on his feet and had the most surprised look on his face. He saw us sitting there and had that "deer in the headlights look" as though he had taken a wrong turn. I spoke to him and said, "Well, hello! I know you are not from here. Where did you just come from?" His clothing did not seem to be different from what we were wearing at the time, but then he probably planned for that before he left. I got the impression that he had made a mistake and ended up there instead of where he was supposed to go. He never said a word to me, but suddenly just popped out about ten feet from where he had popped in. I just sat there for a moment, talking to myself by saying, "Wow! We just had a time traveler." I asked Richard if he had seen him, and Richard said that he had not. No surprises there. Richard rarely sees or experiences what I am seeing and experiencing. I have had two-or-three-time travelers pop into this house too, but when I see them, they leave.

Something else we must remember is that the ancient stargates we find around the world today were built at the time of the Sumerians or before. Time travelers have been using some of those gates since they were built.

Additionally, there are many you tube videos of alleged time travelers that have been captured on film. Of course, we should look at those with a skeptical eye, for the most part, only because photos can be doctored in so many ways, but every once in a while, there is one or two that look absolutely real, and I presume they actually are. I have, myself, seen quite a few that I feel pretty sure are real. And why not? We have been actively experimenting with this technology for over a half a century and maybe even longer.

Chapter 28

Project Pegasus, Darpa, and Time Travel and Teleportation Experiments

The total number of minds in the universe is one. In fact, consciousness is a singularity phasing within all beings.
—Erwin Schrodinger[12]

When I was writing my doctoral dissertation in 2003-2005, I became aware of a project of our United States military intelligence division, DARPA, which is an acronym for Defense Advanced Research Projects Agency, called Project Pegasus. The Project Pegasus mission statement is: "*Project Pegasus was the classified, defense-related research and development program under the Defense Advanced Research Projects Agency (DARPA) in which the US defense-technical community achieved time travel on behalf of the US government-the real Philadelphia Experiment.*"

What the mission of Project Pegasus was, had to do with studying the effects of time travel and teleportation on children. Additionally, it was to send important information about past and future events to the United States President, the intelligence community, and of course, the military.

Andrew D. Basiago, an attorney based in Washington, began

telling his story of a top-secret organization called Project Pegasus. Basiago claims that from 1968 to 1972, he participated in many unusual experiments that took him on trips through time, space, and potentially into parallel universes. He was seven years old at the time. Children were selected, according to Basiago, specifically for their ability to "adapt to the strains of moving between past, present, and the future." Also, an Army veteran by the name of William White Crow, claims that he trained Basagio in the fifth grade in karate and aikido to prepare him for his training for time travel in Project Pegasus. Apparently Basagio and White Crow met again ten years later on Mars. While on Mars, White Crow said that he and Basagio were involved in an incident where they had to protect themselves and another jumper, William Stillings, from an attack by pterodactyl type birds who were dive bombing them. White Crow was a shaman and a seer who allegedly saw the future events of 911, the collapse of the St. Louis Bridge, the Mt. St. Helens volcanic eruption, and Fukushima. He claims that he was in many secret limited access programs. In a quote by William White Crow, he says that "we have to choose whether we are going to become a part of the sixth great extinction which is taking place now, or advance to a higher level of humanity as a species spiritually, intellectually and technologically. It's all up to us."

He claims that there were several time devices used during these travel experiments. However, he said, that the majority of his time adventures was using technology from Nikola Tesla. After Tesla's death in 1943, documents were retrieved from his New York City apartment. These documents contained a blueprint for a teleportation device. Basagio claims that this device would produce what was called 'radiant energy,' which would create a "shimmering curtain between two elliptical booms." This radiant energy was capable of bending the fabric of space. He said that his first journey was to be teleported to New Mexico's state capital, but he remained in the same time period. He did this for a while for just a few hours back in time to get used to the feeling and sensation of traveling.

When he passed through this shimmering curtain of energy, Basiago said that he would enter a vortex tunnel that would send him to his destination. He said the other teleportation devices included a plasma confinement chamber in New Jersey, and a jump room in El Segundo, California. Basiago also said that there was some kind of "holographic technology," in which the person could travel both physically, but additionally, virtually.

These tunnels were not always safe, however, when they first started using this technology. Alfred Webre, one of Andrew Basiago's friends, claimed that one time when a child returned from his time-travel voyage, his body returned before his legs did. Webre said, "He was writhing in pain with just stumps where his legs had been." He also said that those bugs have been ironed out and repaired. Basiago described his traveling experiences through the vortex tunnels as a "rough and turbulent experience."

Andrew Basiago claims that several of his trips took him to the 1800s. One time he jumped into the Gettysburg address on November 19, 1863, given by Abraham Lincoln. He also time traveled to the Ford Theatre on the night that President Lincoln was assassinated. He claims to have traveled to Gettysburg multiple times, running into himself on two occasions, but he said he never witnessed the assassination.

Basiago also noted that each trip was just a little different than the last, which he believes that there was more than time travel at work there. He was being sent into slightly different alternative realities on adjacent timelines.

Back in the early 1980s, I remember hearing about Project Pegasus and their trips to Mars. When I was a teacher, I had written to the Jet Propulsion Laboratory in Pasadena, California, to request any slides they had in their teacher materials packet. I received back several slides of the terrain and atmosphere of Mars, which always appeared as a reddish atmosphere. With the exception of one slide which showed a very Earth-like atmosphere of blue, and I questioned JPL about that and they passed it off as false color photography, but I did not buy it then, and I don't buy it now.

Basiago claims that when he traveled to Mars in the 1980s, he used the jump room to teleport to Mars, with the expected mission to act as an ambassador to the Martian civilization already there. The people who allegedly traveled with him were William Stillings and Barry Soetero, who of course, is President Barak Obama. While doing the research for my dissertation, I read stories that Barak Obama had been involved in these experiments.

According to Alfred Webre when talking about the history of Mars, said that there was a solar system catastrophe in 9500 BCE in which a fragment of the super nova, Vela, entered our solar system and hit Mars, making it a barren planet flattened at the poles. It destroyed its surface ecology and the civilization that was there, and then ran into the Earth as well destroying our ancient civilization of Atlantis. Webre insists that the term, "Atlantis" refers to the whole civilization of Mars and the Earth, not a single place.

Before the flood in which Noah built the ark, about 10,500 BC, Webre explains that Earth and Mars were a single interplanetary pyramidal cultural and society ruled by the predecessors of the Egyptian pharaohs, the conehead Annunaki extraterrestrials. That makes sense to me because the Viking spacecraft that went to Mars in the 1970s discovered the face and pyramids of Cydonia, Mars, which are identical to the Sphinx and the pyramids on the Giza plateau. They had to be built by the same people. Allegedly there are frescos of cone-headed Egyptian rulers on Mars as well as Earth.

On his many trips to Mars, Basiago said that he encountered many extraordinary things. He said that there were huge dinosaurs there and humanoid scorpion men.

In January 1901, the Lowell Observatory at Harvard picked up a 70 second signal sent from the Martians. Also, Nikola Tesla in 1902, built a Tesla machine in New Mexico and began interactive communication with the Martians. According to Basiago, all of this was being reported in the mainstream press at that time.

Basiago goes on to say that in the 1920s and 1930s, the Martians organized tours of Mars for the Earth elites, the dark cabal, and they were conducted through the Vatican with pick-up locations in the American southwest and Brazil. He claims that by 1970, Mars astronauts conducted regular liaison visits to Earth, where Andrew and his father met several Martian astronauts visiting their counterparts in the US Defense department.

We are told that the Earth and Mars built a common defense perimeter against invasion of the solar system by a hyper-dimensional race which were possibly the greys from the constellation Orion and the Draco reptilians. When the CIA activated the Mars jump room program in the 1980s, the executive decision by the United States was made to covertly colonize Mars going against the treaty in place in 1967 called the United Nations Outer Space Treaty.

Basiago says that these devises have quantum access capability which could be divided into two categories. The first is the physical teleportation of someone to the past or to a future event. The second is called chronovision. Chrono refers to the time aspect of it. This would be the ability to create a hologram that works like a looking glass, which would be used to gather intelligence of a specific time and place. The teleportation device was based on the papers of Nikola Tesla that were found in his apartment after his death in 1943, and the chronovisors were developed by two Vatican music people. Both devices were handed over to the U.S. government by Rome afterward. Basiago says the government chose to take both of these technologies and weaponize them as a way to send troops to different times and places instantaneously, as well as using them to gather very important intelligence. It is mind boggling to me that we choose to militarize space rather than making it a welcoming zone for extraterrestrial life to visit peacefully. Buckminster Fuller used the word, "ephemeralization" which refers to the idea that any technological advancement would lead to an ability to do more with less, until you can do anything with virtually nothing.

Today, Andrew Basiago believes that the US government needs to disclose its teleportation technology. In so doing, humanity as a whole would benefit, plus make traveling both on Earth and throughout the cosmos instantaneous, plus being environmentally-friendly. Time travel and teleportation could help reduce greenhouse gases by 60 percent, the biggest culprit being human transportation.

Unless this is all just cleverly orchestrated propaganda, it is hard to imagine that we have not mastered time travel and teleportation. The fact that we have active vortices and stargates around the planet and projects such as the Philadelphia Experiment and Montauk Project and also Project Pegasus, among others, it is difficult for me to believe that this isn't true. Certainly, the Star Visitors who come here regularly did not take several light years to get here as suggested by mainstream third dimensional scientists today.

Chapter 29

Dimensions

Commit yourself to do whatever it is you can contribute in order to create a healthy and sustainable future-the world needs you desperately. Find that in yourself and make a commitment-that is what will change the world.
—John Denver

We now know we are shifting from a third dimensional reality into a fifth dimensional reality. What are dimensions anyway? Dimensions are different planes of existence that are put together according to the rate they are vibrating. Each dimension operates with specific sets of laws and principles that are specific to that dimension's frequency. Each dimension as you go up in number, will vibrate at a higher rate than the dimension below it. In each higher dimension you will find a more clear, wider perspective of reality and a greater level of knowing.

The third dimension is a pretty dense place because the third dimension is stuck in a duality paradigm. In other words, it is set in a time-space and cause and effect duality. In the third dimension, we have a very limited and restricted state of consciousness. In our third dimensional society we are told that the only reality that exists is the one we can feel, smell, taste, hear, and see; in other words, our five physical senses. We are also told to believe that our third dimensional perceptions of reality are the only reality. In the third dimension we lived with rigid beliefs and an inflexible set of rules and limitations. One of these rules we were told is that our bodies are solid, therefore, they cannot merge with each other or even walk through walls. Here, in the third dimension, we are limited by the force of gravity, our psychokinetic skills are very weak if we have them at all, so we cannot make physical objects disappear, and we cannot read another person's mind. We are taught that we must work hard in order to accomplish our goals. The ideas of fear, judgment, and separation are the ideas we live under in a third dimensional world.

In a fourth dimensional reality it acts like a bridge for us to cross over into the fifth dimension. We have been told that we will be here for just a short period of time. By traveling through and experiencing the fourth dimension, we are preparing for the fifth dimension.

Many of us have been experiencing the fourth dimension without really being aware of it. When we have times of awakening spiritually or are having experiences where our heart is opening up to a wider reality, we are experiencing the fourth dimension. Other times we are feeling very clear, but also calm and quiet inside. We also experience things around us as lighter and less up-tight. We have times of feeling an expansiveness around us and things seem more lay-back and up-lifting.

One of the things that I have really noticed about experiencing the fourth dimension is that time is no longer linear. It is also speeding up. Once we hit the fifth dimension, there will be no time as we know it now. The laws of time and space change. Time is now changeable and we can work with it. Time can stretch, but it can also condense down. What is kind of cool is that because time is fluid in the fourth dimension, our astral forms can morph naturally. We are able to manifest more quickly in this dimension as well. Our thoughts and feelings create reality much faster than when in the third dimension.

What is the fifth dimensional reality? It is one I am really looking forward to. We will be living in the Unity Consciousness, but we are still allowed to experience ourselves as I, like an individual within a group. Consciousness is not bound in the fifth dimension by linear time and space. There is no illusion of separation or limitation as we had in the third dimension. Everything in the third dimension is created by illusion. In the fifth dimension, there is a constant and steady experience of the Oneness of everything. In order to qualify for the fifth dimension, you must have cleared up all mental and emotional baggage. Mastery over our thoughts is a prerequisite for getting into the fifth dimension, because what we think becomes reality immediately. As we know, all thoughts are measurable energy waves. If our thoughts are measurable, then they are also tangible which means they are manifested in a fifth dimensional reality. A fifth dimensional being will show no fear, anger, hostility, guilt or suffering.

When living in the fifth dimension, all of our actions will be based on love because fear cannot survive the higher vibration of the fifth dimension. One of the reasons we do not want to have fear or lack of confidence is because our vibration would drop, and our consciousness would be lowered, almost instantly, to the lower levels of the fourth dimension. Also, in the fifth dimension, we will be living under unconditional love, unconditional forgiveness and unconditional acceptance.

In the fifth dimension, manifestation occurs immediately. Your thoughts become realities. People communicate mostly telepathically, and they now have the ability to read each other's feelings and/or thoughts with ease. As I mentioned before, how we experience time will be very different. Everything is happening at once. Because you are living in an expanded dimension, we won't distinguish between the past, the present, or the future. You may go anywhere and experience whatever time you want to.

If you are having dreams of being in the fifth dimension, that is great! These dreams will give you hope for our future and keep us moving through the fourth dimension. As we begin to ascend to the fifth dimension, we will see that all consciousness is multidimensional.

In our present year of 2019, we must take the opportunity to decide which dimension we wish to be in. We all need to look at our mental, emotional, spiritual, and also physical selves. Is there anything keeping us stuck in the third dimension? If so, are we willing to change those?

Suzanne Worthley wrote an article entitled, *Ascension Energies,*

Signs, and Symptoms in 2019, in which she lists third dimensional energies in 2019 and fifth dimensional energies in 2019. I think these are worth mentioning.

Third dimensional energies in 2019 will be experienced in the following ways. Mentally: limited thinking, the inability to see the possibilities, repeating anxious mental patterns, difficulty sleeping and boredom. Emotional symptoms being expressed are anger, having the need to be right and also feeling that others are judging you, trouble in relationships by repeating or bringing up issues you had previously resolved, experiencing conflict both internally and externally, having excessive fear or worry, usually regarding not having enough. Physical symptoms include feeling tired all the time, aches and pains that appear and then leave for no apparent reason, headaches or perhaps ringing in the ears-tinnitus, having trouble with balance, being nauseated or the feeling of being bloated, and either having no appetite or overeating. Spiritual symptoms in the third dimension are a feeling of isolation or cut off from God, a feeling of being disconnected from nature and humanity, and having an ongoing sense of fear or dread.

Fifth dimensional energies in 2019 will be experienced in the following ways. Mentally: You will have new ideas, creatively express yourself, and you will understand new information you are receiving. You will have new and improved problem-solving skills and more clarity in your life. You will have an ability to see opportunities, and will set goals to achieve them, and you will have mastered the ability to rest and do nothing without feeling guilty. Emotionally, you will find that you are happy for no reason, you will have that true sense of abundance and have the sense that you have enough. You will be able to handle challenges more easily, and you will be able to self-regulate your moods and will have a feeling of being balanced. Additionally, you will show more gratitude for what you receive and what you have, and you will be in fulfilling relationships. Physically, you will feel balanced and will be eating a healthy diet. You will also feel an increase in energy and exercise, and you will spend more time in nature and also see and pay attention to nature in your everyday existence. You will discover your body has an increased flexibility and more range of motion in your joints, your head and your thinking will be clear, and your skin will give off a vibrant glow. Spiritually, you will be connected to the collective unconscious, you will see signs and symbols in your daily life, you will have an overall sense of being aligned and feeling in the flow of life, and you will have a sense of personal awakening or knowing.

We each must take the responsibility of what we are going to experience. We do have a choice. We must embrace the duality that is here and then work hard to transcend it. Everything has two sides. One is driven by love, and the other is driven by fear. Additionally, we are all a part of the collective unconscious. We are all one! One person does change the world for the better because the collective unconscious is all one frequency.

Let's look at the fifth dimensional ascension timeline. I know in 2012, I was under the impression that the transition would be almost instantaneous. As I wrote about first landing and the transition to the fifth dimension, one must remember, that is only one possibility. That is what the Beings from the Planet Sirius have said could happen if everyone was vibrating at a higher frequency. Everything is fluid at this time. We have lots of variables to consider, we have free will, and our paradigm must shift.

That being said, I looked at the research from Diana Cooper's book entitled, "*Birthing a New Civilization: Transition to the New Golden Age in 2032.*" What she says, basically, is that there are four major phases of our ascension process. The first, is our initial transition, from 2013-2016, which we have completed. The second, is the mass cleansing, from 2017-2022, which we are in the middle of now. The third, is creating the fifth dimensional template, from 2023-2032, and the fourth, is settling in our new Earth, from 2032-2042.

Looking at these phases individually, the Initial Transition was from 2013-2016. The Golden Age of Atlantis ended in 2012, which gave birth to the Age of Aquarius. The date happened to coincide with the end of the Mayan Calendar on December 21, 2012, the solstice. This was the end of a 5,126-year cycle for the Mayans. At that very instant, we officially began our next 26,000-year cycle of the precession of the equinox. According to Collins.com, precession of the equinoxes is defined as follows. "the occurrence of the equinoxes earlier in each successive sidereal year because of a slow wobble in the Earth's axial spin which shifts the equinoctial points slightly westward along the ecliptic: the wobble is caused by the pull of the sun and moon on the Earth's equatorial bulges and makes the poles move around a center point, the axis of the ecliptic, taking about 25,800 years to return to the same orientation with the stars."

During these years, 2013-2016, we were laying the groundwork for helping the transition to be easier. We are also moving to a more heart-centered and holistic world. Some things that occurred in those four years were the debut of the program, *Cosmos: A Spacetime Odyssey* on many networks, and it won a Peabody Award too; adult coloring books of a spiritual nature became popular which led to an increase in people actively participating in meditation; organic food continued to become more popular. Sales for Organic foods reached $43 billion in the United States in 2016; This set the stage for the mass cleansing as the United Kingdom voted to leave the European Union with Brexit; police shootings against unarmed Black men put systemic racism to the forefront in the United States; and Russian athletes and coaches were penalized for systemic doping.

During the years of 2017-2022, is the mass cleansing. We are right in the middle of this phase now, since it is 2019. What we are seeing now in the world is oppressive political, economic, and cultural systems collapse. This is making way for new growth. With this mass cleansing, we have been witnessing the worst in our society and will continue to do so in order to learn to recognize the oppressive laws and structures that are being perpetrated on all of us so that we can change them. But, along with this, we will also see the parts of society that truly values holistic health, healing modalities such as Reiki, more compassion, better educational opportunities, more exploration, here and in space, and freedom. During these five years, we are already witnessing the start of a severe economic crisis, which causes people to focus their energies on things that inspire hope.

Some 2017 highlights included meditation apps as people became more interested in mindfulness. Bernie Sanders remained a popular politician, even though some people blamed him for Hillary Clinton losing the 2016 election because he pulled potential voters away from her. Donald Trump became the President of the United States, in spite of the fact that he made several racist and sexist comments during his political campaign. A mass shooting occurred in Las Vegas, Nevada, which brought gun control to the forefront once again.

Some important highlights for 2018 were thousands of U.S students led demonstrations throughout the country to protest our gun policy after a massive school shooting in Parkland, Florida. In Madison, Wisconsin, thousands of students marched around the state capitol. Governor Rick Scott signed a very aggressive gun control reform bill after the Parkland shooting. Tariffs were placed on steel and aluminum not manufactured in the United States which forecasted a trade war. At the same time, the stock market and housing market showed increasing instability. People, in general, became more introspective and focused more energy on the spiritual aspects of life.

Some important highlights for 2019, which we are now half-way through, are that Warren Buffett vowed to give away the majority of his wealth before he dies. He is giving huge amounts to the Gates Foundation and other charities as well as non-profit organizations. The program, *Cosmos: Possible Worlds* hosted by Neil DeGrasse Tyson airs on Fox and National Geographic, leading me to wonder if disclosure is about to happen. By the end of this year, progressives will become more organized politically. Mindfulness is now being taught in our schools. There is an economic slowdown happening, and in general, the world is finally realizing that we cannot continue this way. The United States is on the edge of a recession and/or depression this year, and with some hope, we may avoid it, but it is shaky.

What do we have to look forward to next year in 2020? Reiki, the hands-on healing technique becomes mainstream. That makes me happy because I am a certified Reiki II Practitioner and hands-on healer, techniques that I learned long ago from the Star Visitors when I was taken to the cosmic classroom. These types of healing modalities will start to show up on more local, regional, and national news segments. There will be a huge explosion in the number of holistic wellness practitioners. On the physical level, the Earth will begin to move physically into the fifth dimension. Spiritual awareness and consciousness will continue to increase. Electric cars will continue to be purchased more and more, and Tesla is planning on producing at least a half a million vehicles in 2020 alone. In 2020, Harriet Tubman will appear on our $20.00 bill, which replaces Andrew Jackson. In many parts of the United States, solar energy will become more cost-effective than electric. My sense is that the electric companies are not going to be very happy about that. Additionally, the year 2020 will bring the World's Fair to Dubai, United Arab Emirates. My hope is that because Dubai is already a good example of a cosmopolitan city where people from all over the world live and work in peace and mutual respect, more of the world will be able to witness that first hand. Although an Islamic country, other religions are allowed to practice their faiths there in peace and understanding. Having been to Dubai at least six times in the last two years, I can attest to the fact that Dubai is a place we could learn from. My hope is that the World's Fair will bring it to the forefront.

What can we expect in the year 2021? Activism is at an all-time high. People have had it! The United States starts to become sustainable on a much larger scale. Holistic healing practices continue on the rise. Our country is also more peaceful. There will be a mass production of self- driving cars that starts in China. Personally, from what we have observed in 2019 so far, self-driving vehicles are a scary thought. Hopefully, the technology will have improved in the next two years. The stock market will become unstable once more and the effects of climate change intensify. This will include the melting of the permafrost.

The last year of this phase is 2022. During this time, it is predicted that the country of Denmark will move to a cashless society, which is the first step towards having a shared economy where money and finances are irrelevant. During this time, more devices and accessories will become connected to the internet.

The third phase of moving into the fifth dimension is from 2023-2032. It is where we are to create the fifth dimensional template. This is a ten-year period when women will move into leadership roles, and a female will become President of the United States. The United States will not be a superpower any longer like it has been since World War II. There will be two trends that will continue moving forward. Those are a movement towards simplicity where people will grow their own food, they will walk and bicycle more often, and the population will be less interested in the celebrity culture. The other trend is that there will be a significant increase in technology with virtual reality entertainment becoming mainstream. Driverless cars will also become the vehicles of choice, and internet access will become a human right. Artificial intelligence and data automation will play stronger roles in how business and governments are handled and run.

Something else wonderful happens during this time. Hatred, racism, and the intolerance of others will become totally unacceptable. The human race will become more peaceful and loving and accepting of others. More and more people will continue to be more interested in spirituality. It is predicted that we will have a huge influx of Rainbow Children being born here. Just a reminder, Rainbow Children are the newest group of Star Kids that have come to Earth to help humanity ascend. Rainbow Children were almost all born after the year 2000. They are born primarily to Crystal Children who came as early as the 1980s. Rainbow Children are from the ninth dimension of consciousness. They are highly evolved and spiritually advanced souls who are here to use their special skills and abilities to teach peace and harmony, and to help raise the vibration for all of humanity. During this time, Western medicine will be heavily supplemented, complemented, and supported by holistic healing. Any social, economic and cultural structures that still remain during this time that are not for the greatest and highest good for all, will be eliminated.

The final part of our ascension process will be from 2035-2042. It will be all about settling into our new Earth. By the year, 2032, we all will have adapted to what will be the new normal on Earth, including the climate shifts. The world's population will have dropped somewhat, and people living modestly will be considered dignified. During this time, materialism will no longer be important, and we will see governments start to disappear. Cities may still be fairly large in 2042, but the trend for the longer term will be to have smaller, high-tech, sustainable, rural communities appearing all around the world. Crystals will once again be utilized to cleanse and purify water. At this time, holistic healing will be an integral part of our society and considered more important than Western medicine.

Having a general overview of what will be happening in the next 25 years is great, but it is not worth much unless we use it to look at our present daily behavior, and to start now creating this world together. We can bring this world to us sooner by focusing our behavior on the things we are choosing for our new Earth. We can become a conscious consumer of food, water, fuel, and other products. We are currently such a 'throw away' society with pre-packaged food, plastic, and non-recyclables. We can began composting, reducing unnecessary waste, reusing or upcycling what we can, and recycling are all important ways to help our Earth navigate through this time more easily. We should learn how to grow our own food, donate to charitable causes, and become a volunteer if we are not already doing that. If we do all of these things now, we will be able to hasten the arrival of our fifth dimensional world which is being built on cooperation, unity, and love.

This transition will be challenging, for sure, but it should encourage all of us to grow in ways we never thought possible. It will be necessary to support each other and work together in the next 25 years. This journey, however, should be amazing, an inspiration to all of us, and absolutely wonderful!

My thanks to Kelly Noel Rasmussen for writing these phases out for us on March 24, 2018 in an article called, *Ascension.*

In Chapters 21 and 22, I talked about the possible ascension process that the Sirians' said would be a choice for us if our vibrations could handle it. That is when we would go into the metamorphosis chamber and in three days come out with our light bodies. If this process does not happen, there are phases we go through to get to that sacred state of being. For the people consciously moving towards their light body state, the process will go more quickly, but it is still a slower process.

In this longer process of light body ascension, at first, your DNA and chemical make-up will start to undergo subtle alterations. The brain will be the first part noticed where restructuring starts to heal the groove between the left and the right brain. Also, the new head chakras including the pituitary and pineal gland chakras, will become larger. When this starts to happen, a person may get symptoms such as digestive problems, muscle and joint pains, and in some cases, even rashes or spots.

Next, a person might feel disoriented because light is unlocking from within, and the merkaba in our bodies starts to spin more quickly than before. As you continue to move through the phases, colors will become more vibrant, smells will be more pungent, and your taste in food could change literally overnight. At this point, a person can no longer go back to their previous phase. Light has been unlocked within you and you are moving towards ascension.

In the next phase, physical symptoms may occur, from headaches, blurred vision, nausea, and maybe even chest pains for some individuals. What is happening now is that your senses will be realigning in order to perceive higher dimensions. You may experience that feeling you get when you step out of a roller-coaster after a wild ride.

In the middle phases of this process, you will start to tune into the frequencies of the spirit realm and your dreams may become more lucid. In addition, your thought processes will alter and you and others may notice a shift in your personality as the concept of yourself begins to shift. You will be looking at your relationships in a new light, and you will start to reevaluate which ones are positive and which ones no longer serve your highest good. You will find your social life more chaotic as your attitude towards it begins to shift.

As your ascension energy increases more, you will find you have more emotional clarity and that you are more honest. You also begin to see yourself as a higher dimensional being. At this phase, one starts to dissolve the ego and look at what is best for the group rather than oneself.

At this point, a person will start to feel physically different because you are starting to inhabit you growing light body. Your soul starts making all kinds of connections and you get a feeling of being connected to the entire Earth. Now you become one with God/Source. This mutates the DNA causing it to open up ten more strands and your ancestral DNA as well. At this point, the merkaba is fully formed.

At the end of your metamorphosis, your light body will be activated and your regeneration of your cells will be complete. Merging within you will be time, space and dimensions, and you now have access to-all of them. At this point, for the rest of your journey, you continue to do the healing work on your light body.

Many of us are already well on our way to achieving our light bodies. Many are just beginning. It is neither good nor bad; it just is. Wherever we are on our individual paths is where we will start, perceive and react to these shifts in consciousness.

Part X

New Information

Chapter 30

Disclosure

I believe that we are here for each other, not against each other.
Everything comes from an understanding that you are a gift
in my life-whoever you are, whatever our differences.
John Denver

I think most people would agree that we are not alone in the Universe. In fact, many Star Visitor races have been visiting us for decades that we know of for sure, but probably much longer. These star visitors have given us technologies, that had they been used the way they were supposed to be used, our planet and its people would look very different today. But what happened in the 1940s and 1950s is the formation of the military industrial complex and the pigeon holing of black projects into highly classified programs and limiting access to way above top secret and the need to know. The need to know goes way above the President. These programs are orchestrated by the dark cabal, the top 1% of the wealthiest people on the planet. Their goal is to create their New World Order and gain complete power and control over the entire planet. The way they hope to accomplish that is to create such a level of fear in all of us that we will look to them to save us. However, thanks to programs such as CSETI, The Center for the Study of Extraterrestrial Intelligence, people like Steven Greer, MD have worked with thousands of citizens world-wide to create a group of ambassadors who regularly make contact with highly intelligent and evolved extraterrestrials, reaching out in peace. People who have trained with Dr. Greer then go back to their cities and form their own groups and teach them the protocol. I trained with Dr. Greer and the CSETI group on many occasions from about 1994 to 2012. I can say first hand that the Star Visitors who came to our groups were highly evolved, intelligent, and very peaceful. I recall, in 2012, a group joined our circle who were very small, about 3 feet tall, and at first, we were told, they were afraid to visit our planet because we are so violent. They have no weapons, wars, hostilities on their planet. I recall how happy they were when they found us so loving and kind and willing to reach out in universal peace and love. They were humanoid, not homo sapiens.

Ending the secrecy about alleged UFOs and ETs is really needed now. I use the term, 'alleged', because our military industrial complex has back engineered spacecraft that look exactly like the ET craft. It is my understanding that they have their own armies who answer only to them as well, and have created so-called alien abductions and much more.

Dr. Greer published an article in 1999 entitled, "*When Disclosure Serves Secrecy*" and he raises some excellent points. Having known Dr. Greer since 1994 and participated in about eight week-long trainings, I trust what he has to say. There are those out there who are trying to discredit Dr. Greer, but I have seen him interact with these highly intelligent, sentient beings, and he is telling the truth. He has also been privy to many of the people in Washington who have something to do with these programs, so I listen to him when he speaks about the subject. This article is excellent and it gives us possible scenarios to solve this issue in a peaceful, loving way. I am going to summarize Dr. Greer's article, but also encourage you to go on the CSETI website and read it or download it.

He starts out by saying that disclosure is long overdue. Done properly, disclosure would change our world in ways we probably cannot imagine yet. But, because of the political climate, it can be very dangerous. The covert projects that have been in charge of these programs for the past 60 years, are only interested in the type of disclosure that does not upset their status quo. The dark side (my term) has the power and connections to do their type of disclosure if they choose to.

Dr. Greer, in his newest book, *Extraterrestial Contact: The Evidence and Implications,* explains what kind of disclosure the world needs now. That would be an "honest and open one, and one which would replace the secrecy with democracy. It should be a disclosure that is peaceful, scientific, and hopeful." I would certainly agree with that, but that kind of disclosure does not serve the needs of the dark cabal.

He goes on to say that the kind of disclosure the people in power would love to see would be a disclosure that is manipulated and done in such a way as to create as much fear as possible. It would be done in a way that would create chaos so that the people would be looking towards the government, aka Big Brother, to take care of them.

Dr. Greer is writing this as a warning to us to pay attention and to realize they have unlimited resources to carry off whatever they choose because there is no oversight committee watching them. He points out that many of the people working for these programs have no idea of what is really going on because they only see what they are working on and not the whole picture.

Dr. Greer states in his article, "Confusion and lack of clarity serves the larger covert goal of keeping it off the long-range radar of society." Their disclosure will only serve them. You can bet that there will be a spin on it that could prove dangerous to all of us. Their disclosure would be akin to the fox guarding the hen house.

Dr. Greer is warning all of us to be very careful. Theirs will be a false flag disclosure, selfish and greedy. They have a huge greed for total power, for control, and for domination over everything and everyone.

Well-informed citizens will be able to see through the lies and deceit that will be perpetrated on us. But beware! Hopefully, these same informed citizens will recognize that the dark side's disclosure will have a major spin to it, one that only serves the dark side. Every citizen needs to know that with disclosure done the proper way, good will and universal peace will come to society. Also, though, the informed citizen must realize that the cabal will spin it until they get the desired results.

Dr. Greer gives a positive scenario that could occur for the higher good, where humankind and our planet benefit in ways we cannot yet imagine. This is a quote from his paper, "*When Disclosure Serves Secrecy!*" He says that

> "the UFO and Extraterrestrial subjects are acknowledged in a way in which is scientific and hopeful. Excessive secrecy which lacks executive branch and congressional oversight is ended. Humanity begins to entertain open contact with other civilizations with peaceful engagement as the goal. Technologies which are currently suppressed are allowed to be disseminated. Pollution ends. An economy of abundance and social justice is firmly established. Global environmental destruction and mind-numbing world poverty become a faint memory. Zero-point based energy devices transform the world. Electro-gravitic devices permit above ground travel without paving over the world's precious fertile farm land."

This is the disclosure we should want.

However, this kind of disclosure could have happened in 1950. But it did not. We may ask ourselves why? A disclosure like this would lead to the total transformation of the status quo. Centralized energy systems would become obsolete. Oil would be useful for only lubricants and synthetics, and would no longer be utilized as it is today for automobiles, heating and the like. The geo-political arrangement we have today would be a thing of the past. Every country and its citizens would be so advanced that every nation would be sitting at the global table. Power would be shared by all countries. There would be peaceful acknowledgment of life elsewhere in the universe. The trillion-dollar global military-industrial complex would end. It might also bring the beginning of a universal spirituality. We must keep in mind, however, there are huge, powerful interests who are fearful of this scenario because it would be the end of the world as they know it. It would signal the end of centralized elite power, the end of the controlled geo-political order of things, which today, leaves 90% of the people on Earth "barely one step out of the stone age." They do not want to share the power that they have and they are willing to do whatever it takes so that they do not have to. It is up to us to stop them.

Dr. Greer, in his paper, goes on to describe the disclosure that these covert controlled programs want to see. This would be the false disclosure which has only one objective: the "further consolidation of their power and their paradigm." It is based in fear and not love. It is based with war and not peace. It is based on division and conflict and not unity. It is the dominant paradigm now, but it is slipping away from them slowly. Therefore, a very carefully orchestrated disclosure of their facts about the UFO and ET subjects would probably secure their power. This is the dreaded disclosure and we must be careful. It is already happening.

Dr. Greer goes on to say that he has met with many top-level people, covert operatives, who have worked in these programs or related fields. The power that this has is huge and it is hidden from us right now. Our government of "We the People," has been made irrelevant on the issues of UFOs and ETs. The theme has two main parts. One is the eventual covert militarization of the subject of extraterrestrials, and a bizarre covert religious group that will emerge. What is strange about all of this is that aggressive combatants and militarists are working together with industrialists because they share the dark view of the future which features an extraterrestrial Armageddon, or at least a threat of it happening. The whole idea is to get an expansion of the arms race into space.

Framing the disclosure of UFOs and ETs in a threatening manner is from the perspective of the military-industrial complex. President Ronald Reagan in the 1980s, used to say if the entire world could be united around the need to fight a universal threat, it would bring us all together for one common goal. Of course, this would ensure for them that the multi-trillion-dollar military-industrial spending would be in full swing well into the twenty-second century, and probably beyond.

Backwards and extremist religious groups both have a vested interest in fulfilling the promise of Armageddon. An end-of-the-world paradigm is well-ingrained into the belief systems of the people who run these covert UFO projects, and it is supported by the acting out of a cosmic conflict in space. And just like that! Now there is the necessity of spinning this issue as those evil invading aliens, or demons in religious terms. This has already been accomplished in part. The civilian UFO community and the tabloid media have certainly made this possible. Let's face it! All media has been hijacked by the dark side, so we are never privy to the whole truth about anything.

Additionally, where does racism come in? Already they have created the myth that there are good aliens and bad aliens. The good aliens are described as the Pleidians who are handsome and beautiful, white with blue eyes; Aryan types. Sound familiar? Of course, then, those evil aliens are darker, shorter, look funny and smell unusual. It sounds like Adolf Hitler himself has reached down and influenced the dark side. In my own encounters with the Star Visitors over the years, I have met many highly evolved and sentient beings who appear as though they could have been taken directly from the bar scene in the Star Wars movie. Imagine what we must look like to them! Dr. Greer says in his paper that he had one very long meeting with a multi-billionaire who said that he had given huge support to UFO activities, such as the alleged alien abductions scenarios, that would send the message to the public that aliens were a threat. This person later told Dr. Greer that those demonic ETs were the very cause of every setback in human history since Adam and Eve. Oh my God! Really? Sounds familiar, doesn't it!

These military interests have a shared goal of disparaging the UFO and ET phenomena. They are heavily involved in covert projects which hoax extraterrestrial events, such as human military-controlled abductions of people and making them look and feel like extraterrestrials are doing it. As a clinical hypnotherapist specializing in working with people who claim to have had experiences with extraterrestrials who want to know more about what happened, I devised a method to break through the barriers placed in their minds by hypnosis or other mind controlling techniques. What I discovered was that my clients had experienced a very positive encounter with Star Visitors and were starting to keep diaries, write about their experiences, and talk to people about their experiences.

I believe that when people start to listen and follow the experiencer, these covert operators come in and stage a very scary 'alien abduction' scenario and then block the memories of the good experience. This, of course, provides the long-term need to provide a rationale for an ever-expanding global military. Even if world peace would happen. Under the idea of the entire world uniting as one against a common enemy, 'world peace' could happen. It would be more like 'peace on Earth,' though.

Dr. Greer points out that under this planned scenario, we would get peace on Earth, but we would be exchanging it for interplanetary conflict. He also points out that this strange combination of militarists and religious cults are happening. In the Reagan years of the presidency, the Cabinet Secretary for the US Department of the Interior, James Watt, made some comments that were not supposed to be overheard. Not realizing that his microphone was open said that we did not need to worry about all of our environmental problems because Armageddon was coming soon and the world would be destroyed anyway. This, coming from a leader who shaped and applied policy for the Interior Department of the US Government. Even though these beliefs may seem bizarre on the surface, they are in fact shaping covert development on the subject of UFOs.

What is unnerving about this is that this combination of military war mongers and bizarre religious fanatics are the dominate forces forming both the civilian UFO community and the planned spin on UFO disclosure. We must pay attention.

To people who are rational and sane, these ideas may seem ridiculous. The normal person would query, "Why would anyone who is in his/her right mind want a cosmic war in space? Armageddon? And the destruction of our beautiful Earth mother who has nurtured us and sustained us from the beginning? Just look at the mind-set of people such as James Watt and you will see their thinking. Why worry about deforestation, air pollution, and areas of our oceans that are dead if the entire Earth is going to be destroyed in a couple of years anyway. Going even beyond this though, Armageddon is supposed to bring Christ back to the Earth according to Christianity which will save all the 'good' people. I wonder who they think those good people are?

It could also be that these extremists and war-mongers that are wanting a cosmic war really only want all of us to think there is a threat so they could justify a reason to be in existence and also the ridiculous sums of money that comes their way if there is a perceived threat from space.

It seems that there is a coming together between the civilian UFO community and the covert policy-making group. The covert group has infiltrated the civilian UFO community to a great extent. There are actually projects which on the surface seem innocent, but which in reality are totally controlled and financed by off-shoots from ultra-secret projects. What makes this so dangerous is that those covert operatives are working with civilian think tank heads, with very wealthy business people who are wanting Armageddon and they are being advised by civilian technologists and scientists. These people, too, are proponents of the bizarre religious belief systems involving the end of the world and extraterrestrials.

This is the group that will make the disclosure, but they are owned by the dark cabal and the power brokers who do the bidding of the secret entity that runs these black projects to begin with. It all looks like a civilian initiative. It looks innocent and well-intended, and scientific.

It is important for all of us to not be deceived by them. We need to understand the dark scenarios which some would like to initiate on the world. However, there are alternatives. This is important: if a disclosure is given to the world that is xenophobic (prejudice towards groups of individuals), militaristic and terrifying, then it is coming from the people spinning the story to meet their agenda. Even though the individuals or the group may look and sound respectable, they are not. That kind of disclosure just gives us a new group to hate so we can keep the war machine going.

One way the military industrial complex can pull off a false flag alien invasion is to use the back-engineered space craft that were made by humans. They will have it well-orchestrated all for the purpose of disclosing the truth with the desired militaristic spin. Most of humanity will be deceived into believing that the threat from space has finally arrived, and that if we are to survive, we must fight them at all costs.

The false flag alien invasion has been set up and proposed through Project Blue Beam. The idea of Project Blue Beam came about in the 1980s when the conspiracy theorist, Serge Monast claimed that there was a top-secret program that was run jointly by NASA and the Pentagon, to stage a false-flag extraterrestrial threat to trick the world into ceding power to the global elite who would set up the New World Order. This New World Order would be a godless world, totalitarian and liberal. In other words, the global elite (the dark cabal) would try to convince the world to all agree on a proposal that says a single world government is the only way to save humans from an alien invasion and takeover.

One way to make this happen is through something called 'predictive programming.' What this does is to familiarize people with the idea of alien invasion and to test a mass reaction to it before the entire Project Blue Beam is implemented. Look at the dominant themes of media and Hollywood movies. The global elite have promoted the idea of an alien invasion by sponsoring such movies as an *Independence Day* sequel, and by reshowing old movies such as *The War of the Worlds*.

Former Canadian Defense Minister, Paul Hellyer, made a claim that the world governments were under the control of the New World Order-Illuminati global elite and they were covering up information about contact with extraterrestrial civilizations. He said that there were groups who work to ensure that relevant files remain classified. Additionally, these groups organize efforts to intimidate and/or eliminate whistle-blowers. He named some of these groups as allegedly New World Order linked organizations. He said the Trilateral Commission, founded by David Rockefeller, the Council on Foreign Relations, and the Bilderberg Group, were three such groups.

Here is another thought: Instead of waiting for the dark side to unleash one of these scenarios on us, why don't we, the people, do it ourselves in a way that resembles the first scenario described above? It would be an honest one that will lead to peace, not war. It would lead us to a sustainable and pristine world which would be free of pollution, overflowing with abundance, in every way. This type of disclosure allows us to reach out and explore the unknown. We do not need to be shooting particle beam weapons into space.

Dr. Greer's new movie, *Close Encounters of the Fifth Kind,* is due to be released this fall, 2019, and it should be a game changer. All of the extraterrestrial technologies are tied into consciousness. By getting quiet and connecting to consciousness, we will make benevolent, higher dimensional contact with these beings who have been waiting for us to figure it out, and to reach out to them in unconditional love and peace. This is our disclosure! Connecting to consciousness is so powerful that the dark side pales in comparison.

"Evil steps in when good people do nothing. This is a lesson taught through thousands of years of human history. We stand at the beginning of a new time, and a new world awaits us. But we must embrace it, and help create it. For if we are passive, others will have their way-at least in the short run." Steven M. Greer M.D.

Part XI

Connecting to The Middle East

Chapter 31

A Psychic's Story

Throw your dreams into space like a kite, and you do not know what it will bring back, a new life, a new friend, a new love, a new country.
—Anais Nin[13]

I am sharing the next story because it is amazing how our lives can change. When I was 40 years old, I thought I had my entire life figured out, when I would retire from teaching, how I would go full time in my hypnotherapy practice, how one day I would write that book, and the exotic places I would travel to. Richard and I were planning well for our future, so I figured that I could do anything I wanted.

I retired from public school teaching in June of 2008, just about the time the stock market crashed taking millions of people down. We were one of the casualties. We lost everything and then the housing market crashed. We had a second home in Gardnerville, Nevada, where I thought we might go to retire, but we lost that. Then in 2011, Richard had to have open heart surgery to replace his aortic valve, and the bills started piling up. Ultimately though, the saddest thing for me was that we lost our beautiful home of 45 years that we had almost completely remodeled, including going to solar energy, because the bank was foreclosing on it. We ended up selling it below market value just because we had to get out of it. Any money we made on the sale went to pay off the loan to the bank and to the IRS for taxes. But, on the bright side, I am grateful that we were able to at least do that. About that time also, I was really seeking a spiritual partner, my special soulmate. So here I was, no house, no money except for what I made on my retirement check every month, and also, I was finally writing that book I always wanted to write. And I was subconsciously seeking something that seemed like a far-off dream.

Then in 2014, about August, a wonderful young man asked me for a friend request on Facebook. He had been attracted to my Facebook page because it was very spiritual. It took me about two or three months to respond to him and accept his friend request, but then we started chatting. This man was tall, dark and handsome and was living in Dubai. He was a lot younger than I, but that did not seem to matter. Now hold those thoughts as I go back in time to about the year 1985.

In about the year 1985, my friend and I were attending a UFO convention in Los Angeles, California, and we were staying the weekend in the hotel where the convention was being held. I remember it was right by the airport, LAX. It was late in the afternoon and my friend and I had been listening to lectures all day and were a little tired, but we decided to go through the concession room where they had products to buy, people reading tarot cards, taking Kirilian photographs, and there was a psychic in the back corner of the room. There was no one else around him so it gave him privacy to do a psychic reading for someone. As with anything, some psychics are very gifted while others not so much. He was very interesting looking, about middle aged and he had an accent that suggested Russia or Poland or someplace like that. He observed me watching him and he smiled and beckoned me over. He was charging twenty dollars for a 20-minute reading and so I decided to let him do it. I figured if nothing else it would break the monotony and I might learn something.

He held my hand just to get the energy, I guess. He did not read palms or anything like that, but he was clairvoyant, I think because he just started telling me things. He told me that I had an amazing life still ahead of me and that it would be full of surprises and would take me to places that would be magical. I thought, *Okay! That's cool. I figured that I would travel extensively someday so it sounded real.* Then he said, "*You are going to get married in December of 2018 or 2019.* I laughed and told him that I was already married. He said, "*No, this is someone different!*" Then he told me that I was going to meet a man who was tall, dark and handsome, much younger than I, who would love me deeply, would become my spiritual partner and soulmate, and is possibly my twin flame, and would be from the Middle East. So, I told him that first, in 2018, I would be in my 70s. I thought to myself, "*Why would a much younger man want to marry me?* Although, one thing that often happens when twin flames meet in an incarnation, one of them, often the woman, is much older. However, it does not matter. Since he was not completely sure about the twin flame part, I put that part out of my mind. I then said, if he is from the Middle East then we will never meet because I will never go to the Middle East. I had been brainwashed about the Middle East like many Americans have been.

He laughed and told me that when I was in my 70s, I would still be young and beautiful. I would still be working, teaching and writing. I had not told him anything about me, the fact that I was a teacher, but not a writer yet. That came later in my life. I have been blessed by always looking younger than I am. When I was younger, I hated it, but now, of course, I embrace it. He also said that I would start making big money when I was about 77 years old. I figured that I would have my teacher's retirement and other investments and that must have been what he was referring to. I also asked him what would become of my current husband and he did not know, but said that I would be single and could marry if I chose to.

The 20 minutes were up and I was very intrigued and decided to write all of that down when I got back to the room. I was sure nothing would ever come of it, but I kept it just the same.

Now we fast forward to 2014 and the sudden appearance of this beautiful, spiritual man, who is tall, dark and handsome and living in Dubai-The Middle East. Everything this psychic in 1985 told me was coming true, with the exception of getting married in 2018. We are waiting for immigration to grant him his Visa status and then he will be here and we can make plans. People talk about their twin soul, and

I believe he is mine. He feels the same way. If we are not twins, we are very close to it.

You may be wondering what this little story has to do with everything. This psychic was truly gifted because he put the thought into my head about the Middle East, a place I thought I would never go. As it turns out, there are active stargates and portals there as we have already seen. I had been involved with the stargates in the Valley of the Fire, Nevada, and so it makes sense that the Universe, over time, was going to put me in the proximity of this history. What has been unfolding in my life since is truly amazing and 'magical', as the psychic had said. Along with the magic, however, are life processes that can be painful sometimes. Releasing, letting go, choosing, setting boundaries, and simply growing. The Universe chose to bring the joy into my life late, at the dawning of the age of Aquarius, when my skills would be most needed. So, I have had to make a huge change in my life-letting go of material things, releasing people from my life who no longer serve my higher good, the toxic ones, the takers! The best part and most rewarding has been expanding my spirituality, living the idea that we are all one and that unconditional love is the answer. Love really is all that there is. Bringing people into my circle of friends who are like me-the dreamers, the seekers, the changers, the teachers and those who will join the challenge to help our beautiful Mother Earth transition into the fifth dimension along with those of us who raise our vibration and frequency high enough to go too. It is in our destiny if we choose to accept it.

Chapter 32

Converting to Islam, Mecca, Saudi Arabia, Cairo, Egypt and The Giza Plateau

Learn how to see. Realize that everything connects to everything else.
—Leonardo da Vinci

As my young man and I talked, over time we realized that we were falling in love with each other. He was Muslim and I was Christian, which is acceptable in Islam for a Muslim man to marry a Christian woman. As I was falling more and more for this guy, I wanted to know what made him tick. I did not say anything to him, but I bought a Holy Qur'an in Arabic with the English translation. I found out which English translation of the Arabic was the best and ordered that one. It arrived about a week later.

At that time, I shared with my special friend that I was going to read it and I would let him know what I thought. He was very excited that I was going to do that and he thanked me for trying to understand him. Because I was searching, I read about 50 pages a night until I was done. When I was complete, my friend suggested that I should go and visit my local mosque. I had lived in this area for about 40 years at that time and

I did not even know where a mosque was. I just had not paid attention, plus with the brainwashing that has been perpetrated on the public about what Islam allegedly is, I was a little uneasy. However, I also did not believe the propaganda that we were being fed about Muslims. I had taught Muslim students in my classes at the high school and they were very respectful, helpful, kind, and enjoyable to have in class. Their parents were also very respectful as well. So, I decided to see for myself what this religion was all about.

I called for an appointment to visit my local mosque, The Islamic Institute of Orange County, and spoke with their outreach coordinator, and told him that I wanted to visit the mosque to see what Islam was all about. My appointment was for four days later, May 17, 2016. I was nervous because I did not know what to expect and I knew women were supposed to wear head covering, but I only had a scarf. I called them and asked if it was okay and I was told it was fine. I could have actually gone in without head covering because I was not Muslim, but I wanted to be respectful so I wore a scarf. When I arrived, I was greeted so warmly. Seeing my nervousness, one of the sisters came over and introduced herself to me too and made me feel right at home. I was very impressed with the Mosque, the prayer rooms, the elementary school there, the classroom and lecture facilities, and just the overall warmth of everyone I met. After my tour, it was time for the midday prayer, and I was asked if I wanted to stay and watch the prayer. I said that I did. The first thing that happened was that the prayer was called over the microphone. The call to prayer is actually very beautiful, almost chant like, and it is the same all over the world. If we had been in an Islamic country, the call to prayer would have gone out over the loudspeakers to tell everyone it is time to pray. We cannot do that here in the United States because we are not an Islamic country and it would disturb our neighbors, so it is done inside the mosque. I was drawn in by the beautiful chanting sound of it. I had recently been worshipping with the Hindus and I loved the chanting part of it. I was doing group meditation and yoga with them.

The caller of the prayer sat down and there was a wait of about 15 minutes to allow people to arrive for the prayer. In this particular mosque, the men prayed in the front of the prayer room and the women in the back. I asked why that was, and there actually is a very good reason for it. Women are dressed very modestly and when one has to prostrate herself during the prayer, the forehead goes down and touches the floor, leaving your behind up in the air and kind of vulnerable to looks. With the men in front, that doesn't happen. On the Friday service (Like Sundays for Christians) since there are more people at the service and prayer, the women and small children are upstairs and watch the sermon (khutbah) in Arabic, and prayer on the monitor. Not all mosques are like this one. In some mosques, men and women are separated into two different rooms, and in some Islamic countries, women do not go to the mosque at all, only the men.

When the prayer was finished, my guide sat with me and explained about the prayers and important dates in Islam. As he was talking, I became aware of a sort of familiarity with what he was saying. When I was taken on board the spaceships in the past, the spirituality I was being taught was a lot like some of the premises of Islam. I felt very comfortable with it. After I had all of my questions answered, I asked him what one had to do to convert to Islam. I figured you would have to take a series of classes to orient yourself to the religion and then it would be kind of like confirmation in the Lutheran religion that I grew up in. It isn't like that at all. I was asked if I was doing this of my own free will, and I responded that I was. I was told to repeat after him what they call the Shahada. It means faith. The Shahada is the Muslim declaration of belief in the oneness of God and on Muhammad as His final Prophet, peace be upon him. Recitation of the shahada is one of the Five Pillars of Islam for Muslims and is said daily, and all Muslims have to follow in order to become a Muslim. I did that and became a Muslim on the spot. I was given a prayer rug, a book about Islam, and a book on how to pray including what I had to memorize, which was quite a bit. I was paired up with a mentor who would teach me about the prayers and Islam.

I felt wonderful after that. I was told to go home and take a shower, a ritual for washing away all of your past sins and starting anew. When I arrived home, Richard asked me how it was and I told him that I was now a Muslim. He was not all that surprised because he already knew that if I had gone so far as to read the Qur'an and visit a mosque, that there was a strong possibility that I would convert. He did tell me that I should be very careful how I told my family, if at all. I called my special friend in Dubai and he asked me how my visit was. I looked at him, smiled and said, "I'm Muslim now!" I watched his face go from one of surprise to total happiness and acceptance. It was a beautiful moment for both of us.

As the year moved forward, my special friend and I were growing more and more in love with each other. We talked every day while I continued learning the prayers in Arabic and studying about Islam and the Prophet Muhammad, peace be upon him. In January, 2017, I decided to apply to California Islamic University in Fullerton to their bachelor's degree program in Islamic Law and Theology. I started by taking two classes.

It was during this time that my mentor told me of a trip to Mecca, Saudi Arabia for Umrah, the minor pilgrimage, and would I want to go? I thought it would be interesting, but expressed that I did not feel I was ready to go. I spoke to my special love in Dubai about it and he told me that I must go. He expressed to me that when God gives us an opportunity to do something, that we take it. The trip was to happen in March, just two months later. I signed up for the trip. We would spend six days in Mecca and then go to Medinah, the burial place of the Prophet Muhammad, peace be upon him, for three days and then on to Cairo, Egypt and spend four days more.

Here I was being thrust into the holiest place on Earth because the Kabba, God's house, is there, and Mecca is the only city in Saudi Arabia that you may not enter unless you are a Muslim. Saudi Arabia is also very strict when it comes to following the rules, and for women, the dress. A woman must be completely covered. The only parts of her body that she does not cover are her face, feet and hands. As the weeks went by, I began to remember what that psychic so long ago had said to me, and now it was all coming true. I pondered why God put me into the Middle East and why did this beautiful man come into my life now. I knew that I was to learn about the Kabba, the history of the area around Mecca, and then visit the pyramids in Egypt, a place I had remote viewed myself into before. I knew I had at least one past life in Egypt so this was very exciting. It was also during this time that I decided that I was going to make a trip at the end of May to Dubai to meet my special guy face to face and we would see if there really was chemistry between us or not. I chose the end of May because it was the start of Ramadan, the holiest month in Islam because that is the month that God handed down the revelation of the Qur'an to the Prophet Muhammad, peace be upon him. During the month of Ramadan, my university did not hold classes, so I had the time to go. We were both very excited about that and were looking forward to it.

On the day that my mentor and I left from LAX for Mecca with our tour group, the excitement was building in me. I was going to the place where it all began and I knew that something in my destiny had been set probably before I came into this life. There are no accidents as we all know, and here I was on my way to the Middle East, a place that I swore I would never go to. It was during this time also that I had been learning about the stargates and my trip into the Valley of Fire, Nevada, had also taken place. It was exciting to me to be in the area where these stargates were, even though I knew that I would never be allowed to go anywhere near them.

We flew into Jeddah Airport in Saudi Arabia. I realized then that it was a good thing that I had been working out so hard with my trainer at the gym because the amount of walking we did would have been hard had I not been in pretty good shape. We were bussed into Mecca. Airplanes cannot fly over Mecca because of the electromagnetic energy coming from the Kabba. The Kabba is a sacred structure built in the middle of Islam's holiest site and its amazing history predates Islam itself. In Arabic, Kaaba translates to cube and it is considered by Muslims to be the house of God. It is within the Grand Mosque of Mecca. The Kabba was built by Prophet Abraham and his son, Ishmail, peace be upon them. They built it as a monotheistic house of worship. Believers around the world face the direction of the Kabba during the five daily prayers each day. Muslims do not worship the Kabba; it gives all Muslims a direction to face as they worship God. I knew that when I saw the Kabba for the first time, it would be a life-changing experience. The energies coming from this structure are amazing, and as I mentioned in the chapter on sacred geometry, the healing powers coming from this sacred place are very powerful.

Of course, when I did see the Kabba for the first time, it was exhilarating and powerful. As I was walking around the Kabba performing Umrah, I could feel the energy in every cell in my body. I knew I was walking in the footsteps of the Prophet Muhammad, peace be upon him, as well as the other Prophets before him. I knew that my being there was no accident; that this event had been placed into my consciousness and set up by that psychic some 30 years before.

There were over 1,000,000 people there performing Umrah during that time. Because Muslims are required to go to Hajj, the major pilgrimage, at least once in their lives if they are able, often people who are very sick come if that is the time they set aside to be there. Because there are so many people circumambulating around the Kabba at once, you are shoulder to shoulder with others. So, if you are next to someone who is ill, you could get very sick, which is exactly what happened to me. I started feeling sick the day we left Mecca by bus to travel to Medina, the city of the Prophet Muhammad, and the place where he is buried. The flu-type infection I had, took about three days to incubate so our entire time in Medina, I was coming down with it. Several other people in my group became ill as well.

By the time we flew to Egypt, I was really starting to get sick. This upset me because I wanted to be able to go to the pyramids, see the Sphinx, and experience the city of Cairo, its shops, people and restaurants. Fortunately, we visited the pyramids the next day. Because of the political environment at the time, we had to have an armed escort with us at all times. When you see the pyramids for the first time in person, you realize the immensity of them and it does make you wonder how they were built and who built them. I was also very surprised at how small the Sphinx appears. It must be the angle of the photographs that are taken that give it the perspective of being much larger than it really is. It is still amazing and beautiful though. And to know that there is another structure and pyramidal area on the planet Mars that is almost identical, is stunning.

Before we left for the Sphinx, we visited another pyramid area, where there were guards there because people had dug up under a couple of the pyramids, stolen the historical objects buried with the Egyptian people, and then sold them on the black market. When we got to this pyramid, we were allowed to climb up to one of the false doors on the side of the pyramid. Many did that but I chose to stay at the base of the pyramid and just soak in its incredible energy.

While I was just sitting there, I closed my eyes and started to feel this very strange energy, almost like feeling the energy of the pharaohs buried there. Since no one was sitting there with me, I closed my eyes and started focusing on the pyramid itself. I began to access the akashic records of the place. Akashic records are a conglomeration of all human events, thoughts, emotions, and intent that has ever occurred in any particular area on the planet in the past and the present. These records are believed to be encoded in a non-physical plane of existence known as the etheric plane. The akashic records also exist beyond our human ideas of the human structure of time and space. These records are timeless, which is exactly why we can utilize them to retrieve past life information.

Sitting there I started to go into an altered state of consciousness. I began to have flashbacks of a time long gone. This area was alive with workers building the blocks that made up this tomb. There were camels and a few horses that I could see, and I looked around to see these amazing people everywhere. As I opened my eyes, I could see that I was back in the present time, but my entire body tingled with the excitement of what I had just seen. Why did the ancients build these pyramids here and like-ones on other planets? The feeling I had there was electrifying. We left this pyramid area and drove on to see the Sphinx.

Like I mentioned earlier, I was startled by how small the Sphinx actually appeared. We were not allowed to go walk around it and the area it was located in. They are continually repairing and restoring the Sphinx, we were told, so that is probably why people are not allowed to walk up to it. It made me wonder just how much of the monument may still be buried under the desert sand. We walked around and took pictures with the Sphinx in the background, and sat down under the beautiful Egyptian sun for a while.

One of the things that Egyptologists have been studying in the last century is how old the Sphinx really is. It was thought to be built by the Egyptians living there during the last rule of the pharaoh, but I do not think that is so. If Mars and Earth were both ruled by the same civilization, Atlantis, and there are these monuments that are identical on both planets, then the Sphinx has to be much older than what was thought.

In the 1920s, two scholars, R. A. Schwaller de Lubiuz and John Anthony West noticed that the body of the Sphinx has distinct markings of water erosion. They wanted to know if these water erosion marks could prove that the Sphinx was constructed before 2,500 B.C. It is now thought to be a civilization much older than that. In an abstract written by Vjacheslav I. Manichev and Alexander G. Parkhomenko, they reported that after their visual investigation of the Sphinx, there was an important role of water which partially flooded the Sphinx with the formation of wave-cut hollows on its vertical walls. The shapes of these formations are very similar to the hollows formed by the ocean in coastal zones. This led them to conclude that the destruction of the Sphinx was the wave energy that was there at one time rather than the sand abrasion. If one looks back at the geological records of the area, there is confirmation of long-lasting fresh water lakes in various periods in the past that coincide with the Sphinx being there. These lakes were in the areas next to the River Nile. The highest mark of the upper erosion hollow of the Sphinx coincides with the level of water surface which took place in the early Pleistocene era when these lakes were there. The Egyptian Sphinx had already stood on the Giza Plateau by that geological, historical time. It is believed now to be a part of a civilization far older than was once thought. This erosion could have carved out these marks on the Sphinx as far back as 12,000 years ago, at the end of the last ice age. When else could the Sphinx have been exposed to 1,000 years of very heavy rainfall? There was no rainfall like that in the time of the pharaohs either. The Giza Plateau was as dry

4,500 years ago as it is today. But still, here we have a structure that has been heavily weathered by rainfall which fell on it for a very long period of time. One must go back 12,000 years to get the clouded conditions in that part of the Sahara Desert that would have been capable of causing that level of erosion on the Sphinx. Apparently, the erosion is most visible on the trench surrounding the Sphinx. No one has bothered to restore that part. I was not let close enough to the Sphinx when I was there to see that part.

This is where it gets interesting for me. It has been said that the face of the Sphinx was actually that of the pharaoh who was in power in 2,500 BC. I could see that a narcissistic pharaoh could have re-carved the face of the Sphinx to make it look like him. But I think it is more likely that the Sphinx was really a lion, just as the face found on Mars in the area known as Cydonia is. If you think of the Sphinx as a lion in the age of Leo at the end of the last ice age, circa 10,000 years or so BC, the Sphinx was facing his own image in the sky, the constellation of Leo, on the vernal equinox. This was probably incredibly significant, because it marks the precessional cycle for 12,500 years, which would be 25,000 years plus before that. The age of Leo only recurs every 25,920 years. The astronomy doesn't exactly commit us to the date of 12,500 years ago, but the geology does. Using modern computer software, it is possible to look at the ancient night sky during any period we choose.

If we look at the Sphinx and the pyramids on the Giza Plateau as though they are connected to each other astronomically, you will see that the Sphinx is perfectly aligned on due East. That has to be the work of people who were studying the night sky. If one looks at the ancient skies in 10,500 BC, and you go to Giza, you will find two constellations are modeled on the ground there. The constellation of Orion, with the stars in Orion's belt aligned with the three pyramids, and the constellation of Leo with the great Sphinx looking due East. None of this works if we take the date 2,500 BC when the monuments on the Giza Plateau were supposed to have been built. You must go back 12,500 years to get Leo locking perfectly with the Sphinx at dawn on the vernal equinox. It is the age of Leo. It is as though the lion-bodied Sphinx is looking at its own celestial counterpart in the sky, and the constellation of Orion due south on the meridian exactly the pattern of the three pyramids on the ground. That only would have happened 12,500 years ago. I would love to know how the Martian Sphinx aligns to these two constellations from Mars.

We need to ask ourselves what would be the purpose of such a marker at the Giza Plateau? Is there, perhaps, an unseen power there that future generations tried to capture? Is it possible that it is a different kind of power that we have not yet been able to understand that is attached to the Sphinx and the Giza Plateau? Why is the Sphinx uninscribed? Wouldn't its creators want us to know its purpose?

When John Anthony West and Robert Shock were allowed access to the Sphinx to study it and run some tests, they did a sonar survey around the Sphinx. What they found under the left forepaw of the Sphinx at a depth of 30 to 40 feet, is a very large man-made chamber. As soon as the Egyptian government found out what they were doing, they threw them off the site. They were not allowed to continue their work. Since then, apparently, there have been a lot of drilling projects under the Sphinx. The Egyptians claim that they are just relieving the ground water under the Sphinx, but my sense is that it is much more than that.

What if one of the things in that chamber is actually the records of that civilization that existed on Earth in ancient times? The Greek Philosopher, Plato, said that the Greek Law Maker, Solon, went to Egypt to speak with one of the Egyptian high priests. Solon asked him about the history of the Greek people. He said that in the beginning, humans were created. Then, there was a big flood, a big catastrophe which wiped out the humans. After that, humans were created again. The Egyptian high priest told him that you Greeks just remember the last one. He said that there had been many before that. He said to Solon, "You lost the records of these earlier histories. We have those records of those earlier histories." Solon asked the Egyptian priest, "Who built these things?" The reply was, "They were built by the crocodile kings." That might be a description of the Annunaki because there are a lot of depictions of them with reptilian features. Perhaps whoever built the Sphinx and pyramids buried these records in that chamber and it might be a hall of records of the Egyptian priesthood. If we were to gain honest access to that chamber we might find writings from them on tablets depicting ways of using knowledge that they knew we would not be able to get to until a certain point in our evolution where we would be able to get down to these chambers and pull out what is down there. If the Sphinx does mark the gateway to secret knowledge of our planet left by an ancient higher civilization, and by design, is not to be made available until our modern civilization is ready to see the universe differently, would make sense to me. Graham Hancock, a British writer and journalist who specializes in theories involving ancient civilizations, suggests that this question is partially answered by understanding the symbolism in Egyptian art. The ancient Egyptians had a beautiful way of looking at human life. This was a culture that was forgiving in nature. They understood human frailty and that humans are not perfect. We are going to make mistakes. However, the question is, "Do we learn from these mistakes?" What do we do with the lessons that duality has to teach us? Do we integrate those lessons into our lives and make them better, or do we choose to simply ignore them and keep life as it always has been?

If the ancient knowledge is below the paw of the Sphinx and it remains inaccessible, is it possible that this same knowledge exists in a different location? Or even in a different frequency, so that only higher evolved people would be able to access it? If the Sphinx and the Great Pyramid are just the beginning of our understanding of humanity on Earth, perhaps it is a reminder for us to dig deeper, not only physically at the site, but spiritually as well. When, if ever, will this knowledge be available for all of us to see? For all of our technology and all of our progress that we have made, we still live in a very fractured and very dangerous world right now. The entirety of human achievement could be put in jeopardy. We have the technology, the toys, to blow ourselves to bits, but I am concerned we do not have the spirituality to stop it. Only through a raising of mass consciousness and living the kind of lives we want to see on our fifth dimensional Earth, and unconditional love towards one another, will we stop from blowing ourselves back into the stone age in a matter of days. We don't really know why we are here or what we are doing. We seem to still only have an illusion about what that is. That illusion is locked away deep in our past where it all began, and we need to recover that truth about ourselves.

By the end of the day I was feeling very sick. I knew there was a Nile riverboat cruise planned for the next night and I really wanted to be part of that so, I went to bed and then slept through the next day until dinner time.

Chapter 33

The Annunaki, The Bible and The Holy Qur'an

Awakening is not changing who you are,
but discarding who you are not.
—Deepak Chopra

As you may recall in Chapter fourteen, I wrote a story about our original history and where it all began. I stated that, at the time of this writing, I did not have the religious texts to back some of this up, and so I wrote the story as I had been taught over the years of working with the Star Visitors, Sheldon Nidle, and others. As often happens when I am writing, sometimes at night when I am sleeping, I am either visited and downloaded important information or I am taken out to a spacecraft and downloaded the information. Sometimes, I think, they wait until I am ready to receive the information before giving it to me so as not to give me too much to store until I need it. This happened to me a couple of nights ago.

I was asked by a friend not too long ago, how do I rectify this information with the Quran and/or the Bible? I will answer that question before leaving this chapter. I believe my answer will unfold as I am writing this.

We know the Earth is approximately 4.5 million years old. I do not know if the Bible mentions Adam's age, but the Qur'an does not specifically. When I asked my Imam what the thought is about when Adam was created on Earth, I was told that we really don't know for sure, but 10,000 years ago is a pretty good guess. What I am going to say now may shock some of you, but I also know that many of you will agree with me on some level. If nothing else, I would hope that you would think about it.

First and foremost, I believe in God as being the Creator of all that there is. No matter who or what is out there in the universe, God created it. We also know now, without a doubt, that there is intelligent life out there on other planets, other solar systems, other galaxies, and other dimensions. Add to that parallel universes, and you have a lot of possibilities. We also know that God handed down the Holy Books of the three main religions on Earth-The Holy Bible, The Torah, and the Holy Qur'an. This was done on Earth after Adam was created. However, we can go back on this planet to 25,000 years ago and see that there was intelligent life here. One might ask, well if that is true, why didn't God hand down the Holy Books for those people who were here before the creation of Adam? I intend to answer that, but first, let's go back in time.

As we now know, the age of the Sphinx on the Giza Plateau and the surrounding pyramids is estimated to be much older than it ever was before. They can tell by studying the water damage to the Sphinx that could only have been done by deluges of water over long periods of time. Since Giza is very arid today, we have to travel back in our geological history to when we had that kind of climate there. If we go back to right after the last ice age in the Pleistocene era, we find that kind of climate. Therefore, the Sphinx is probably 12,000 to 12,500 years old, plus or minus a few years.

When I was talking about the Stargates that we find around the world, the native peoples who live near them have heard the stories of ancient gods who would travel through them and intermingle with the people there. They were usually described as very tall beings, sometimes with reptilian like features. If these beings were using the stargates to get here, they had to be coming from another planet, star system or dimension. If you believe as I do that God created everything in the universe, and they were here on the Earth before Adam was created, then one might assume that God created them on their home planets at some point in their planet's evolutionary history. I am suggesting that if God sent down his rules for us in the form of the Bible, the Torah and the Qur'an, then perhaps he sent similar books to those on other planets too. I do know that the star visitors I have worked with since I was six years old were more highly evolved than I was. Their planets are far older than the Earth and therefore, their species is also far older than we are and have had millennia to develop and grow spiritually. I will add though, that being a more highly evolved species does not necessarily translate to more enlightened.

I have felt for a long time now, that the human race on Earth as we know it, has been genetically manipulated. The beings from other planets were created by God and many of those species had evolved over the years to be quite advanced, and certainly, would have known how to make test tube babies and clones. That being said, even if that is true, we are still all of the one God, the creator of everything.

The ancient texts are rife with stories of strange gods, machines that fly, weapons that could destroy everyone, and biological experiments. These biological experiments could only be things like genetic manipulation or cloning. People such as Zachariah Sitchen, Erich von Daniken, and others have meticulously gone through the Bible, the Egyptian Book of the Dead, ancient Sumerian tablets, the Qur'an and other ancient texts, and have told us a huge amount of information about extraterrestrial gods, wars that were fought, their spacecraft and their genetic manipulation. Keep in mind that the people of Earth at that time might see these extraterrestrial beings as gods because of the way they got here, through stargates and portals, and the advanced technologies they came with might look like magic to the people of earth at that time.

The Qur'an has been studied the least in this, mostly because of the poor quality of many Qur'anic translators, which would contribute to scholars not wanting to read through it. According to what I have read, the translations that existed, at least in the English, have not translated the nuances and sometimes mystical sense that the Arabic language has. There is much advanced scientific knowledge and technical knowledge in the Qur'an. As an example of a poor translation, the Qur'an said that Allah "sent down water from the sky," which would probably be understood as rain. However, if that same person read that in the Qur'an, stated some 1,500 years ago that Allah sent down water from the asteroid belt, that would be different.

In Arabic, the word, 'Sama' is translated into English as sky, heaven or even cloud. There are several possibilities for the translation. However, the word, 'Sama,' came into the Arabic language through the Sumerians. The meaning of 'Sama' to the Sumerians was "hammered out bracelet." That is how they referred to the asteroid belt. They thought this because they believed that the asteroid belt was 'hammered out' by a collision of two planets. One planet was called Nibiru and the other was a giant water planet known as Tiamet. Allegedly, this collision shattered half of the planet, Tiamet, which became the asteroid belt, and the other half was knocked into a new orbit and became our Earth, which, of course, is a water planet. Even the scientists at NASA say that it is probable that the asteroid belt was created because it was once a planet and it collided with a large body and broke up, but those pieces of the planet remained in the proper orbit around the sun exactly where the planet should be. The Qur'an says that water originates from outer space. Now, 1500 years later, scientists are thinking the same.

Over the past 50 years, there have been new theories proposed about human's extraterrestrial origin. In his Earth Chronicles, Zechariah Sitchin seems to make sense based on what we have been told so far. His theory is based on his interpretation of Sumerian and Babylonian clay tablets which had preserved scriptures like The Epic of Gilgamesh, The Enuma Elish, and the Tale of Adapa.

Many mainstream scholars of today would probably call these stories myths. But I have always looked at myths as ancient happenings that were handed down from word of mouth from one generation to the next. Things that really happened. That is my personal opinion regarding myths. Zechariah Sitchen believes these myths to be actual, factual reports of what our ancient civilizations actually witnessed, experienced, and learned from the people they referred to as gods.

The theory proposed by Sitchen is that billions of years ago a planet called Nibiru, and its moons entered our solar system from deep space. After the collision of the two planets, Nibiru's moon, Kingu, became the earth's moon. Because of the wide elliptical orbit that Nibiru takes around our sun, it comes by earth every 3,600 years. When it has passed by the earth before, its gravitational pull was so great because of its immense size, that it caused disasters on the earth, such as floods, and possibly the poles to shift.

The story goes that Nibiru's people were an advanced intellectual society and their king was named Alalu. He was overthrown by a person named Anu. Alalu escaped from Nibiru in a spaceship and landed on the earth. At that time, Nibiru's atmosphere was deteriorating and huge amounts of gold were needed to sprinkle gold particles into the atmosphere to shield the planet's people from the sun's deadly radiation.

Alalu sent word back to Nibiru that he had found gold on the earth. This was approximately 400,000 years ago. Anu sent his oldest son and a crew of 50 to the earth to mine the gold. Enki, the son, went to south Africa and set up gold mining operations there. Even today, there is evidence in south Africa of advanced mining technologies that were used over 100,000 years ago. None of the earlier species of humans living on earth at that time were capable of doing that.

These people from the planet, Nibiru, were the Annunaki. They lived incredibly long lives. Because of that, those assigned to work the mines felt like they were in hell and so they rebelled. Anu arrived and agreed with the miners. It was proposed that they create a primitive worker to do the slave labor to work on behalf of the Annunaki.

What they were doing was genetic engineering and cloning, something our society today is only beginning to understand and duplicate. There were many failures, lots of trial and error and many experiments that failed, but finally they created the perfect prototype.

To make this prototype, Enki mixed some of his own DNA into the mix with homo erectus, early man, to create this first cloned child. Enki's half- sister, Ninhursag, who was the medical officer, carried the mixture of DNA in her own womb. Later, the Annunaki birth goddesses had to carry the clones. Remember, they were creating workers to mine the gold for the Annunaki because the Annunaki did not want to do it anymore. After a while, the demand was so great for these clones, the women no longer wanted to carry these human embryos in their wombs. Therefore, Enki did another major DNA manipulation that allowed hybrid clones to procreate.

When the female population of workers grew, the Annunaki who were orbiting the earth decided to come down and mate with them. This absolutely infuriated the leader because he did not like the mixing of different beings. Knowing that the planet Nibiru was approaching the earth in its elongated orbit around the sun, the Annunaki decided to let all the workers and the Annunaki hybrid mixes die when the gravity from the passing planet caused the great floods on the Earth.

This is where the story gets interesting. Enki was able to get word to a human disciple, Utnapishtim, and taught him how to build a submarine. He also told him to collect the seeds of all the animals so they could repopulate after the flood waters receded. Doesn't that sound like the story of Noah's ark? Noah was given the dimensions of the ark and told to collect a male and female animal of each species on earth so that after the flood, they could repopulate. I never understood until I got older that Noah could not have taken two animals of each species onto the ark. What he took was the sperm and egg from each species on earth.

Utnapishtim and his family survived, just as Noah and his family had survived, and the Annunaki had a change of heart and decided to let the humans re-procreate because their offspring were needed to feed the gods and to work the mines.

Remember, in chapter 14, I talked about the galactic wars that took place. Look at the similarities of that story and this one.

The Annunaki trained priest-kings to be in control over the workers and to act as the intermediaries between themselves and the worker humans. These kings were half Annunaki and half Annunaki-human hybrids. Enki genetically modified many of the wild plants to make them suitable for the Annunaki to eat.

However, there was discontent among the gods. In the past, a god named Zuen stole all of the computer discs, weapons systems, and civilization programs from the Annunaki, and a huge war happened to try to repossess these stolen items.

The god, Marduk, wanted to build a spaceport in Babylon to rival the other gods. The main spaceport had been located at a place called Sippar, but it was destroyed in the flood. They rebuilt it in the Sinai at the site of a stone landing platform at Baalbek. When the Annunaki leader found out about what Marduk was doing, he flew over Babel, the gate of the gods, and destroyed the launch tower and the entire space program. A few of the stargates were referred to as gates of the gods.

I mention all of this because there are so many stories out there that seem to confirm these myths. I do believe that there has been genetic manipulation over the centuries of our species. It has also been strongly suggested that members of the dark cabal, the elite that is ruling planet earth right now in the banking industry, oil industry, pharmaceutical industry, education, and is orchestrating the hatred that we are being bombarded with on a daily basis through our movies, television programs, video games, our hand-held devices that we are all attached to, and the controlling of the media and what we are allowed to hear and learn, are descendants of the Annunaki and have stayed in this ruling class ever since the Annunaki were here long ago.

If you are interested in finding out more about all of this, I suggest you read the Earth Chronicles by Zechariah Sitchen. In it he gives Bible verses and Qur'anic verses that seem to support all of his ideas. It can be rather compelling, but for me I hold to the belief that our one God, Allah, is the only One who created everyone and everything in the universe. I think it is important that we all stay spiritually strong and know and believe that we and our beautiful planet Earth, are shifting into a higher dimension, and all of the darkness that we have lived with for centuries is finally coming to an end. While I believe that we do have a unique history that has been kept from us for thousands of years so that this ruling species could control us, our religions have been manipulated to suit their needs and to scare us into compliance, we all know on some level that we have been lied to. I, for one, want to know the truth. That is all I have ever wanted. As we continue to awaken to who we are and really begin to come together in unconditional love knowing that we are all one, our lives will all change for the better. Love is the answer. It really is all that there is.

Chapter 34

Twin Flames

Have you ever felt really close to someone? So close that you can't understand why you and the other person have two separate bodies, two separate skins?
—Nancy Garden[15]

I felt it was important to talk a little about twin flames because I have been blessed with mine finding me. People often use the term soulmate and twin soul or flame as one in the same. They are, in fact, different. A soulmate is a partnership that is mainly an energy relationship. This kind of relationship is intense and at times, extreme, but it does not go into that deep spiritual connection that occurs between twin flames. An energy relationship usually develops because the person you are attracted to has a shared soul pattern with you.

You will share a deep connection with this person in all aspects of your life, which will include intense attraction and mutual chemistry. The reason for this is because of your shared soul pattern. Because you share this soul pattern, you will express many of the same behaviors. But, in actuality, you will not be the same. Your life experiences create who you are, so the way your soul pattern expresses itself will be different from your soulmate. Throughout your relationship, hopefully, you will align yourselves to each other and find a balance between you, which allows you to grow together.

When you meet your twin flame, there are several things that happen to you which will help you identify him/her. When you meet him for the first time, your heart chakra will react strongly. You will feel a flutter in your chest area, like butterflies, and a warm feeling that spreads throughout your body. Also, your eye contact with each other will be intense. Remembering that our eyes are the windows to our souls, you put each other in a trance-like state. Your souls recognize each other through your eyes and you suddenly feel like you are the only two people on Earth as you connect.

You immediately feel accepted for who you are. You feel as though you have known each other forever, because you have. Intuitively you know this person is important to you and your future. Because of the intensity of this first meeting, all of your chakras will become active at once. You will have the sensation of floating, being light-headed, and maybe even tingling. You feel intense magnetism towards them that is a physical feeling and it makes it very difficult to leave their side. You do not want to be without them. All of a sudden, you will feel that you are fulfilling your destiny. My twin and I experienced all of that intensely.

Speaking from experience, twin flames dominate each other's thoughts. You find that you have a strong psychic connection. You fall in love with each other easily because, "you are they, and they are you." You mirror each other. Whenever twin flames unite on a spiritual level, it opens up many channels of energy, and there is a ripple effect felt throughout Earth and the entire universe. There is a psychic connection between twins that allows you to feel and sense what is going on with your counterpart physically, mentally, and emotionally. There have been many times I have been having a hard day, and at the moment I start thinking about my twin, he will text me and ask me what is wrong? He heard me psychically and, as an empath, he feels what I am feeling. This all happens through our heart chakra.

Twin flames are the half souls of each other. It is thought that one's twin flame is destined for them in their last lifetime. I do not know about that. When you meet for the first time, you will feel an unexplained bond between you. It feels like you have met before and you will know that he/she is the one. You feel it in your heart, your stomach, your emotions, and your mind. There are also moments when you feel intense genuine love between the two of you. This feeling will be so strong that your souls feel as one and you will be feeling your twin's soul inside of yours. Moments such as these will make you know for certain that you two are meant for each other, and no matter what happens, you will not be broken apart.

A relationship with your twin flame should make you grow as an individual. You begin to realize that you will develop new ideologies and ways of life as the result of your twin's influence on you. Your relationship will enable you both to reach your highest potential in the world.

Twin flames join at the heart chakra. When this occurs, it opens the heart to an expanded feeling of love. This love is very inspirational which encompasses everything, and this feeling will send remarkable energy into the universe which will ultimately lead to God!

Distance is not a barrier between twin flames. My beautiful twin and I have lived apart for five years now and we are trying to get him to the United States through legal immigration, but it is a very slow process now. With us, telepathy and empathy are very common. At any time of the day or night, we will hear each other's thoughts, and sometimes we may finish each other's sentences. Often, we find ourselves texting or emailing each other at the exact same time.

Twin flames almost always have a strong physical attraction to each other and the sexual chemistry is electric. However, the spiritual and emotional chemistry between them helps to create a romantic relationship that is far more exciting and fulfilling than a regular relationship between two people who have a romantic one.

It has been said that more and more twins are going to find each other and come together during this time period. Twin flames are meant to join in this lifetime. The reason is that it will encourage others who are around them. It is true that the more twin couples who rejoin one another, the higher the consciousness is raised on our planet and that is when change happens. I hope that those of you reading this will find or will have already found your twin flame. It is not uncommon for twins to be twenty to forty years apart in age. Sometimes certain cultures do not approve of the age difference and make it difficult for you to be together, but even that can be overcome. The twin flame relationship is made for lovers, and when factors that come into play to make a relationship difficult to be together, push through the red tape and enter into your full relationship through marriage with your twin. Giving up is not an option!

Conclusion

Education is the passport to the future, for tomorrow belongs to those who prepare for it today.
—Malcolm X

So much has happened in my life since those first experiences I wrote about in my first book, *Caught Between Two Worlds...A Journey Through Time.* I have received some answers about some things that happened to me and I want to share those with you. The first is about my grandma, Nonnie, whose farm is where I had all those wonderful experiences from ages 6-12, in Antelope, California. I wrote in my first book that I could not understand why she reacted to me in such an angry way when I told her about the first time my Star Visitor friends landed and took me on board their spacecraft. She was so mad and upset at me that she told me never to speak of it again. So, I did not.

As often happens in my life, I receive information while I am sleeping or meditating, or sometimes it is simply a telepathic message I receive when I am sitting very quietly. A couple of years ago, I was thinking about my book, and my mind took me back to 1951. It was a dream like reflection that I was having when I felt the presence of my grandmother. She has been a guide for me ever since she crossed over in 1956. It was a wonderful feeling, her nearness to me, and I just allowed the feeling to wash over me. It was then that I heard her voice in my head. She said, "*Judy, I have watched you all of these years and am so proud of you; all that you have accomplished, and how you have handled what happened to you so many years ago on our farm. I partly reacted to your story from a place of fear, not a fear associated with the little people, but the fear associated with what others might think. You see, the same thing happened to me when I was small, and from your description, I believe it was the same group of little people. You were right with everything you were saying but I was afraid to let you know that it had happened to me too. In the early part of the last century when my encounters occurred, it was a very different world then. The time was a few years before World War I, and my family was poor. My parents had a farm and we all worked very hard, even the children. I made the mistake of telling people about what happened to me and people thought there was something wrong with me, like I was a little crazy. I was treated very differently by kids in the town and at school and I did not want that same thing to happen to you. My way of handling it was to yell at you and try to scare you away from it. As we both know now, you did not stop, you just became secretive about it."* I could hear her laughing a little in my head. She continued, *"That's my girl! You were stubborn, and I think it is that stubbornness that has been one of your biggest assets in your life because you never give up. I still want to say to be careful because you still have an innocence about you that believes you can't get hurt, but you can if you are not careful."* I heard her say, *"I love you,"* and then she was gone, leaving me to ponder and process what had just happened.

The next person I want to update you on is Bob, the hobo, who rode the rails and befriended me when I was so little. I somehow always knew that there was something very special about Bob and I have thought about him from time to time all of these years. Bob, I know now, is an extraterrestrial who has been assigned to watch over me and give me guidance along the way. As an adult now, I can look back on the incidents that I ran into Bob, and I know that is exactly who he was. Bob was the hobo who rode the trains when I was in Antelope, California, in 1951, who befriended me and gave me those wonderful marble-like balls and the special rock with the cross on it. When I asked him what they were for, he told me to put them in a safe place and someday when I was a lot older, I would know what to do with them.

The next place I ran into Bob was on August 8, 1991, when Diana and I walked into the Little Aly Inn in Rachel, Nevada on our way to area 51. Bob was the old cowboy who I sat down next to at the bar. He was the one who was giving me advice about where to go to watch the lights at night and what to watch out for. I can look back on that now and know he was the same person because of the way he felt, warm, friendly and wise beyond words.

The next time I saw Bob, he took on the persona of a homeless guy who just appeared out of nowhere, literally, to help me. I was by myself and driving into Los Angeles in the wee hours of the morning, around five am. I was driving my Jeep and after being on the freeway a couple of minutes, I had a blow-out on one of my tires. I was not in the greatest part of town, and being a lone woman driving in the dark, I knew better than to stop on the side of the road. I could see a Chevron station at the next offramp on the other side of the freeway, so I drove my car very slowly until I was able to get there. Upon arrival, I discovered that there was only one young man attending to the station, but his job was only to monitor the pumping of gas. He came out to me and told me that there would not be anyone there to help me until eight am. I had to be in L.A. at six for an appointment. So, I decided to call AAA, The Automobile Club of Southern California, and have them come out and change my tire for me. But before I could call, this old homeless guy just appeared out of nowhere. There was nothing else around this station but barren land, and I saw him approaching. He truly just walked into the area as though he came through a time portal. When he got to me, he said, "*I would be happy to change that tire for you for a pack of smokes.*" I looked at his eyes and saw a gentle soul so I agreed. It only took him about ten minutes to do the task, and all the while we were talking about things like unconditional love and taking care of each other. It was pretty amazing. When he was finished, I gave him twenty dollars and thanked him. He was very grateful and turned and walked back towards the place where I first saw him. When he reached that spot, he simply disappeared into thin air. There had to be a place there that he stepped into and teleported himself back to where he had come from.

The next time that I know of that I ran into him was not a physical encounter but a spiritual one. This occurred when I was out in the Valley of Fire working on the stargates. Jeanne Love, who is a gifted medium, told me he was there and had some things to say to me. He told me that he was proud of me for how I turned out and how I figured out how to use those balls and special stone. I will explain that next. I asked him if I would ever see him again and he said that I would, but it would be a few years into the future from then. That was in about 2013 or 2014. It is now 2019 as I sit here writing, and as far as I know, I do not think I have run into him yet. I think I would know if I had.

When Bob gave me those four marble-like balls and the special rock when I was about seven years old and I asked him what they were for, he told me to put them away in a safe place, and when I was older, I would know what to do with them. So, I did that. Over the years, I would take them out and look at them and try to guess what they were for, but never really hit on it. I figured the marble-like balls would be used for some kind of healing, and I could not guess what the special rock was for. But, when I went out into the Valley of Fire, Nevada, I put them in my pocket and took them with me. I really don't know why I did that, but the feeling to do that was very strong. When I got to the site where I was to work on that stargate, I took out the balls and I held one at arms-length and aimed it at the stargate. As I did that, the ball came alive in my hand. It connected in the sky with the stargate, which shimmered as I held it up there. It started to spin really fast, like an atom with the protons and electrons spinning wildly around it. I could feel this vibration all the way up to my shoulder and it made my heart beat fast. After about five minutes, the stargate made a big flash and the vibration and spinning in the ball stopped. As I looked at it in my hand, it was just quietly lying there now, although it was hot in my hand, and my arm and heart went back to normal.

As far as the special rock goes, I learned that I could use that rock like a 911 call if I found myself alone and in trouble. I simply had to hold it, and telepathically send out an SOS in my head, and one of the Star Beings would come along to help me. Sometimes when I carry it in my pocket, it starts to vibrate all of a sudden, and I take that to mean that they are just letting me know they are near should I need them.

In 2016, my life changed dramatically. Our home of forty-five years went into foreclosure and we could not get the banks to work with us. We were able to sell it at a much lower price than it was worth, but we had no choice. The sad part for me was that when my dad had passed away in the house in 1993, he opened up a portal which I just left open. I kept two guards from the other side guarding the portal so only beings of the Light could enter. When we had to leave, I closed those portals so as not to scare the socks off of the new owner. I knew she would never be able to handle anything like that, so I lovingly closed it up and sadly left it all. I had beautiful fairies in my courtyard, which I have a picture of somewhere, and experienced so many amazing encounters there. The beautiful birch tree that I had planted fifteen years before was now big and beautiful and brought such peace to the courtyard. For those of you who are experienced with talking to the trees and listening for their answers, I had that kind of relationship with that tree. When I knew I had to leave, I remember going over and hugging it, like I had done so many times before, and I could feel a sadness coming from the tree. There are some of you who are going to know exactly what I mean, while others of you, not so much. It's all good. Sadly, I drove by the house about a year later, and the new owner had cut down that beautiful tree. I had designed my courtyard from a vision that I had. I wanted to create an area of peaceful contemplation and where I could also teach classes if I chose to. When people walked into the courtyard, usually they would feel the energy and not want to leave. However, I think the new owner could not handle the vibration there because it was very high, so she began eliminating the things that made her uncomfortable. It broke my heart, but thank God I have the memories and some good pictures.

Now I know that this chapter in my life had to close in order to allow in the next chapter. For that I am very grateful. I am sharing this next part with you because I know many of you have experienced the same thing. We were in the position we were because we had most of our money in the stock market, and when the market crashed in 2008, we lost most of it, and foolishly we left the rest in there thinking it was going to bounce right back, but of course, it did not. Then Richard had to have emergency open heart surgery to replace the aortic valve in his heart. I became his caregiver which meant I could not work, and so no money was coming in. We had a two-acre ranch in Gardnerville,

Nevada that we bought to retire to, but the housing market also crashed, and we lost that.

At this same time, every appliance in the kitchen and laundry room went out and had to be replaced. Because our credit rating had always been in the high 700s, I had a lot of credit available on credit cards. So, I had no choice but to use them, and you know the rest. With no income because I could not work, our financial world came crashing down. I never would have dreamed that could happen to someone who had planned for a comfortable retirement, that they would lose it all. But we did. There were a lot of things that ultimately caused the snowball effect, but we just had to deal with it.

As the time for our getting out of our home was fast approaching, we quickly learned that we could not get anyone to rent to us because our credit was in the toilet, as you can well imagine. Even though I could prove that I made enough each month to pay the rent, it did not matter. Finally, my current landlord took a chance, with the stipulation that I pay the rent for the whole year. The only way I was able to do that was because there was a little left from the sale of our home. The rest went to pay back taxes. So, I am now in Placentia in a cozy three-bedroom house. I am just grateful that everything fell into place.

I have been here two years now. It is a struggle, but I am determined to get back. As sometimes happens in a marriage, even a marriage of fifty years, the two people discover that they are not on the same page anymore. Richard was happy just sitting at home and not doing much, but I was not ready for that. I still have so much to do, so much to see, so much in the spiritual realm to accomplish. I had hoped that he would be my spiritual partner as I went about doing my work, but that was not to be. Although Richard has grown a lot spiritually over the years, he was not interested in joining me in my endeavors. It just happens sometimes. I am still his care giver because now he has Alzheimer's disease. Even though it has been difficult, I know that God never gives us more than we can handle. It is heartbreaking to watch this horrible disease eat away at Richard's brain. It makes me really sad. We are still special good friends who have a special love that will always be there. It comes from being with someone for fifty years. Richard is happy for me and wants me to be taken care of after he crosses over, whenever that will be.

What is interesting is that I was not going to put any of that in this book, but, as I was writing, it just started to appear. I'm guessing one of my writing guides on the other side thought that it was important to share with the world. Maybe it is to show that this could happen to anyone. I never dreamed it would happen to me because I had saved and invested well and had a lot of money. But my life was missing something very important and I had to let go of all of my past in order to be ready to receive it.

Remember back in chapter thirty, the psychic's story? Well, all of that has come true except for getting married on December 18, 2018. None of it could have happened if I had been still carrying around all of that stuff. So, for me, it has been about letting go. That has probably been the hardest thing I have ever had to do, but I'm doing it. It feels good. My fiance' is still not in the USA, but we are going through the legal immigration process to get him here. Richard will probably live with us after my fiance' and I are married so that we can take care of him. That is totally my fiance's idea because he sees Richard as family. He and Richard have met and an interesting bond has formed. My life has never been normal, so it does not surprise me that this chapter we are writing now is not normal either.

One of the things I was missing living in Placentia were the active visitations I used to receive all the time from the star visitors, angels, an occasional time traveler, and an occasional enlightened spirit. After being here for about a year, I went to bed one night and the whole bedroom was glowing pink. It woke me up. As I opened my eyes, there were about fifty orbs in the room, moving about everywhere. I could reach out and touch them and feel their essence. The room was filled with such a high vibration that it created an atmosphere of pure joy and love. I interacted with them for over an hour before falling off to sleep. That is the only time here that it has happened like that. Sometimes when I awaken the next morning, I know I was taken, but I am remembering nothing. I have also had an occasional time traveler that seems to pop in once in a while.

I have a lot of telepathic communication with star visitors, however. I am starting up a new CSETI contact group to teach them the CSETI protocol and to make contact with the benevolent star beings who are here. I know that Steven Greer is correct when he says that the disclosure about the reality of star visitors on our planet must and will come from the general public who cares about what happens to all of us, our planet, the galaxy and beyond. We cannot leave it up to the government to tell us by putting their spin on the whole thing to lure us into submission.

As I get back to my hypnotherapy practice, my teaching, my writing, and field work, plus completing my bachelor's degree in Islamic Law and Theology, I see that it is time to teach others all that I have learned. I am still learning, still experiencing, and still making contact, and I believe that all of us who wish to, will assist our beautiful Mother Earth in transitioning to the fifth dimension, and will join her as we help create our new earth, alive with new technologies, no more diseases, beautiful relationships with each other, living on a beautiful and pristine planet where there is no famine, no diseases, pure water and air, all of us realizing we are one, and advancing our spirituality beyond what we can even imagine. We will be allowed to join an amazing galactic community that stretches through the galaxy, and our universe; a membership that we have been barred from for so long due to our warring and violent ways.

I know I am ready! This is our chance to create that world that we have worked so hard to create over these past decades. By modeling the behavior and living our lives according to how we want the people on our new earth to be, we will manifest our Heaven right here on Earth.

Epilogue

Do not let the memories of your past limit the potential of your future. There are no limits to what you can achieve on your journey through life, except in your mind.
Roy T. Bennett[14]

As I finish writing this book, I feel as though I am sending my child off to school for the first time. It has been so much a part of my life and now it is done! My amazing experiences continue, but my place in it has changed somewhat. All of my experiences, encounters, my jobs, my studies, my adventures, and my contact with beautiful and enlightened galactic beings, have brought me to the next step. I have been taught so much by these beautiful Star Visitors, time travelers, angels, my Earth teachers, my hypnotherapy and angel clients, and my thousands of students that I have taught over the years. Now it is time for me to teach others what I have been taught.

At this point in our lives, we are sitting at the edge of a precipice. Our future could go either way-to the dark side and complete and total control of the dark cabal over us, their famous *New World Order,* or we could step up and take our place in the beautiful galactic community for which we have earned the right to join, but only after we raise our vibrations and frequency to the level of the fifth dimension. Without that, our bodies would never be able to handle the increase in vibration and we would perish.

How do we do that? I know that as we look at the state of the world right now, the task seems daunting. That is because we are constantly bombarded by the ugly side of life through the media mostly. The media, as we know, is completely controlled by the dark cabal. No matter what the story, the media is told how to spin it to make it in their favor. Most of us now are fighting for our survival and many do not even realize it. Our economy has been manipulated to the point that groceries are at an all-time high, the cost of fuel for our vehicles keeps rising, our medical system is such that doctors have become symptom relievers and push medications on us because they cannot do anything else. The medical industry, the insurance companies mete out surgeries and life-saving medicines to those they deem as worthy to be saved. God forbid if you are over fifty years old, or unless you are very wealthy. Then none of the negative touches you. Let us not forget the tobacco industry who recently created vaping geared at young, teenage smokers. We were told that was safe and now we know it is actually worse than smoking tobacco. They are still allowed to sell this poison. Now because we have a whole new age group addicted, the pharmaceutical companies have the "opportunity" to create more treatments for getting someone to stop smoking. What a racket! Then, we have the utility companies who keep raising their rates so that if you are strapped for money, you cannot turn on your air conditioner and you suffer in the heat and humidity. Likewise, in the winter, you are forced to ration your fuel for heat. I am talking about this to remind us all about how we have been brainwashed almost into complete submission to the New World Order. It is only by understanding what is happening that we can change our behavior, and not get taken in.

The book, *1984,* by George Orwell, published in June, 1949, is worth taking a look at now, 70 years later. In his story, he was predicting what life would be like in 1984, but if we look at 2019, it gives one a very eerie feeling. Orwell was a democratic socialist and he wrote the book as fiction. However, many aspects of this dystopian novel have come eerily true. Dystopia is an imagined state or society in which there is great suffering or injustice, typically one that is totalitarian. It is from this book that the phrase, *"Big Brother is watching you!"* came from. The society shown in "1984," is one in which social control is achieved through disinformation and surveillance. The technologies and techniques used in the novel are present in our world today.

Surveillance is achieved in the book through technology. They use a "telescreen," which is very much like our televisions today. The telescreen has a single channel for news, propaganda, and wellness programming. There are only two differences between telescreen and our own television sets. It is impossible to turn telescreen off, and the screen also watches its viewers. Telescreen is a combination of television and surveillance all rolled into one. Actually, when I think of it now, our smart TVs have a camera that is capable of watching us. In the story, the character by the name of Smith never is sure whether or not he is being monitored through the telescreen. Technologies of television were created before World War II, so it really wasn't science fiction. Germany had a working videophone system in the 1930s. Television programs were being broadcast in parts of the United States, Great Britain and France. 1984 has been said to be a prediction of what could happen.

Scholars have said how clearly the book, 1984, is a prediction of what was to come. In 1949, Americans watched as an average, four and a half hours of television a day. In 2009, those statistics had drastically changed. In 2017, watching television was slightly down to eight hours.

Television in the United States teaches a different kind of conformity. In the novel, telescreen is used to create conformity to the party lines. Mark Miller, a scholar in media studies, opined that television produces conformity to a system of huge consumption by using advertising for the general public, but focusing on the rich and famous. He said further that watching television promoted endless productivity. Subliminal messages being flashed on the screen regarding the meaning of success and the many virtues of hard work, are being fed cognitively to an unknowing audience. Television allows people to look into the program and watch strangers without being seen. Scholar Joshua Meyrowitz says that the type of programming that dominates television in the United States have made this easy. The news, sitcoms and the dramas that are played out in front of us each day and night, have made it normal to look into the private lives of other people.

Reality TV actually started in the 1960s with programs such as "Candid Camera," "Real People," and "Cops," to name a few. These programs have made it seem normal to look into people's lives and accept a certain kind of video surveillance.

One of the programs that I cannot stand and I have never been able to watch unless I was at someone else's house and they were watching it, is "Big Brother." I had not even thought of that until now about the title of the show. We have become such sheeple that we, as a whole, just accepted it. The show is kind of acknowledging the novel in a sense by naming it Big Brother. The hidden message is really like, "We are watching you. We will take care of you."

As a reality show, Big Brother is also an experiment in a fishbowl, so to speak. It is about controlling and modifying behavior. Because the actors are asked to put their lives on display, it encourages self-scrutiny and behaving in such a way that they are following perceived norms. Sometimes it is even roles that challenge those norms.

The Big Brother show now has a team of psychologists that are there for the actors because they have to perform 24 hours a day, 7 days a week.

Reality television can actually be traced back to the work of social psychologists who did behavioral experiments after World War II. A famous study was done by Stanley Milgram, a psychologist from Yale University. Milgram was actually influenced by the show, "Candid Camera." His subjects were not aware that they were being watched or that they were even part of an experiment. Milgram wanted to know if he could force large numbers of people to simply follow orders and participate in acts of genocide. His experiment focused on the conflict between obedience to authority and one's personal conscience. What Milgram looked at were the justifications used for acts of genocide by those who were accused at the Nuremberg War Crimes Trial after World War II.

What Milgram concluded from his experiment was that people would go against what they thought was morally right in order to obey people they saw as authority figures. Here is what Milgram said about his study. "They will obey orders from what they think is legitimate authority even if they are ordered to do terrible things." Milgram had the lab set up such that one group was the control group and the other group, the experimental group. The control group was to administer shocks to the experimental group in another room. This group was told to play like they were being shocked when they saw a light come on at the desk where they were sitting. The control group really thought they were shocking the other group. As the control group kept being ordered to turn up the power and increase the shocks, the experimental group was told to yell louder as though they were really receiving the shocks. The results showed that sixty-five percent of individuals administered the final electric shock even after the person had expressed significant pain and distress followed by a continuing silence. The Milgram experiment was deemed unethical because the subjects were subjected to a significant amount of stress. The experiment was set up to trap people psychologically into a situation, where as far as they knew, they helped torture and kill another participant in the experiment. Many were traumatized from their participation. What this shows us is how easily we can be manipulated if we think it is for a good reason as told to us by someone we see as an authority figure. I guess that is how war works.

While reality TV shows today do not order the players to hurt each other, they are often set up like a social experiment that involves intense competition and sometimes, even cruelty.

Lastly, let us look at surveillance in our daily lives. Video surveillance is already here. You cannot go anywhere without a camera picking you up somewhere. Closed circuit television exists in just about every area of American life. Transportation centers and networks, schools, grocery stores, hospitals, and even public sidewalks. Plus, law enforcement officers now wear body cameras and their vehicles are often equipped with surveillance equipment.

Surveillance footage from these various cameras are often used for programs like, "America's Most Wanted," or the local news. Viewers just accept it as normal. Reality television can be seen as the friendly face of surveillance. These programs make the audience think that surveillance only happens to those who choose it or to those who are breaking the law. We are lulled into complacency, and this is when those in control can make their move on the public before we know what happened.

We, as a society, are provided with so much technology in the forms of smart phones, I Pads, laptops, electronic music, the list is long, that we do not pay attention to what is going on around us. We talk on the phone for hours, text each other, do social media such as Facebook or What's App? We walk into light poles on the street because we are texting and not looking up, get hit by cars because we step off of curves while talking on the phone or texting and we aren't paying attention. Laws are put into place without our knowledge because we do not participate in paying attention to what our lawmakers are proposing. What I am saying is that we need to wake up to the realities of life, but more than that, we need to wake up spiritually. Only a raising of mass consciousness will stop this insanity. It begins within each one of us. We need to treat others the way we want to be treated, create the world that we want to see, look at each other as our brothers and sisters because we are all one. We must give unconditional love and we will receive it back, forgive each other and ourselves, and all work together to achieve peace. We now have the technology to blow ourselves to bits, but we also must have the spirituality to ensure that we do not.

As our beautiful planet moves into the fifth dimension, we may go with her but only if we are vibrating at the fifth dimensional level. We do that by raising our own consciousness and frequency through meditation and prayer, doing charity, helping each other, and being thankful. We have been offered an amazing and peaceful existence if we reach out and take it. We are going to create through our own levels of consciousness what we experience. I believe that we will. Love is the answer! It really is all that there is!

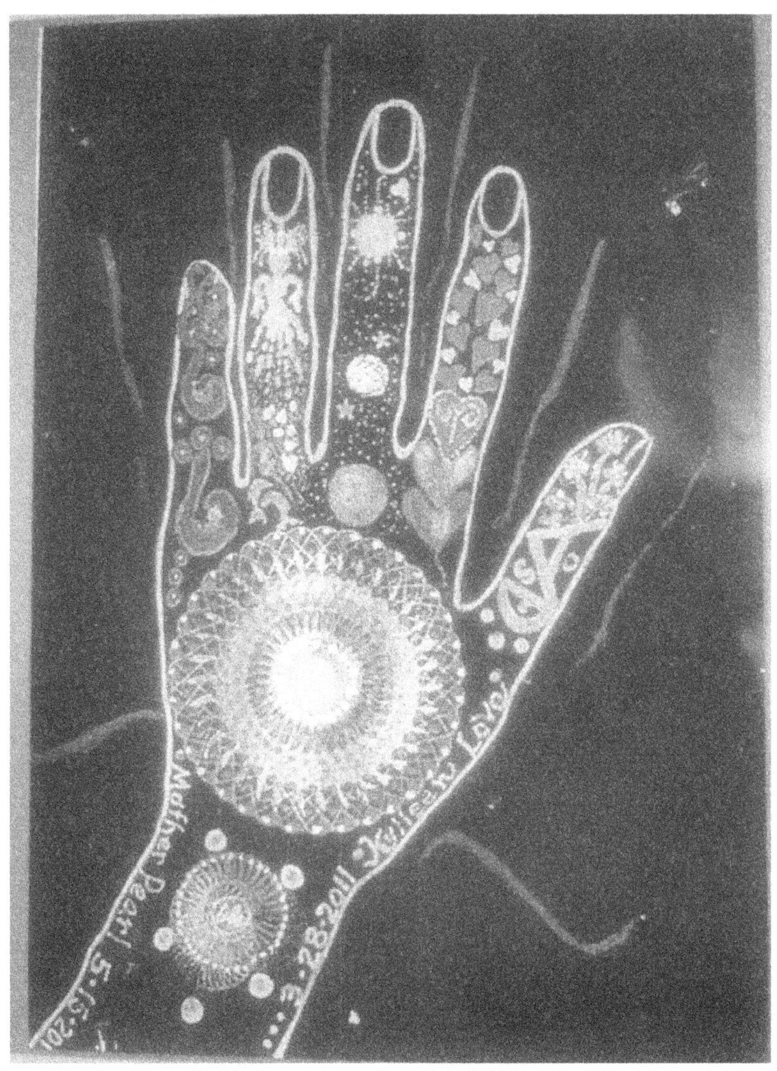

Picture of the hand blue-print encoded with stargate information, mentioned in Chapter 26. My two blueprints are the middle finger and index finger.

Endnotes

1 1977 Broadcast from the Ashtar Galactic Command at http://www.goldenageofgaia.com/2012-history-4/1977broadcast-from-the-ashtar-galactic-command/

2 Stephen Jay Gould was an American paleontologist, an evolutionary biologist, and historian of science. Born in 1941 and died in 2002, he was the most influential and widely read author of popular science of his generation.

3 David R. Hawkins, M.D., Ph.D., is a well-known authority within the fields of consciousness research and spirituality.

4 Robert Lawlor is a writer and film producer living in Australia who has studied aboriginal culture firsthand. He published, *Sacred Geometry: Philosophy and Practice* in 1952.

5 Ibid, note 1.

6 Neale Donald Walsch is an American author of the series, *Conversations with God.* He is also an actor, screenwriter, and speaker.

7 Martin Buber was an Austrian philosopher known for his philosophy of dialogue which is a form of existentialism centered on the distinction between the I-Thou relationship and the I-It relationship. He was influenced by Friedrick Nietzsche, Immanuel Kant, Sigmund Freud, and Soren Kierkegaard.

8 Sol Luckman is a well-known author of fiction and nonfiction and a pioneering ink painter whose work has appeared on mainstream book covers. His books include, *Conscious Healing* and its sequel, *Potentiate Your DNA.*

9 Charles Caleb Colton was a famous writer from England who lived between 1780 and 1832. He was also a priest and an art collector. Later in life, an illness required an operation which he did not want to do. He killed himself instead.

10 Brian Greene is an American theoretical physicist, mathematician, and a theorist of string theory. He was born in 1963 and is a professor at Columbia University since 1996 and chairman of the World Science Festival since co-founding it in 2008.

11 Jim Bishop was an American author and journalist who wrote the book, *The Day Lincoln was Shot.* He was born in 1907 and died in 1987.

12 Erwin Schrodinger was a Nobel Prize winning Austrian physicist whose groundbreaking wave equation changed the way we looked at quantum theory.

13 Anais Nin was a French-Cuban American diarist, essayist, novelist, and writer of short stories and erotica. She was born to Cuban parents in France and was the daughter of composer Joaquin Nin and Rosa Culmell, a classically trained singer.

14 Roy T. Bennett wrote, *The Light in the Heart.* He loves sharing possitivities and creative insight that has helped many people to live a fulfilling and successful life.

15 Nancy Garden was an American writer of fiction for children and young adults. She is bet known for her lesbian novel, *Annie on my Mind.*

Bibliography

It's not differences that divide us. It's our judgments about each other that do.
—Margaret Wheatley

Books:

Beckley, Timothy, Psychic and UFO Revelations in the Last Days, New Brunswick, NJ: Inner Light Publications, 1989.

Borysenko, Joan and Borysenko, Miroslav, The Power of the Mind to Heal, Carson, CA: Hay House, Inc., 1994.

Bruce, Alexander, The Philadelphia Experiment, New York: Sky Books,2001

Buchanan, Lyn, The Seventh Sense-The Secrets of Remote Viewing, New York, Simon and Schuster, 2003.

Cayce, Edgar, Atlantis, New York, Warner Books, 1968.

Evans, M.J, PhD, Zecharia Sitchen and the Extraterrestrial Origins of Humanity, Bear & Company, Rochester, Vermont c. 2016

Greer MD, Steven M, Disclosure, Crozet, VA: Crossing Point, Inc., 2001

Greer MD, Steven M, Extraterrestrial Contact: The Evidence and Implications, Crozet, VA: Crossing Point, Inc., 1999

Greer MD, Steven M, Hidden Truth Forbidden Knowledge, Crozet, VA: Crossing Point, Inc., 2003

Haleem, Abdel M.A.S, translater Qur'an The, Oxford University Press, c 2016

Keyes, Ken, The Hundredth Monkey Theory, 1981, no copyright Travel. Evanstar Creations, New Zealand c. 1993

Lamb, Barbara, and LaLich, Nadine, Alien Experiences, Claremont, CA: Light Technology Publishing, 2008 +

Lamb, Barbara, Crop Circles Revealed, Claremont, CA, Light Technology Publishing, 2001

Nidle, Sheldon, Your First Contact,

Nidle, Sheldon, Your Galactic Neighbors,

Orwell, George. 1984, Secker & Warburg Publishers, c 1949

Price, John, Roswell: A Quest for the Truth, Truth Seeker Co., Inc., 1997

Sitchen, Zecharia The Anunnaki Chronicles, Bear & Company. Rochester, Vermont 05767. C. 2015

Sitchen, Zecharia There Were Giants Upon The Earth, Bear & Company Rochester, Vermont c. 2010

Zimmerman Jones, Andrew String Theory for Dummies, Wiley Publishing inc., Hoboken, New Jersey c. 2010

Websites:

https://aligningwithearth.com/welcome-fifth-dimension

https://awakening5dhealing.com/2019/04/01/energy-update-dna-upgrades-portals-and-ascension-symptoms https://archive.org/stream/AmirFatironAliensintheQuran/extraterrestrial Aliens and reptilian Gods-9-djvu.txt

http://www.bibliotecapleyades.net

http://www.exopolitics.org

http://www.exosciences.angelfire.com

http://www.galacticconnection.com

http://www.galacticfederationoflight.com

http://www.mindpowerworld.com/cropcircles

https://www.mintakahealing.com/2018/03/24/5d-ascension-timeline/Rasmussen,KellyNoel.Ascension

http://www.ocspr.com

http://www.index.php/star-union/ww-are-the-stargate

http://www.siriusdisclosure.com

https://medium.com/we-are-not-alone-the-disclosure-lobby/why-extraterrestrial-disclosure-matters-5df5427ba8ea

https://www.strangerdimensions.com/2014/02/13/time-travel-teleportation-experiments-project-pegasus

https://www.sworthley.com/author/suzanne-worthley/2018/31/12

http://www.thrivemovement.com

My Personal Notes Taken At:

Cobra Conference Notes, Laguna Beach, CA, 11/23-11/25/2012.

Planetary Activation Organization, Nidle, Sheldon, Webinar 24: Ascended Masters

Planetary Activation Organization, Nidle, Sheldon, Webinar 35: First Contact/Disclosure

Planetary Activation Organization, Nidle, Sheldon, Webinar 36: Full Consciousness/Reality Shift

Planetary Activation Organization, Nidle, Sheldon, Webinar 37: Galactic Society

Planetary Activation Organization, Nidle, Sheldon, Webinar 41: Fulfilling Our Life's Contract

Articles:

Williams, Matt A Universe of 10 Dimensions, Universe Today. December 11, 2014

Youtube Videos:

Holy Guardian Angel, Youtube 9-20-17

Labay, David. How to open a Stargate Portal. Youtube 3-20-14

Zohar Stargate Ancient Discoveries, 6-11-19

DVDs and Movies:

Gamble, Foster and Gamble, Kimberly, Thrive, Thrivemovement.com 2010

Greer MD, Steven M and Kaleka, Armardeep, Sirius, Siriusdisclosure.com

Greer MD, Steven M, Unacknowledged

Nidle, Sheldon, DVD 701: Consciousness, Heaven, and Physicality, Planetary Activation Organization

Nidle, Sheldon, DVD 703: The Conscious Universe, PlanetaryActivation Organization

Nidle, Sheldon, DVD 704: Galactic Federation Ships, Part 1, PlanetaryActivation Organization

Nidle, Sheldon, DVD 706: Galactic Federation Ships, Part 2, Planetary Activation Organization

Nidle, Sheldon, DVD 709: N.E.S.A.R.A. Shifting The Planet, Planetary Activation Organization

Nidle, Sheldon, DVD 714: The Truth About Right Now, Part 1, Planetary Activation Organization

Nidle, Sheldon, DVD 715: The Truth About Right Now, Part 2, Planetary Activation Organization

Nidle, Sheldon, DVD 719: Landings 101, Planetary Activation Organization

Nidle, Sheldon, DVD 720: Inner Earth Your Future Home, PlanetaryActivation Organization

Nidle, Sheldon, DVD 726: Back To Being Galactic Humans, Planetary Activation Organization

Nidle, Sheldon, DVD 727: Meet Your First Contact Team, Planetary Activation Organization

Nidle, Sheldon, DVD 728: Zero Point, The Endless Sea of Energy, Planetary Activation Organization

Nidle, Sheldon, DVD 729: Shifting Gaia and Humanity, Planetary Activation Organization

Nidle, Sheldon, DVD 731: Ascension and Inner Earth, Planetary Activation Organization

Reference Verses in the King James Bible:

Job 1:6 Regarding-The devil refusing to bow to Adam

Revelation 12:9 Regarding-Satan and his angels being cast out into the earth

Revelation 12:7-9 Regarding-the war of the Annunaki and other alien gods in the asteroid belt

Reference Verses in the English-Translated Version of The Holy Qur'an by M.A.S. Abdel Haleem:

Qur'an 18:50

Qur'an 7:12 Regarding Iblis refusing to bow to Adam

Qur'an 72:12 Regarding Qur'anic Jinn

Qur'an 6:129

Qur'an 21:32 Regarding the real Star Wars battle

Pictures and Images:
NASA public domain pictures, nasa.gov/publicdomain

1. Pioneer Plaque
   Picture creation: Carl Sagan and Frank Drake
   Artwork: Linda Salzman Sagan
   Manufacturer: Precision Engravers, San Carlos, California
2. Wow Signal Dr. Jerry Ehman, SETI, Ohio State University

My Photographs:

1. Landing spacecraft, picture taken in Arizona
2. My biography photograph
3. Blueprint picture of the hand

Drawings:

1. Our new head chakras, drawn by artist Haifa Dagachi
2. Cross sections of Inner Earth, drawn by artist Haifa Dagachi

About the Author

Learn to light a candle in the darkest moments of someone's life. Be the light that helps others see; it is what gives life its deepest significance.
—Roy T. Bennett

Judith L. Cameron, PhD, is an educator, a writer, a clinical hypnotherapist, close encounter therapist, second degree certified Reiki Practitioner, hypno-anaesthesia therapist, and spiritual angel therapist. She is also a trained ambassador to the universe, teaching others to make contact. Through seminars and classes, she teaches about sacred geometry, meditation, and the raising of mass consciousness. Judy also teaches people how to make contact with the sentient Star Visitors who work with the people of Earth to invite these extraterrestrial civilizations to Earth in peace. Teaching how to reach out in unconditional love and peace will put us on a positive path to create the fifth dimensional Earth that we are hoping and striving for. By us ordinary citizens reaching out and making positive contact in peace, disclosure of the hidden truth will come out. We really cannot wait for the dark cabal to do it because it will not be in our favor or in the Earth's favor if they do.

As an extraterrestrial experiencer from the age of six, Judy's life has followed a unique and special path. As a teacher in public education for forty years, teaching elementary school, then high school for the last thirty years of her career, she has taught thousands of students. Her subjects in physical and space science, psychology, developmental psychology, and relationship psychology, plus special education at all grade levels has given Judy a chance to meet and work with a wide variety of students. They have enriched her life beyond measure is what Judy would say if you asked her. She is well-rounded and has an amazing understanding of humans and our behavior.

Answering the call in 1985 for NASA's Teacher-in-Space Program, Judy became an International Faculty member for the Challenger Center for Space Science Education, and a part-time flight director at one of the Challenger Learning Centers in Southern California. Carrying on the mission of the Challenger crew after the Challenger exploded after lift-off, Judy had the privilege of working alongside astronauts, astronomers, and other gifted teachers to teach children, teenagers, and adults about the shuttle program and living and working in space. She also worked on projects about one day colonizing Mars, our nearest neighbor in space.

In 1994, Judy received a special invitation to the East Room of the White House as a representative of teaching in the United States. She was one of three teachers selected for this honor. The event was for the twenty-fifth anniversary of the Apollo 11 moon landing. While there, Judy met Neil Armstrong, Buzz Aldrin, and Michael Collins, plus other astronauts, astronomers and scientists. In addition, she met President Bill Clinton and First Lady Hillary Rodham Clinton.

In 1988, Judy received her doctorate in clinical hypnotherapy and psychotherapy and started her part-time private practice. She began specializing in working with people who had experiences with extraterrestrials and inter-dimensional beings. As an on-going experiencer herself, Judy knew and understood what her clients were going through. In 1994, Judy began training to be an ambassador to the universe with Steven Greer, MD, the founder of CSETI, The Center for the Study of Extraterrestrial Intelligence. Dr. Greer has trained thousands of such ambassadors now around the world to create their own contact groups and reach out to these beautiful beings. To study the phenomenon further, Judy enrolled in the doctoral program at St. John's University and earned her PhD in parapsychology in 2005. Her dissertation was about studying ET contact and spiritual development.

In a lucid dream in 1989, Judy was told that she would be a liaison for first contact between Earth humans and extraterrestrials. Knowing that we are all One and mass consciousness is increasing every day on planet Earth, Judy is helping to co-create our New Earth and teach others about our collective future.

Knowing that there are no coincidences, in late 2014 to early 2015, a life described to her by a psychic, that seemed very far-fetched at that time in the 1980s, started to materialize. Meeting her twin flame and galactic counterpart, her life began to change dramatically. Judy converted to Islam, enrolled in the degree program at California Islamic University in Fullerton with the goal of receiving a bachelor's degree in Islamic Law and Theology, and has made extensive trips to the middle east. This has led her to look further into the Sphinx and the pyramids at Giza, Egypt, the sacred geometry of the Kabba and surroundings in Mecca, Saudi Arabia, to learn more about potential stargates in Iraq and Egypt, and to learn the interesting connections of Dubai, United Arab Emirates to all of this history.

Judy has appeared on several radio programs and has written several articles for various hypnotherapy journals. Her first book, *Caught Between Two Worlds...A Journey Through Time,* allowed people to look at the idea of extraterrestrial contact in a safe and interesting way. She teaches seminars and workshops in meditation, sacred geometry and the universal connection of everything, and our future on Earth and how we can help raise mass consciousness. Judy has recorded numerous CDs, CDs for special programs, as well as meditation CDs.

Judy lives in Placentia, California and takes care of Richard, who is living with Alzheimer's. She has two indoor cats, Einstein and Patches, and six somewhat feral cats, Baby Cat, Fluffkins, Ebony, Apollo, and Midnight, who have found their way to her for food and love when they approach her. Her yard is also filled with squirrels, a couple of raccoon families, an opossum or two, and lots of birds. She is an amateur astronomer and loves to hike and be in the outdoors. Being out in nature or under the stars, and connecting to the cosmic consciousness that we all have access to if we meditate and consciously reach out to it, allows Judy time to rejuvenate and stay balanced. Judy loves volunteering at her local mosque and out into the community to help with the homeless situation. Judy loves her music and plays her guitar every chance she gets. You can catch up on what Judy is doing by checking her web profile at JudithCameron@Cambridgewhoswho.com. You may e-mail her at etdiplomat@gmail.com. You may also check her out at cosmicangelenterprisesllc.com.

Some final personal thoughts

The environment is where we all meet; where all have a mutual interest; it is the one thing all of us share.
—Lady Bird Johnson

We all have a wonderful opportunity to move into the fifth dimension with our planet, which will be like creating heaven on Earth. In order to accomplish that we must stop all hatred, wars and anything that does not serve our highest good. We must come together in unconditional love, peace, empathy and understanding. We must set a good example for those who will follow us by being compassionate, giving, reaching out to one another with understanding and lovingness, and extending our hearts to our Galactic neighbors to join us in peace and unconditional love. We will then be allowed to join a vast galactic community of evolved beings who come from all over the galaxies, other dimensions, and encompassing the entire Universe. If we follow God's commandments handed down to Moses at Mt. Sinai and stored in the Ark of the Covenant, and also written in three parts in the Holy Qur'an, we will raise mass consciousness and our planet will be an abundant, prosperous, and happy place to live. Love is the highest frequency we can vibrate in, and therefore, the highest state of consciousness. If you are in the pure frequency of Love you will find gratitude, happiness, creation, and Oneness. Love is everything! Love is us!

Judy Cameron, Ph.D.

We are all One!

Love is the answer! It really is all that there is!
Walikum Salaam!
Namaste'!
Peace and Blessings to All!

CPSIA information can be obtained
at www.ICGtesting.com
Printed in the USA
LVHW112150130420
653355LV00001B/226

9 781982 234720